Advance Praise for Sometimes Creek

Florence Rose Krall Shepard has spent her life at the edge. From an Italian family who felt themselves not yet fully American to a vision of America beyond progress, from ranching country where men still shot each other over water rights to academia and the Ph.D., from the last of the frontier where the only good coyotes, eagles and cougars were dead to teaching in the Audubon Center, from the Church to a vision of a 'native' cosmology, she has spent her life on the borders that separate her roots from life as teacher, ecologist, activist and writer. From motherhood to croneship, what for others might be endless brinks is for her just that divide from which mature perspective is gained.

—Paul Shepard

FRK Shepard's *Sometimes Creek* is quite simply a long overdue, much needed contribution to the literature of the American West. Her life story—perennially exposed to the harsh yet gorgeous realities of life at the edge of wild nature and perennially nourished by the fierce, strong lineages of human love—is also, and most importantly, a woman's story. Listen carefully. Then, listen again. An archaic wisdom is speaking and its message is urgent.

—Casey Walker, editor of *The Wild Duck Review*

Sometimes Creek is a strikingly vivid and artful historical memoir in which Florence Shepard brings readers happily along with her on a soulful remembrance of what it was like growing up on a remote family ranch back when Wyoming was still the Old West, with all its bristle and bark still on. This beautifully written book is also a lifelong naturalist's portrait of the best of what's left today of yesterday's natural American West.

—David Petersen, author of *On the Wild Edge*

A lovely, eloquent memoir that lopes along with grace that is nothing short of inspiring for what's seen, felt, heard in the landscape over the course of the 20th century American West. Flo Shepard's lyrical sense of place transports us to a Western America that lives only in the rare mind able to depict with clarity the shape and feeling of the land, the fresh scent of a home-cooked meal, the joy of family, the anguish and realities of loss and, most of all, the progression of a life so generously lived and shared.

—Bernie Krause, author of *The Great Animal Orchestra: Finding the Origins of Music in the World's Wild Places*

SOMETIMES CREEK

Sometimes Creek

• A WYOMING MEMOIR •

Florence Rose Krall Shepard

Flo Shepard

Raven's Eye Press
Durango, Colorado

Raven's Eye Press, LLC
Durango, Colorado
www.ravenseyepress.com

Shepard, Florence Rose Krall.
    Sometimes Creek./Florence Rose Krall Shepard.
    p. cm.

1. Twentieth Century--Memoir
2. Natural History--Wyoming
3. Early Twentieth Century Immigrant Family--Biography
4. Woman Rancher--Wyoming
5. Sheep Ranching--Wyoming
I. Title

ISBN: 978-0-9840056-1-1
LCCN: 2012936970

Cover & interior design by Lindsay J. Nyquist, *elle jay design*
Cover photo by Susan Marsh
Back cover author photo by Kathryn Ann Morton

Printed in the United States of America
1 3 5 7 9 10 8 6 4 2

• • •

Dedication

This book is dedicated to:

The memory of
Matt and Matilda Bertagnolli,
my parents who gave me life,
and
Paul Shepard,
who enriched my life;

Sisters,
Barbara Wagner and DJ Kominsky,
who shared my life;

My progeny who have made life worthwhile,
Kathryn Ann, Matthew, Lisi, Bobby, Jason, Meredith, Phil,
Brandon, Francis, Brady, Jared, Makayla, Jordan, Addy,
Florence Isabella, and Kaden.

Table of Contents

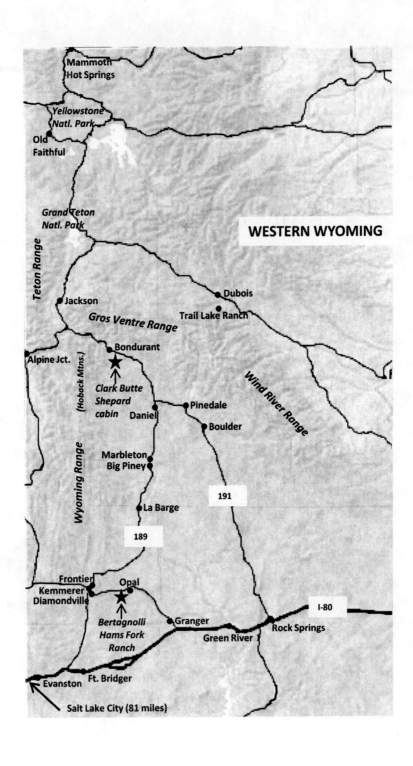

WESTERN WYOMING

Mammoth
Hot Springs

Yellowstone
Natl. Park

Old
Faithful

Grand Teton
Natl. Park

Teton Range

Jackson

Gros Ventre Range

Dubois

Trail Lake Ranch

Alpine Jct.

Bondurant

(Hoback Mtns.)

Clark Butte
Shepard
cabin

Daniel

Pinedale

Boulder

Wind River Range

Wyoming Range

Marbleton
Big Piney

La Barge

191

189

Frontier

Opal

Kemmerer
Diamondville

Bertagnolli
Hams Fork
Ranch

Granger

Green River

Rock Springs

I-80

Ft. Bridger

Evanston

Salt Lake City (81 miles)

· 1 ·

Heartwood

As Lisi's car rounds the curve and disappears behind the willows, I stop waving and walk back into the cabin. Typically, when one of my children departs after a visit, I get to work. For as long as I can remember, work has been a remedy for any ailment in our family. But today I choose another way to fill the void left by departing loved ones. I wipe my eyes, put on a hat, fill a canteen with water, grab a few matches and my walking stick and head for Clark Butte.

The meadow extending from my cabin door is yellow and dry and crackles underfoot. I cross the Query Ditch, excavated when settlers first came into this land. It followed the course of Sometimes Creek, an intermittent stream, which ebbed and flowed with the seasons long before homesteaders filed their claims in this part of the Hoback Basin in Wyoming. The ditch runs along an ecotone between the meadow and Clark Draw, an expanse of sagebrush steppe. To the west, forested Monument Ridge circumscribes the perimeter. And beyond it, the distinctive skyline silhouette of the Hoback Range forms the western horizon.

Across the ditch, I squeeze through a pole stile and step out onto United States Forest Service public land, then follow a barbed wire fence northward up Clark Butte, an island ecosystem rising about a thousand feet above the basin floor. Contouring up the ridge, I pick my way through the sagebrush steppe, a diverse vegetative community of small shrubs, grasses and wildflowers. These resilient plants are perfectly adapted to the harsh environmental conditions in this Wyoming bioregion with its high elevations, frigid winters, short growing seasons and minimal precipitation.

The bleached bunchgrass and delicate dry seedpods are only a hint of the colorful ephemeral bursts of blossoms a few weeks ago. Summer passes quickly here. In June the entire basin is emerald green. In July, the slopes are painted pink with the blush of wild onions with delicate white sego lilies peeping through here and there, followed by the yellow bloom of balsamroot. Now, at mid-August and after the first frosts, the verdant hues have faded to tan, the lackluster landscape masking the vitality and stability of this land.

The hike to the summit of Clark Butte slows me down considerably, more than it did a quarter of a century ago when Paul Shepard and I first came here to spend our summers. Approaching retirement, we decided this would be a good place to build a small cabin and spend most of the year. Excellent fishing drew him; I needed no enticement to return to Wyoming where I was born, grew into womanhood, married and raised my four children.

After considerable contouring, I reach the crest and stop to catch my breath. On the summit I feel like a raptor riding a thermal as I survey the Hoback Basin with its ranch meadows, clusters of homes and the tiny community of Bondurant. Down below is our cabin, one of about a dozen scattered over what was once a homestead. Mountains surround the basin on all sides. The majestic Gros Ventres on the north, the Hoback Range to the west, and the South and East Rims, foothills of the Wyoming Range, complete the encirclement. Over the crest of the East Rim, barely visible in the distance, are the wild and wonderful Wind River Mountains.

From here, I can see far and, thanks to hindsight, I can also look back. In my mind's eye I picture the family sheep ranch, nestled in a sea of sage on the banks of the Hams Fork River, which flowed southeast from the Wyoming Range. The original homesteaders of our ranch had to travel fifty miles by wagon to cut logs near the river's headwaters. They hauled them back to build the house and the pole bridge that crossed the river.

We moved to the ranch when I was three. On the banks of the Hams Fork, our hardworking and loving Italian parents, Matt and Matilda Bertagnolli, raised my two sisters and me. When we daughters—Barbara, three years older, and Dolores (who now prefers DJ), six years younger than me—reached the age of reason and gained a measure of physical strength, we became a part of the working ranch. Our parents' astute seasonal observations, sense of timing, awareness of the progression of the seasons and appreciation of Earth's creations set our roots firmly in nature.

My world expanded exponentially when I began going to school. Our parents drove Barbara and me to a one-room school in Opal, a railroad shipping stop five miles from the ranch. When that school closed during the Great Depression, we were bussed about a dozen miles to the Burgoon School, an elementary and junior high school in the small mining town of Diamondville. Though short on amenities, the school provided ethnic diversity and the opportunity to grow into adolescence among a cohort of interesting children. The bus went on to deliver older students to the high school in Kemmerer, where I graduated in 1944.

Kemmerer played an important part in the history of southwestern Wyoming. With the ending of the Civil War and the onset of the Industrial Revolution, demand for resources—timber to build and repair railroads, coal to fuel the engines and laborers to extract these resources—burgeoned. After serving as a railroad stop on the Oregon Shortline Railroad completed in 1881, Kemmerer was established in 1897 as a service and supply center for the surrounding coalmines.

In 1902, my maternal grandparents, Teresa and Louis Coletti, got off the train in Kemmerer ready to start a new life. They were among the destitute from around the world, recruited by coal and railroad companies. From the French-Italian Alps, they and their siblings came to work in the coal mines. In 1921, my father, an immigrant from Austrian Tyrol, and my mother, firstborn daughter of my grandparents, married. They built a brick bungalow in Kemmerer where I was born in 1926. Three years later our family moved to a ranch on the Hams Fork River, twelve miles downstream from Kemmerer.

Kemmerer holds significance for me personally: when I married my first husband, Bob Krall, we settled there and raised our four children, Kathryn Ann, Matthew, Lisi and Bobby. In Kemmerer I first began teaching school. Thus my life story is a twentieth-century tale of acculturation and accommodation experienced by this immigrant Italian family in the process of becoming American.

The view from Clark Butte affords me the opportunity to revisit the significant times and places of my past, all within two hundred miles from where I stand. The mountains enfold and comfort me; I feel contained and secure. In any direction I can see the boundaries of my existence. I know where I stand.

With these high-altitude thoughts set aside, I work my way cautiously across the summit of Clark Butte through a tangle of shrubs and young aspen clones peppered with fresh excavations. Badgers have been hard at work routing out plump Uinta ground squirrels already in hibernation. The rainbow colors of tall larkspur, lupine, sticky geranium and columbine of mid-summer have been reduced to delicate, dry seedpods that catch the morning sun. Yellow sprays of flowering rabbitbrush now dominate the show. Buffaloberry and snowberry, heavy with fruit, offer a bounty for birds preparing for migration.

As I pick my way across the summit, legitimate residents of the Butte protest my intrusion. Townsend's Solitaires, Olive-sided Flycatchers and Green-tailed Towhees flit nervously in front of me. Clark's Nutcrackers scold as White-breasted Nuthatches and Mountain Chickadees send warnings from the dense canopy of conifers on the north slope. Two Red-tailed Hawks screech and circle above. A twig snaps, and I glimpse a buck mule deer moving slowly away between white aspen trunks into the shadows.

My first destination is a weather-beaten Douglas-fir I have christened Heartwood. Guarded by a stately sub-alpine fir with a majestic spire, Heartwood sits on the north edge of Clark Butte facing the Gros Ventre Mountains. From the first time I saw it, this old tree has enticed me toward a bit of botanical forensics as I try to uncover its mysterious past. Either because of genetics or some injury in its formative stage, Heartwood originally developed as a double tree. Judging from the charred remains, I surmise that one trunk burned and, after standing dead in place for many years, snapped off about twenty feet above the ground, perhaps assisted by a gale-force wind. The old trunk crashed to earth and shattered, creating a perfect seedbed where young trees of various sizes have taken hold. I work my way over the jumble of broken branches sheltering a profusion of new seedlings and stand at the base of Heartwood.

How the living Heartwood withstood the fire that burned its other half is a mystery. Dead and charred trees in the area indicate that fire spread across the summit of the Butte. I can imagine lightning striking one of the two trunks of the living tree and then traveling downward to its roots, the heat expanding and exploding them with a great burst. Perhaps the fire smoldered in the duff for days until a high wind fanned it into a flash fire that raced across the top of the Butte and burned itself out, leaving part of Heartwood singed but still alive. Whatever the scenario, one part died; the other lives on.

On the south side of Heartwood, below where the burned trunk cracked off, a concave shell of the dead trunk still clings to the living tree. Heartwood's trunk leans slightly north but, above where the break occurred, relieved of balancing its weight, the trunk rights itself. It rises straight above with a full and healthy spread of branches bearing a profusion of ripe cones.

Sun shines through empty knotholes in the skeletal remains of trunk number two, casting light on the vertical gray-and-tan striped dead phloem cells encasing rusty, brick-like rows of xylem chambers. The matrix of dead wood creates a network of crevices that collect pine needles and debris, offering shelter and nesting sites to birds and the substrate for an intricate web of life for decomposers and predatory insects. Pitch dripping along the scar where living bark is growing over dead wood leaves a benediction of amber drops on a dead wren lying feet up in an old nest, a clump of yellow green lichen at its side.

The bark on the north side of the live trunk is thick and corky. Where an outer layer has fallen away, a tawny surface, etched with wavy lines of growth, testifies to Heartwood's ability to adjust in untold ways. The thick bark of the Douglas fir is resistant to low intensity fires, thus insuring longevity. Some members of this species survive for over a millennium.

Through the years of visiting Heartwood, I have searched, with some trepidation, for tracks leading into a huge burrow under its roots. Chief, and his wife, Lena, a couple now deceased who at one time lived on the other side of the Butte, told me that in earlier days they often saw black bears here. Holding to the hope that at some future date my heart will leap with fear and excitement when I find tracks of a bear, or see one, I check the burrow repeatedly but have found only traces of small rodents.

A swing, an incongruity in this scene, hangs from one of the branches. Too high for a child to reach unassisted, it is apparently intended to be used with the supervision of an adult to insure that, from the perch, little ones will not catapult over the edge. After a bit of a struggle, I hoist myself into the swing where I sway peacefully back and forth, the movement reminiscent of childhood meditative moments. The swing, like the rocking chair for women, must have been invented to give a sense of movement and passage while staying in the same place, satisfying in the homebound an inherent desire to wander.

As I leave, I give Heartwood a hug and rest a moment with eyes closed and my face against its corrugated surface. Now too old to sit in the presence of grandmother or mother, I lean reassuringly against the weathered bark of this majestic being, a surrogate ancestor of sorts. It has survived the fire that burned its other half and since then has sheltered life and spawned generations of seedlings that now grow at various stages of development in the rich duff of its decaying branches. This magnificent elder, a living metaphor that I emulate, advises me: Patience.

I move across the summit to a sandstone outcrop on the west side of the Butte and light a tiny fire from dry sagebrush I gathered on the climb. Pungent smoke rises as I fan the flame and add a few green sprigs. I've repeated this seasonal ritual each year since my first visit here about six weeks after the death of my second husband, Paul Shepard. I was grief-stricken and his good friend, Carl Hertel, suggested that a simple ritual might help Paul cross over and also help me to cope with my loss. Having left ritual behind with the Catholic Church, I was skeptical. It was late summer in a dry year when fires were burning in the surrounding mountains. Smoke filled the Hoback Basin. Open fires were banned.

I broke the rules and built a tiny fire. As the smoke rose, I asked Paul to please find peace in his new place and help me find strength to survive without him. The simple ceremony somehow broke the cycle of abject despair and hope crept back into my heart. Since then I have come here to repeat the ceremony, sometimes with others suffering from the loss of loved ones, sometimes just as I have today, in thanksgiving.

After dousing the fire thoroughly with water from my canteen, I work my way carefully back across the badger diggings and descend the Butte. Juvenile Mountain Bluebirds with mottled breasts and a hint of blue on tail and wing, flying from post to post, escort me down the trail along the fence. For the past weeks they have been gathering in family groups learning to hover and hunt insects as they prepare to leave for warmer climes.

As one flies from its perch, a least chipmunk takes its place. It is a lovely, diminutive creature, ash gray with tawny sides and black, tan and rufous stripes extending from its face down its back. As I pass, it contemplates me momentarily and then scurries down the pole with tail held high and disappears into the sagebrush, probably into its burrow, where it raised its young and is now storing a cache of seeds and nesting materials for winter survival.

The urgency sensed in animals at this time highlights the fine-tuning of their phenology, their adaptive behaviors timed in response to seasonal changes. Native people who lived in these parts also developed skills for surviving the coming cold. The Shoshones, who were summer residents here before the homesteaders, like birds, migrated to warmer climes for the winter. One branch of the Shoshone, known as the Sheepeaters for their skill in ambushing wary Rocky Mountain bighorn sheep, stayed year-round in the high mountains and lived on their companion animals, the bighorn sheep. With extraordinary provision and incredible skills those horseless natives stoically survived the cruel winter months.

At a deep level, I share the same rhythms felt by the animals that winter here. A response set in our genes long ago, when life began on this earth with its two poles, tilted axis, cyclic rotation and revolution around our bright star, is initiated in me at this time each year. My body responds to the decreased daylight and increased darkness, the drop in temperature, and the slanting rays of the sun. In the hush that hangs over the landscape, I share the expectancy and dread of the next months that may bring hard times. But for now, things are fine. I crawl through the fence and head for my cabin and evening chores.

Cabin in the Hoback Basin

Back row: Bob Krall, Kathryn Morton, Flo Shepard
Front row: Bobby, Lisi, and Matt Krall

Clark Butte (photo by Susan Marsh)

Bertagnolli ranch on the
Hams Fork River

· 2 ·

Harvest

With a cup of tea in hand I step out on my porch to witness the building light. Usually a peaceful time each morning when I ease out of the dream world into the reality of another day, today I am caught up short by a qualitative difference in the ambience. Nothing in particular strikes me at first as unusual. Yet, many small indiscernible changes have been taking place that now add up and can't be denied. With a sense of resignation I have to admit: Summer is ending.

Clinging to the last shreds of summer, I've undoubtedly been in denial. As if awaiting my acknowledgment, telltale changes rapidly fall into place. As the sun moves south and daylight decreases, increasingly slanted rays create a softer quality of light. Greenness gives way to shimmering umber tones of flowers and grass heads gone to seed. Willows turn yellow-green sprinkled with little bursts of gold.

By mid-August we have usually had our first hard frost. Since the last freezing nights were in late June, the math on frost-free days is fairly clear: a month to six weeks in a good year. The euphemism "growing season" takes on new meaning in this part of Wyoming. Domesticated flowers and shrubs that I've planted and coddled in flowerbeds around the cabin give up as the temperature plummets. Native vegetation, however, is amazingly resilient; the first green sprouts make their appearance as soon as the snow thaws in late April, and some plants, like rabbit brush, columbine, mountain hollyhock and green gentian, continue blooming in the forests into September. As daylight hours slowly diminish, temperatures continue to fall. With the first hard frost, blossoms are dulled or nipped in the bud, willows turn rapidly and clones of aspen on the hillsides take on tones from gold to tangerine. I am unequivocally escorted into fall, a bittersweet time when the landscape triggers a change of perspective, one felt by us humans but magnified in wild creatures that must adapt or perish.

From the time I was a young child, the textbook explanations of four seasons never seemed to ring true for me. Not until my travels with Paul in northern Europe did I gain some appreciation for this discrepancy. In a museum in Lulea, Sweden, in a portrayal of the seasons as seen by the Sami, native indigenous people of the Arctic, I saw a clear representation of the seasons as I have experienced them—as eight times of the year. These include not only the four seasons and the days on which each begins, but also four periods called quarter days, six weeks into each season and starting on what are called cross-quarter days. Accordingly, the eight days on which the seasons and quarter days commence are: December 21, the winter solstice or the first day of winter (when the sun begins rising a little earlier each day); February 1, winter quarter days; March 21, the vernal equinox or first day of spring (when daylight and darkness are of equal lengths); May 1, spring quarter days; June 21, the summer solstice or first day of summer (when the sun begins rising a little later each day); August 1, summer quarter days; September 21, the autumnal equinox or the first day of fall (when daylight and darkness are of equal lengths); November 1, autumn quarter days. Interestingly, as Dolores La Chapelle described in her book *Earth Festivals*, pagans celebrated on cross-quarter days, the first day of each of the quarter day periods. Later these days were co-opted for Christian celebrations and still later, as national holidays.

The air, unusually still and warm this morning, portending an approaching storm front, nudges me toward long-neglected gardening. Frosts have sent the chlorophyll underground and left the rhubarb leaves crimson. I cherish the stalks of this plant and harvest them for freezing but am never satisfied with the yield. I always want more for the pies, crisps and jams I make for guests and family. Strawberry-rhubarb pies are my usual contribution to the annual Bondurant Community Club Barbeque and Heritage Day Sale.

I decide to transplant some new starts. The large, fleshy rhizomes are firmly anchored and difficult to dig. I split and transplant them to the beds along the cabin with hopes that more sun and protection will increase the yield. This bent to increase production is undoubtedly inherited from my father, who was determined that our relatively modest ranch would produce to capacity.

Since the first time I dislodged a clump of the tenacious rhubarb rhizomes, I have been intrigued with their appearance, which suggests some deep-rooted history. A little research shows that, indeed, rhubarb is an Old World cold-weather plant used since 2700 B.C. in China for medicinal purposes. Advertisements for rhubarb root extracts and tonics claim everything from digestive remediation to diuretics and purgatives. This ode to rhubarb may seem strange to seasoned gardeners who consider it a weed. But I am sincerely thankful for this amazing plant, pragmatic though my attachment may be. It's the most reliable and useful plant in my garden and it's good to know it also enhances my health.

Next I prune the currant bushes I planted last year, which delighted me this summer with their bounty of jewel-like berries that I processed into ruby-red jelly. The gooseberry bushes were less impressive but show promise for next year. I supplement their harvest with wild gooseberries I pick along the Hoback River. While it's a prickly process, these berries make delicious jelly.

Copious seedpods of lupine, sticky geranium and roadside mustard dangle as dry remnants, reminiscent of their colorful array of deep blue, pink, and lavender summer blossoms. Starts for most of these I transplanted from the roadside or forest. I clip, scatter and save a good supply of plump seedpods, which I'll plant next spring in my continuing efforts to naturalize the meadow. Not a purist, I sow any seed, wild or domesticated, that will grow and bear blossoms.

After years of mowing the meadow around the cabin, I stopped this summer. I've always considered a manicured lawn inappropriate in this prairie environment. Yellow cinquefoil, lavender showy daisies and pink sticky geraniums are already replacing some of the meadow grasses. With luck, perennial shrubs of the steppe—sagebrush, shrubby cinquefoil, silver-leafed buffaloberry, bitterbrush, rabbitbrush and saltsage, to mention only a few plants originally grubbed out by homesteaders—will once more establish their territories. Settlers planted English hay, a mixture of timothy, redtop and clover here, as they had across the United States after they slashed and burned forests and cleared the ground. Now that flower seeds are set, I weed-beat a swath of the tall grasses and flowers around the cabin to satisfy the concern of neighboring firemen, who correctly consider them a fire hazard.

The delphiniums, which offered a bountiful source of nectar for hummingbirds and bees, have been reduced to tatters. Not long ago they were over five feet tall and I could stand eye to blossom with them. Their colors of deep cobalt, purple, robin egg blue, lavender and pink remind me of my high school graduation gown. I had rejected the traditional white for a blue taffeta with a full net overskirt of pink, which, when I danced and twirled, produced all of the colors of these brave sentinel spires. A few days ago a pronghorn buck in rut thrashed the blooming delphinium to bits with his horns.

From my window-filled cabin I first caught sight of him running around the cabin chasing young bucks away from his harem of about twenty does. I followed him from window to window. Filled with breeding frenzy he successfully drove off the young bucks. Then with his horns he proceeded to completely thrash the stand of delphiniums that stood five feet tall. Feeling his power, his horns shrouded in shredded delphinium stalks, he stood on the drain field with his head held high, sniffing the air for ovulating females, claiming his territory triumphantly. His machismo made me laugh. When daughter Kathryn called, as she does each day, I related the scene to her. She suggested I call him Delphinio. The name now adheres to every frenzied dominant buck I see.

After a good workout in the flowerbeds, I load dry remnants in the wheelbarrow and head toward the irrigation ditch to scatter them and where I hope some will take hold. In a confused jumble of vocalizations and fluttering wings, a flock of blackbirds, feeding in the tall grass, explodes into the air.

"Blackbirds!" Dad shouted as he burst into the house. He retrieved his shotgun from the closet, loaded it and called to Mamma and us daughters to follow him. He shouldered the gun and headed for the meadow where black heads were bobbing in the fields near the ranch house. Silently mimicking his stealthy approach, we followed closely on Dad's heels until a huge flock of blackbirds burst in unison into the air and he discharged his shotgun repeatedly into the melee. Birds rained down and, upon Dad's signal, we scattered into the meadow like little retrievers, fetching the birds that had fallen dead or wounded, and delivered them to him. He quickly dispatched those still alive and then beheaded, gutted and de-feathered the lot.

Back at the house with the tiny, decapitated, pink-skinned birds before her, I watched Mamma stuff them with garlic cloves and sprigs of parsley and wrap each bird in bacon. She arranged them on their backs with their little legs sticking pathetically in the air in a large shallow roasting pan, which she then placed in the hot oven of the chrome and blue enamel coal range polished to a mirror-sheen. Rocking back and forth in the old rocker, I waited patiently, savoring the odors of sizzling birds and garlic as I wondered how they would taste "baked in a pie," or if, in fact, how such a feat could be accomplished.

Finally, Mamma called us to dinner and brought the pan of toasty brown, roasted birds to the table, served with boiled new potatoes, crisp garden lettuce dressed with olive oil and wine vinegar and home-baked bread. We ate the little tidbits with our fingers, pulling off the tiny wings and legs and savoring every tender morsel of our ritual harvest feast.

At the end of the repast, the roasting pan was heaped with diminutive skeletons. We enjoyed this once-a-year feast at the end of summer's toils without a twinge of conscience. Killing migratory songbirds—the flock included both Red-winged and Brewer's Blackbirds—is against the law, but in the context of our subsistence on the ranch, we were unaware of such legalities. It seemed absolutely appropriate to enjoy one sacramental feast in thanksgiving for such abundance.

The sun warms my back as I continue working the flowerbeds, digging deeper, thinning and adding fertilizer. The sound of tractors reaches me from across the river from the River Bend Ranch where haying is winding down. They're now hauling bales to the winter storage shed and the sound takes me back.

By about the first of August each year, we had finished haying the main meadow and the hired crew had left the ranch. The remaining cleanup rested on Dad, his girls (I started working in the hay fields when I was twelve) and Joe Abram, an Italian bachelor who lived on the ranch with us until World War II. When the war began, Joe left the ranch to go to work in coalmines that had reopened, where, under one of the benefits of the New Deal, he could earn Social Security credit for his retirement. But during my childhood he lived on the ranch and helped with some of the daily chores from time to time for his board and room. Whenever he took part in seasonal work, like stacking hay, he was paid the going wage. He was also the government trapper, deemed essential by Dad, and he kept the proceeds from the sale of pelts from trapped coyotes, beavers, and muskrats. However, Joe would not milk cows and Dad had to find someone else for this chore when our entire family was away from the ranch.

In addition to Joe, two other Italian friends of Dad's, Joe Dona and Louis Concinni, worked on the ranch from time to time.

During the Great Depression, some of them may have worked just for board and room. All were members of a cohort of Italian immigrants from Dad's region. They enjoyed Dad's company and Mamma's good cooking. At high labor times, Dad sometimes brought in a husband and wife team so that Mamma would also have a helper. I remember Uncle Jimmy, mother's brother, and his wife Aunt Lynn, with special fondness. Uncle Jimmy, a self-taught mechanical genius, was a big help to Dad. He built hay pushers from old cars and electrical wind chargers and snowmobiles from scratch.

We loved Uncle Jimmy's amiable disposition and were entertained by his musical talents. He would somehow jury rig our radio in the front room with a microphone to another room. We would turn on the radio and tune in on Uncle Jimmy playing the guitar and singing cowboy songs. Later when he married Aunt Lynn, a very bright young woman, she came with him to the ranch. While helping with my homework, she once introduced me to the phrase "every walk of life" and encouraged me to use it in an essay I was writing. I've never forgotten that phenomenal moment, as if Aunt Lynn had turned on a light—a time in my intellectual development when I first became receptive to the power of metaphor.

Joe Dona, who had been Dad's partner in some of his early ventures, was with us on the ranch off and on through the years and was like family to us. Unlike Joe Abram, who was a sullen man who didn't seem to like children, Joe Dona, with a wry sense of humor and a bent for teasing, was a pleasure to have in the household. As I think back on that ranch and those childhood days, I see a household filled with a steady stream of interesting workers and friends.

At the end of August, the second crop of alfalfa had to be harvested along with isolated patches of meadow that were too small to fuss with while paying a full crew. Such was Little Meadow, about half a mile up a dusty road, which had been isolated from the main meadows when the Oregon Shortline Railroad was built and bisected the ranch. Though small, Little Meadow produced a stand of hay thick with clover that Dad would not let go to waste. He also cut selective patches within the railroad right-of-way where the hay grew tall and lush. The hay salvaged from these tiny remnants, after being mowed and raked, was loaded on a hayrack pulled by horses or on the truck and hauled to the enormous hay barn. Filled to its tin roof, it provided fragrant cured hay for milk cows and a few horses held in the corrals over the winter.

Raking the patches of hay along the railroad right-of-way, I felt self-conscious and an intruder when trains or section gangs passed on the tracks. Dad, with his entrepreneurial bent, undoubtedly had an understanding with the railroad section foreman. Crews burned grasses and old railroad ties in late summer in order to reduce the danger of fires started by the coal-fueled trains, so I suppose Dad contributed to fire prevention. The foreman generously notified Dad when they were preparing to burn and then ignored our trespasses. We cut and loaded the hay, and with a horse Dad shimmied a good supply of discarded ties across to our property where he later retrieved them for various building and repair projects: They made sturdy corner fence posts and were the major building blocks of many of the ranch buildings he had constructed, including the plant house, ice house, garage and cellar.

The hours cleaning the flowerbeds yesterday were well spent. My muscles are stiff and sore but I'm pleased to have completed the task. Through the years I've learned to discipline my tendency to procrastinate, to put off time-sensitive or difficult tasks to a point of no return—a habit that in my youth brought me much unhappiness. I'm reminded of the time a few years ago when I managed to address such a duty I had ignored for too long.

I placed a long-delayed call to Eileen Dockham, the diminutive, uncontested matriarch of the Bondurant community, whose home was on the other side of Clark Butte. Since her husband's death, she had carried on his legacy as a moral voice. She was the self-appointed historian of the Hoback Basin and kept a written record of important happenings through the years, from daily temperatures and precipitation to marriages, births and deaths. I wanted to browse her archival records but was shy about asking since our last conversation had not gone well.

She had called late one evening and explained that she was speaking for the neighbors down ditch from me who owned a few acres for pasturing their horses. They were unhappy about my diverting much-needed water for my ponds, a series of shallow, temporary containments Paul had constructed to enhance wild bird habitat. During these dry months, she said, they needed water for their horses. I clarified politely that I wasn't diverting water as I do when water is high and overflows from the ponds back into the main ditch. The problem, I proposed, was that it was a dry year and there wasn't enough water to go around. Eileen, unconvinced, ended the conversation with a reminder: "Remember, Flo, horses are more important than ducks."

Putting the past behind me, I called Eileen to ask if I might visit her sometime at her convenience to peruse her journals. She checked her calendar and found it full for the rest of the week.

"How about today?" she suggested.

"Perfect! I'll be right over."

Eileen, neat, pretty and petite, greeted me at the door with apologies about not having things quite in order as she was recovering from heart surgery undergone earlier in the spring. I questioned whether she felt up to my intrusion and she assured me that she was happy I came by. I followed her through the kitchen and past the dining area where her paintings were attractively displayed. On a shelf were packets of cards with reproductions of her landscapes and wildlife. I stopped for a moment to look at them and ordered several packets of note cards and Christmas cards illustrated with her idyllic painting of Saint Hubert the Hunter Community Church, deep in winter snow, with the Christmas star shining above it.

We walked into the parlor with windows facing the Gros Ventre Mountains. The bookcase was filled with references on this area. As a member of the Sublette County Artists' Guild, she had written several historical and biographical essays for the volumes of *Seeds-Kee-Dee, A Historical Folklore of the Green River Valley*, which included the Hoback Basin. After an hour of my reading, leafing through books and asking her questions, Eileen grew weary of my queries.

"Flo," she suggested, "why don't we just drive around the Basin so that I can show you where I've lived through the years."

Delighted with her suggestion, I proposed that, at the end of our excursion, we stop by the Dell Creek Diner for lunch.

We turned off the highway onto the graveled Dell Creek Road that skirts the base of the Gros Ventres Range and wound our way through extensive meadows of the Little Jenny Ranch dotted with bales of hay soon to be replaced by cattle returning from their summer range in the forests. As we passed below the vistas, the backdrop for many of her paintings, Eileen ticked off the names of the peaks: Pinnacle, Antoinette, Corner, Steamboat, Palmer, Triangle, Doubletop, Hodges, Eagle, and Tosi. The road turned away from the mountains at the Elbow, where the jagged fluted cliffs of The Sawtooth trend downward into the Upper Green River flood plain. At the Jack Creek Road turn-off, I asked if she'd like to drive up the road. She seemed unwilling, saying that she thought the road might be too rough. I proposed giving it a try, assuring her we'd turn back if it became too rough.

In a few miles I understood the real reason for Eileen's reluctance. This road was strewn with memories of her husband, Billie, and her family. How well I knew the power of certain landscapes to draw up sweet memories as well as a profound and irreversible sense of loss. In a verdant draw overlooking the meadows below, she asked me to stop for a moment at some old corrals and foundations. She explained that this had been the Quarter Circle XL Ranch, which she and Billie had bought and where they had raised their children. She pointed out the remains of a springhouse where the "water was always so cold and good."

We continued on to where the road ended at well-kept ranch buildings. As I turned the car to head back, Eileen began weeping. I turned off the engine and waited until she could speak. This, she explained, was the family ranch where she and her siblings were raised. Her father was one of approximately fifty-five homesteaders who proved up on land in what was then called Fall Creek Basin. Proving up entailed documenting for the government a homesteader's obligation to build fences and a cabin and provide evidence that the meadows had been extended by grubbing sagebrush, harrowing the land and planting it with perennial grasses. In exchange for proving up, the government granted the homesteader a deed to 160 acres of land. Eventually these small homesteads, too small to support families in this high country, were bought and consolidated into large, productive cattle ranches comprising thousands of acres.

At the apogee of our drive, we headed back toward the highway past the Campbell ranch. Traditional ranchers, they still used horses instead of tractors and stacked their hay rather than bailing it. As we approached the cemetery on a hill overlooking the scattered Bondurant community, Eileen asked if we might stop. I followed her to Billie's grave, marked with a magnificent headstone etched with one of her depictions of a bugling elk. She circled the gravesites and delivered little homilies of family and friends buried there. As we continued our drive and neared the highway, Eileen pointed out the old buildings and land where Benjamin Franklin (B.J.) and Sarah Ellen Bondurant, two of the original residents, settled in 1900. To this pioneering couple, the small community owes its name.

After lunch at the Dell Creek Diner in the Elk Horn Trading Post, I dropped Eileen off at her home. Before leaving, Eileen asked if I might be going to Jackson Hole on Friday when she had a doctor's appointment. Thrilled at the opportunity to return something to her for the gift of her company on this memorable day, I said it would be no bother to pick her up. On Friday, after a busy day of meeting her daughter at the doctor's office and having lunch with an old friend, I left her once more at her home, promising to visit her again when I returned from a quick trip to Salt Lake City.

Upon my return I found a message on my answering machine from Eileen: "Flo, please come on over whenever you have the chance. I have something for you." I drove to her house but, finding no one there, headed back to my cabin by way of the post office. On the bulletin board outside was a notice that Eileen was in intensive care at St. John's Medical Center in Jackson. The next morning I drove to the hospital. No visitors were allowed. Through the partly opened door, I could see her, tethered to life support. It was clear to me she was gravely ill.

Eileen died soon afterward. I was deeply saddened by her death but profoundly thankful for the few hours I had spent with her. In that short time I had learned that although we differed in our disparate values concerning horses and ducks, we also had much in common. Being of the same generation, we both had faced empty houses after our husbands had died. We had been schoolteachers. We understood the tribulations and joy of ranching on the edge of wild country. We had birthed and raised our children in Wyoming where winters are fierce and water, a treasured commodity, is bought and sold, fought over, hoarded and cherished. We lived with the assurance that Sometimes Creek would run again to slake our thirst. But there was something singularly unique about Eileen: She had lived her entire life within the boundaries of this tiny basin bioregion.

Since Eileen's passing, I have thought of how much she loved this place and its creatures, the people as well as the animals and plants. It was not a romantic love, but one grounded in deep care and commitment. The beauty of the landscape reproduced in her paintings, adorning her home and those of others, was etched indelibly on her mind through daily observation. In the past I had watched her with admiration in the meetings of the women of the Bondurant Community Council, the organization she founded, which binds the community through activities and celebrations and helps those in need. Eileen brought a historical and teacherly perspective into each meeting and a moral voice that was heeded and respected as decisions were reached. She was conservative and provincial to the core in the best sense of those words: salt of the earth. She and the others like her resist the onslaught of intrusions that threaten to change the configuration of material life and spiritual values within their home territory. More importantly, she modeled the kind of example that other women can now follow. Even at my age, very near to her own, I learned much from Eileen.

At this time of year as summer ends, weather is variable and difficult to predict. This uncertainty makes me restless. I'd like things to stabilize for a moment. But no two days or two autumns are ever alike. The best way I've found to ground myself in this vertiginous flux is to watch birds.

Summer resident birds are flying helter-skelter in disorganized family groups. At first fledglings resist the push by adults to more independence by continuing to beg for food but are progressively ignored by adults who must prepare for their own journey south. The timing is perfect: Separation from adults is accompanied by a feeling of independence in the juveniles as they test their wings and begin foraging for themselves.

As birds flock and forage, raptors take advantage of the abundance of young birds, mice and voles at their disposal, which help them build strength for their long journey south (some, like Swainson's Hawks, fly all the way to southern Argentina). Red-tailed Hawks and Golden Eagles soar high on up-drafts scrutinizing the landscape for easy prey, while Cooper's Hawks use my cabin roof as a staging place for hunts. An occasional Merlin swoops down to capture a bird. Northern Harriers cruise low over the meadow honing in on the sounds of mice and voles in the tall grass.

Not long ago I watched an avian drama play itself out in gory and unambiguous detail that illustrated the web of life. A mother American Kestrel was feeding a rodent, which she had killed, to a juvenile perched on the fence. Although I doubted that it was possible, the young bird finally swallowed it whole. Its craw was so distended that I feared it wouldn't be able to fly. As soon as this thought entered my mind, the juvenile tried to lift off but unable to get air-born, it plummeted to the ground. I caught my breath and stood aghast, as the scenario I feared dramatically continued to unfold. In a flash, a Common Raven flew in, killed the young kestrel and carried it to another pole on the fence. As the raven tried to tear it to pieces, the dead bird slipped out of its grasp and dropped to the ground. Immediately, a Turkey Vulture swooped down and claimed the dead kestrel as its own. Through this series of exchanges, the mother kestrel frantically called and assailed the culprits to no avail. In the supreme balance of nature, undisturbed by human intervention and left to their own adjustments, these creatures were maintaining nature's balance.

Some mornings I awaken to bursts of unfamiliar melodies. Birds, leaving their summer ranges in the mountains and northern nesting sites—among them the little Northern Water Thrush and mountain-nesting Hermit and Swainson's Thrushes—stop by, leaving trails of sweet songs. In the willows, Evening and Black-headed Grosbeaks add their clear notes and bright colors to the mystery of migration. Their songs, delivered occasionally in short bursts, bring faint memories of the exuberant melodies of spring.

In the quiet of evening light, flower and grass heads gone to seed are bathed in a gossamer haze. Slanting rays of the sun magnify contours and colors. Yellow light on mountain and meadow at sunset turns to heart-wrenching magentas and tangerines followed by lavender and purple-hued twilights ending with blue-black skies. I hold these ephemeral moments close to my heart, knowing they will last only a moment, their beauty inversely proportional to their duration.

Cabin in late summer

Tea on the porch

Pronghorn from cabin window

Barbara, Louis Concinni, and Florence (1930)

Uncle Jimmy (left), Joe Abrahm, and Dad castrating a calf

Truck loaded with hay

· 3 ·

Stocking Up

As I stood on the porch surveying my accomplishments with satisfaction, the whisper of raindrops on parched grass told me the storm had arrived. It had given me just enough time to plant a few tulip and daffodil bulbs and complete the clean-up.

It rained all night and the next morning I awakened shivering under my down comforter as cold air streamed in the open window. I shut the window and dressed quickly in warm pants, a turtleneck, heavy sweater, and wool socks and sheepskin slippers. Bracing myself against the cold blast of air, I chopped a little kindling on the porch and rushed back to build a fire in the heating stove.

Dense, dark clouds obscured the mountains. A cold rain at times mixed with snow fell during the day. A Willow Flycatcher and a Western Tanager, trying to find shelter on the covered porch, perched on the clothesline and repeatedly flew at the atrium doors trying to get in. Ill-equipped to survive the onslaught of wet and cold, they seemed disoriented.

Today, on the third day of stormy cold weather, the clouds lift and the sun shines on the sparkling, white mountains. I walk around the porch thankful for the sunshine, which came too late for the Willow Flycatcher and Western Tanager whose dead bodies lie huddled against the wall. Their deaths are a testament to why birds migrate. Although a few are winter residents, most do not have the physiological ability to adapt to low temperatures.

As the weather clears, those who sought shelter in the willows and survived, begin chirping and regrouping in preparation for flying south. Fledgling kestrels are finally on their own and are making forays out from nesting sites where until recently they begged loudly and insistently to be fed. On windy days the adults have been teaching them the intricacies of hovering and hunting as they ride the air currents on the leeward side of Clark Butte. Migrating raptors continue to move through. Down on Commissary Ridge, at the southernmost segment of the Wyoming Range, Hawkwatch volunteers are counting raptors that funnel through the flyway.

In the evenings, long lines of adult and juvenile swallows and blackbirds sit on telephone wires shoulder to shoulder. Then one morning, they rise in unison, fly off and don't return. The exodus continues each day. The last to leave are second hatches of Mountain Bluebirds, and Vesper and White-crowned Sparrows feeding on seeds along my driveway. A few stalwart Calliope Hummingbirds sit huddled, ready to go to battle with the feisty Rufous, which pass through quickly. But most of the birds have moved on. As the curtain falls on the season, a laggard Western Meadowlark, feeling a resurgence of hormones, sings its last song, a taps to summer days and the opening chords of the autumnal equinox.

Since my journey with Eileen, I feel more grounded and intrigued with this place. Yet even as a child on a family vacation to Yellowstone Park, as we approached the East Rim and then entered the Hoback Basin, the prospect below bewitched me. To this day when driving to the cabin, as I crest the rim, the view before me takes my breath away.

From that gentle divide that separates the watersheds of the Hoback and Green River Basins, the highway follows the contours of the foothills, occasionally cutting through the soft sandstone outcrops that slough off into the borrow ditch. The road works its way downward through a succession of plant communities from higher elevations to the basin floor: from conifers to aspen groves, over foothills covered with sagebrush, to the riparian vegetation along Fisherman Creek where the huge dark heads of moose sometimes peer out above the maze of willows and beaver dams. This area provides a perfect habitat symbiosis between the little dam builders and moose, whose browsing produces copious new shoots for beavers to store for winter food and for other moose to browse on during the following year.

As I round one last curve, the road levels off and the Hoback Basin unfolds. Although ranch country, the basin has not been domesticated to the extent of excluding those other tribes of creatures that, at this time of year, are preparing for winter. Since before explorers came this way, herbivores have found their particular niches from mountaintops to basin floor. In summer, mountain sheep graze on craggy heights, elk occupy the alpine meadows, mule deer and moose browse on forest and willow ecotones and pronghorn favor the sagebrush foothills and meadows.

Mountain sheep are not deterred and remain through the winter. Moose, whose long, flexible front legs are adapted to lift high out of deep snow, also stay on. But deer and pronghorns follow old migratory routes south to the lower Green River Basin, where strong winds scour the snow from the steppe habitat where they browse. Elk, historically migratory, now are enticed to stop midway at feeding grounds. The Wyoming Game and Fish Department maintains these to replace winter habitat that has been usurped for other purposes by humans. An array of mammals—beaver, mink, weasels, skunks, squirrels, muskrats, wolverines, foxes, coyotes, bobcats and mountain lions, an occasional wolf, cottontail and jack rabbits, snowshoe hares, a few raccoons, porcupines, and recently confirmed Canada lynx—remain here and are active through the winter. Black and grizzly bears fall into winter sleep and Uinta ground squirrels and pocket gophers hibernate. But a plethora of mice and voles remain active and forage in their subnivean world. Fish and amphibians—cutthroat, brook and rainbow trout, toads and frogs, garter snakes and rubber boas, and horned toads—have evolved various methods of over-wintering to avoid freezing.

Hundreds of summer birds pass through but a good number are permanent residents. Snow Buntings, Horned Larks and Black Rosy-finches summer in the far north or above timberline and use the sagebrush steppe as their wintering grounds. Rough-legged Hawks, after breeding and raising their young in the Arctic, winter here, where they feed on snowshoe hares, rodents, and road kill. Uinta ground squirrels emerge in April at a fortuitous time for these raptors. The Rough-legged Hawks fatten up on the Uintas in preparation for their journey back to the Arctic where they will again nest and raise their young.

As interesting as the great diversity of animals and their symbiotic relationships in this region is their phenology; that is, their seasonal cycles timed to fruiting and dormancy of plants and the birthing of their prey. Unlike the animals whose survival through the long, cold winters is the consequence of evolved inter-relationships, ours on the ranch was dependent on the carefully laid plans of our parents.

The rumble of a vehicle across the pole bridge alerted the dogs, and they barked furiously as Mr. Sardok drove his truck into the yard. At the peak of the Utah fruit harvest each year he went from farm to farm, loading his truck with produce, which he later sold in mining camps and ranches in southwestern Wyoming. After a polite exchange with Mamma, he set out bushels of peaches, pears, plums and tomatoes for her inspection. Calculating the ripeness of the fruit against the time it would take to process each bushel, she made her final selections. Mr. Sardok always added a few more choice pieces of ripe fruit to fill the bushels to overflow-ing before continuing on his way. The bushels were stored in the icehouse, and the kitchen became a steamy, fruit-scented process-ing center.

Since we daughters had entered school by this time, Uncle Richard, Dad's uncle who lived with us during these years, helped Mamma with the canning. Although he was only about sixty at the time, I remember him as an elderly gentleman, quite dignified and reserved, who helped Mamma with the household chores and yard work. As far as I know, he was the first of the Bertagnolli family to immigrate to Wyoming at the end of the nineteenth cen-tury. Uncle Richard settled in Rock Springs where he learned to read and write English and clerked in a merchandise store. Short-ly after arriving in America, he married Emma Saches, a German woman, and they had two children, Richard and Lizzie. Lizzie died as a young woman and left two infant sons, Alex and Paul.

Emma died a year later, purportedly of a broken heart. Apparently Uncle Richard was unable to cope with these deaths within a short time of each other so Dad brought him to the ranch to live with us. When I think of Uncle Richard, I see him sitting on the porch, reading the paper and smoking a pipe whose aroma was more pleasing than the smoke from the Bull Durham cigarettes rolled and smoked by most of the men. All of them contributed to more than my share of secondary smoke.

During canning time, Uncle Richard helped Mamma prepare the fruit, which she washed, blanched and peeled before packing it into quart jars. Adding prepared syrup, she sealed each jar with canning lids and rings and then processed them in a boiling water bath. Over-ripe pieces of fruit were simmered into jams, preserves and conserves to spread on homemade bread or eaten as a condiment with the rich cottage cheese she made weekly.

After processing the fruit in boiling water, Mamma placed the peach, purple plum, creamy pear and orange-red tomato jars on a counter to cool and seal, where they remained on display. Aesthetic to behold, they were a clear testament to Mamma's work that most often went unnoticed. I looked forward to canning time for another reason. Each afternoon, home from school, I'd go to the icehouse and select choice pieces of fresh fruit for after-school treats.

This was the time for setting up stores for the winter, for filling the cellar as well as the hay barn. Dad harvested root vegetables—carrots, turnips, beets, and potatoes—which, with our diligent weeding and his regular cultivating and irrigating, produced a great provision. To add to these stores, he made a yearly trek to Brigham City, Utah, to bring back cabbages, onions, squash, winter pears, apples and more potatoes.

We anxiously awaited Dad's return from these journeys, usually after dark, always with something special, like honeycombs, to surprise and delight us. On one trip he outdid himself and asked us to wait in the kitchen before he unloaded the truck. He soon appeared at the door leading a tiny Shetland pony into the kitchen. Dad had forgotten his name so we called him Brigham. Barbara claimed him as her own, but he was handed down to DJ and me in due time. He was a feisty little creature who would lie down and roll over whenever we piled on him and he felt overloaded.

Harvest time was also wine making time. Dad bought a permit and ordered a truckload of concord and muscatel grapes. He washed the grapes and placed them in a huge wooden vat, to which was added Joe, our perpetual boarder, wearing thoroughly scrubbed rubber irrigation boots. He tramped the grapes to a squishy pulp that was placed in barrels to ferment. A cup of the new wine was siphoned off and tasted periodically to see if it had reached perfection, when it would be transferred to more wooden barrels to age further in the cellar.

Wine, never served regularly with our meals, was reserved only for holiday dinners or for visiting guests. However, when Dad was called away from the ranch for some purpose, Joe would siphon off a little to measure its progress and share it with Uncle Richard. They were never what one could call good friends, since Uncle Richard expected to be treated with deference, and Joe deferred to no one. This invariably led to quarrels, which Mamma stopped when they became too heated and sent them off to bed.

The grape dregs were stored until a dark winter night when Dad and a friend, who still owned a still, would surreptitiously break the law and distill their yearly supply of *grappa*. This was Dad's favorite liquor, which he enjoyed as a coffee royal each morning and in late afternoon to fortify him for the ranch chores. Mamma, having witnessed Grandpa Coletti's excessive drinking, wouldn't touch a drop of wine or grappa.

The cellar was our principle food storage area and essential for our subsistence. The harvested root vegetables from our garden were stored along one wall in bins filled with sand that Dad had hauled from the riverbanks where it collected. The bushels of vegetables and fruit bought in Utah were also stacked along that side. A long low bench ran along the opposite wall supporting barrels of wine, a crock for sauerkraut and one for cheese, which aged into something like Gorgonzola. At the far end were shelves, one side for cheeses made in early summer and the other for Mamma's canned fruits and preserves. Later in winter, cured and smoked bacon, ham, salami and sausage would hang from the rafters.

Built with a double thickness of railroad ties, double doors and a thick sod roof, the cellar was frost-free and carried the ambiance of an underground root cellar. Mamma frequently recruited me to retrieve preparations for meals from it. Strict rules were set for entering the cellar in order to keep out the freezing cold of winter or summer heat. The huge outside door had to be closed before the inner one was opened and a light bulb turned on to cast a dim light over the shadowy interior. The period of darkness when I stood between the two doors was terribly scary, a heart-pounding adventure for someone afraid of the dark. I hurriedly gathered foodstuffs in the dim, musky, tomb-like interior, always wondering if someone, not realizing I was in there, might come along and latch the outside door. How long would it take, I wondered, before Mamma noted my absence and came to my rescue?

As a young girl, during this season, my soul was not stirred with thoughts of the past as they are today. I left to the adults the bittersweet work of sorting through tangled memories as they completed the harvest and set things in order for the coming winter. Amidst the closing activities of summer, my preoccupation was the prospect of school and the pleasure of playing with old schoolmates and meeting new ones. My mind was kept astir by the challenge and fear of living up to expectations, especially my own, and the anticipation and dread of the unknown. With unabated excitement and apprehension, I awaited that first day of school.

I began each school year with three new cotton dresses, each costing $2.98, which I had chosen from the vast array in the Montgomery Ward Catalog. I pored over the selections until Mamma finally sent off the order, after which I waited expectantly until the big brown paper-wrapped package arrived in the mail and I could try on the dresses. In preparation for school, we also drove to Kemmerer for a day of buying new shoes and school supplies—spelling and ruled tablets, colored crayons, a small pencil box with pencils, a pencil sharpener and an eraser.

My schooling began in the one-room school in Opal. Miss Anna Beyda, the teacher, provided the perfect early childhood transition from my sheltering mother. The white frame schoolhouse she presided over had no running water and was heated by a big coal-burning stove that stood out from a corner in the back of the room. A bucket and dipper provided drinking water. Along the north wall were windows and a sand table—built low to accommodate young children. Its top was a shallow-sided box filled with sand, placed so that students could gather around. At the head of the room were the teacher's desk, a blackboard and a door that led to the teacherage, the living quarters for Miss Beyda.

About twenty children in six grades made up the student body. The desks were movable and the arrangement varied according to the particular activity. My desk, with a drawer under the seat for books, crayons and a pencil box—whose contents I examined endlessly before school had started—was a nest of sorts that gave me a sense of security, ownership and standing. Under the desktop was another compartment for storing current assignments. I gave careful consideration to arranging my belongings in this tiny personal space.

Reading groups gathered around the coal-fired heater, stoked by the boys. Judging from my report cards, I was not a stellar reader those first years. This may have been due to the fact that Dad could barely read Italian and very little English, though he developed some literacy late in his life. Mamma, busy from morning to nightfall, had little time to read to us regularly. Nonetheless, she instilled in us the importance of books and the value of reading. She had stored in her trunk a bound embossed-leather set of *The Junior Classics*. On summer days or on weekends during school when time permitted, Mamma brought the books out of her trunk; they carried the rich scent of knowledge, which one finds in old museums and libraries, overlain with that of mothballs. Sitting on her bedroom floor, she gathered us around and we listened enraptured to poems about "going up in a swing so high," adventures of Little Orphan Annie and stories about a brownie who lived in a cherry tree.

Mamma treated the books with great care and her obvious delight in reading told us all we needed to know about the value of words. But the ceremony and gravity of the scene also told us this was a luxury one did not resort to often. Coming as she had from a home with no books, she conveyed the belief that these were precious objects she had purchased at great sacrifice and were not play things to be used indiscriminately.

I've concluded that Mamma must have cultivated a rich fantasy life since she perpetuated the myth of the brownie. She told us that one usually dwelled in each house and she surmised that ours probably lived in the coal shed. She suspected that the little fellow might be hungry and would appreciate sleeping in a clean bed and suggested that we make up a little bed in an old matchbox and set out milk and graham crackers for him at night. In the morning, the food would be gone, and the bedding, made from pieces of old sheet, was ruffled and dirtied with coal dust. Skeptical by nature, I suspected that Mamma had contrived this little fellow and I examined the porch carefully to see if I could find the brownie's tracks coming from the coal shed. I didn't share my skepticism with Mamma since I didn't want to deprive her of the pleasure of creating the fantasy. Later, when I had outgrown the brownie phase, I was recruited to rumple the bed and eat the crackers and milk in order to perpetuate the myth for DJ, six years younger, who was enthralled with the little fellow.

Thanks to Miss Beyda's acceptance of differing abilities, I did not see myself as a slow learner. My enthusiasm for school never waned and remained a fascination, as much for the opportunity to associate with others as for what I learned in books. Although we passed from grade to grade in a traditional manner, the one-room school was essentially an un-graded classroom, one through six. Reading or mathematics exercises were individualized or conducted in small groups according to ability. The entire congregation of children participated together in project-oriented social studies units. Somewhat like a tribal culture, this mixed-age arrangement, rather than the same-age segregation common today, accommodated our varying abilities and needs and enhanced our social and moral development. Walking about the room quietly observing others, working at my desk, or warming myself by the heating stove, I felt secure and unencumbered by strict rules.

Miss Beyda must have lived a solitary life in the small adjoining teacherage. She was single, which was the norm for most teachers, both women and men, at a time when school boards favored unmarried teachers with no other loyalties. She was undoubtedly a disciple of John Dewey, the educator and philosopher with a bent for replicating society through child-centered experiential learning. During the year, we created dioramas in the sand table. With materials at hand—construction paper of all colors, pieces of cloth, cotton, twigs, leaves, scissors and a big jar of paste—we spent fun-filled days creating the various cultures we were studying in our social studies unit. This activity provided the opportunity for making decisions through democratic social interaction negotiated among children of various ages. Our creativity was challenged when we were each given a straight wooden clothespin to take home to adorn with clothes and faces to represent actors in the cultural scene we had created.

During the construction and display of these miniature dioramas, as we studied the cultures of our depictions, my child's mind dwelt in each as a separate universe. The brightly feathered tribal people with their little teepees and horses lived in peace in our sand table. Eskimos in their white cotton world inspired me during the winter to try to build an igloo. At the end of each unit we wrote and illustrated essays about what we had learned. Thinking back on the unit on Japan, I actually feel I visited that country, walked past pagodas and crossed little streams on tiny bridges. These miniature cultures, with players and components that could be arranged and rearranged, far surpassed anything else in my schooling as a rich source of fantasy and learning, pleasure and inventiveness—except for recess.

Unsupervised, and with a minimum of play apparatus at recess, we divided naturally into gender groups as we created an ongoing saga of "Westward, Pioneers." The older girls, including sister Barbara, were self-appointed mothers and we younger ones, the children. I adored my "mother," Pearl, who was kind but stern. We set up our households with old furnishings gathered from a nearby rubbish heap and arranged them in an old shack on the school grounds where we prepared make-believe meals, sometimes augmented with crackers smuggled from home. We were a family making our way across the prairie while "the men," with their homemade wooden guns loaded with strips of inner tube ammunition, fought off Indians on the periphery. Unfettered by fear of injury or liability, we played to our hearts' content, reinventing the Wild West.

Into this child's world came my first best friend, Evelyn Rae Roberson, whom I admired unconditionally. She had a radiant personality with a quick wit and engaging smile, an animated way of talking, a bent for criticism and confidence galore. We were constant companions and I missed her terribly when vacations came. She represented all the things I longed to be and possessed all the things I wanted to have. One Christmas vacation she sent me a letter each day printed with her new printing set. Since we didn't go to Opal to get the mail regularly, they all arrived in a heap. This correspondence, a sign of love and loyalty, was a most treasured gift. Perhaps the anticipation and joy of receiving her missives initiated in me the value and pleasure of communications with friends and loved ones.

Rae's paternal grandparents were English-speaking homesteaders. Her maternal grandmother was a schoolteacher and became county superintendent of schools, an elected and prestigious position in her day. She had taught her daughter Evelyn, Rae's mother, well. A quiet and unassuming man, Oscar, Rae's father, ran a successful ranch with a spread of good meadows and pastures and a large herd of cattle inherited from his father, one of the first homesteaders in the region. Mechanically inclined, Oscar had rigged his own little water-powered electrical generator and was always willing to help when Dad asked for mechanical advice. The Robersons were good neighbors but never on a first-name basis with my parents; they addressed each other as Mr. and Mrs. Roberson and Mr. and Mrs. Bertagnolli, the formality belying their status.

Rae had many worldly possessions: a bicycle, pretty clothes, and lunches with Hostess cupcakes, canned fruit held in an empty Ponds face cream jar and sandwiches made with store-bought Wonder Bread. Even as a young child, it was clear to me that the material and ethnic differences of our parents translated into standing in the community. Cognizant of the disparity but not envious of Rae's privilege, I participated vicariously in her life, fantasizing a different way of living.

Although I accepted our different family means, one Christmas I was painfully reminded of how that played out in benefits. Miss Beyda believed in celebrating holidays and each year we had a Christmas play. As she read the play to us, I visualized myself as the fairy and was convinced the part was meant for me. But in the end, Rae was the fairy all dressed in filmy cheesecloth with tinsel in her hair and a wand wrapped in tinfoil. I was an orphan child dressed in an old, faded dress that had to be torn here and there to make it completely ragged. The contrast and disappointment were almost more than I could bear and contributed to my growing sense of inferiority. Given Rae's chubby, rosy-cheeked, cherub countenance and my skinny body and sallow skin, we were probably appropriately cast. I would have made an unconvincing fairy.

STOCKING UP • 57

The following year, Miss Beyda redeemed herself somewhat when at Thanksgiving she cast me as a pilgrim daughter of mother Pearl. Although I had no speaking part, the black dress with tight bodice, long skirt and white cap and apron were some compensation. In another play I was a little brown bird hopping around the stage and was very pleased with this acting part.

Patriotism was not ignored in School District Number Two, which included schools in most of the mining camps in the area. Each year, one school was chosen and the children transported to the other schools to present a program. In our Armistice Day program, when schools celebrated the ending of World War I, I was the sound-effects person, more precisely, the bombs bursting in air. I stood back-stage at the piano and hit the two lowest keys on the keyboard while holding the foot-pedal down so that the sound boomed and reverberated. This was a very satisfying role for a shy child who probably would have frozen in a speaking part.

The most enchanting of these performances by schools in our district was a puppet show of Little Red Riding Hood presented by the Oakley School, which must have taken considerable work and practice to execute. We gasped as Red Riding Hood naïvely sallied into the cabin where the wicked wolf, masqueraded as her grandmother, was lying in bed ready to grab and eat her up.

As it happened, my association with Rae not only emphasized our different social standings, but also introduced me to the dark side of life. She had two siblings, Ione, a pre-schooler, and Charles, a year younger than herself, who attended school with us. Their ranch was half a mile from the school and in good weather, Rae and Charles walked home after school. Charles had the habit of dallying a bit along the way so that they rarely arrived home together. One day, he was unusually late in arriving. Alarmed, Evelyn drove up the road toward the school to look for him while Oscar searched the ranch. The road crossed a canal, which brought water to the little hydroelectric plant he had designed, and Oscar found Charles's dead body caught in the water wheel. Tagging along behind Rae, he apparently had fallen into the canal and was unable to get out of the swift-flowing current.

The shock of this tragedy shook the small community but was especially difficult for Oscar, who had built the generator that took his son's life. Upon my family's visit to pay our respects, Rae took me into the dimly lit parlor, appointed in deep-toned plush furnishings, where Charles lay in a casket. Dead. The meaning of the word came home to me full-force. Two of my uncles and one aunt, siblings of my mother, had died within less than three years of each other during my childhood. But their funerals seemed to be gatherings of visiting relatives, with death somehow obscured.

Charles's death was quite different. His body in the casket in the parlor made it crystal clear in my child's mind that something could happen to any of us that would end our lives and take us away from this world and all of our loved ones. The finality and mystery of death was fearsome and incomprehensible.

After our silent viewing, Rae and I went upstairs to her room where we tried to distract ourselves with her worldly possessions. Failing, we sat on the landing. Two little girls caught in the throes of life's vagaries, bewildered by the incomprehensible event, we sat with our arms around each other and sobbed. An unanticipated intruder had entered our lives. The spring rush of water had brought death along with the life it nourished. The aftermath was a wasteland of broken hearts and shattered dreams.

This tragedy occurred at the critical time in my development when I was separating from my mother, and it magnified my concern for what happened to us after we died. At times this kept me from sleeping and my whimpering would bring Mamma to my bedside with concern, asking what was wrong. My reply was always the same.

"Nothing, Mamma, I'm just thinking about the end of the world."

A monster she could have handled deftly, but the end of the world?

Mamma would stroke my head gently, tuck me in and assure me, "You don't have to worry; it's a long ways off."

This explanation did not allay my fears and told me that Mamma was also concerned with this future catastrophic event.

The dark cloud of the coming millennium seemed to permeate my childhood. I wonder now about its origin that perhaps came from that particular time in our social history. Or, perhaps, it arose from folk theology carried by my mother about Judgment Day, when we'd all confront God's final reckoning.

I have outlived all of the principle actors from that time in my childhood. Thinking back makes me more aware of my age, the passage of time and the stark reality, not of the end of the world, but of my lifetime. As many have written, the diversions we seek as well as our altruistic deeds and concern for others are often ameliorations for our fear of death. In the former case we try to forget death exists. In the latter, we seek to leave a bit of ourselves that will continue on after we're gone.

There are timely deaths, like Paul's, that came after a full and productive life with enough warning to prepare us for his parting. But to have a child taken is a great sadness to all who treasure the gift of life. The Roberson family never recovered from the death of Charles and eventually sold the ranch and left Wyoming. Almost a half-century later on a sunny autumn day I stood by Rae's coffin. I had not seen her since we were girls and she had changed beyond recognition. From my point of view we were still young women, "noon in the fullness of summer," at a prime time of our lives. Like Sometimes Creek with no refreshing tributaries at the end of the summer, the flow of her life had ended.

Opal one-room school and Miss Beyda. Barbara (third from left, back row), Rae and Florence (second row on left).

Best friend, Rae

Barbara (left) and Florence on first day of school

Mamma and DJ (in buggy), Barbara and Florence (1933)

New Shetland pony

· 4 ·

Fledging Among Women

In the aftermath of the first storm of the season, the weather has turned toward Indian summer. The snow has melted and days are mellow. By checking the position of the sun as it rises I can estimate how far it will move south each day—about the width of my thumb, held up at arm's length to the horizon over the East Rim. Just as the constant changing of the moon always startles me, the movement of the sun brings me a sense of engagement with the cosmos and a concrete reference for the passage of abstract time. It joins me with the hunters and gatherers of yore, who may have looked at the position of the rising sun on the horizon to calculate when they should start their migrations. I am not a sun worshipper, but here in this place with an unobstructed view of the horizon around me, it seems proper each day to pay homage to our brightest star, the source of light and life on our planet.

The migration of birds seems analogous to our life journey in that it is a manifestation of cohorts made up of individuals responding to a common stimulus. Of paramount importance in this inspiring and vexing mix is the positive response of humans to each other. In war, mutual concern for each other is paramount. But as Paul Shepard asserted in *Coming Home to the Pleistocene*, in our ordinary life cycles—from learning to walk, to being a student, to facing old age and death—we humans need others who share and support our concerns and challenges. Moments with others, some fleeting, such as my encounter with Eileen, have caused me to look at my life in a new way. Of special importance have been women, who entered my life at key times as if sent to take me by the hand.

Foremost among these women was my mother. Of humble birth and means, hard working, bright, and with a mind of her own, Mamma tempered Dad's lofty ideas and was a moral support for us daughters for as long as she was able. She expressed her love explicitly by creating a comfortable and aesthetic home, preparing delicious meals and showing concern for our health and needs. As I matured and my life became complicated by problems she had never experienced, she continued to support my efforts, although she didn't understand my challenges.

Isolated on the ranch without a telephone and easy access to doctors until after we were grown, she relied on folk remedies taught by her mother. Cod-liver oil was a part of our daily diet as well as some not-so-common homeopathic remedies. She mixed honey, sugar and lemon with Homenta, a patent medicine, for coughs. For dad's chest colds, she made mustard plasters and for my chronic tonsillitis she applied slathers of Vicks ointment and wrapped my neck and chest in lanolin-rich wool sheared from our sheep and held in place with pure woolen cloths salvaged from Dad's worn-out long underwear. She bought bricks of camphor from the pharmacy and wrapped pieces in a handkerchief and placed them in my pockets or pinned them to my underwear. I went off to school each morning saturated with the smell of menthol and to bed at night feeling like an itchy stuffed rag doll. If it had any preventive effect, the vapors that enveloped my being and permeated the schoolroom protected my schoolmates as well.

Eventually I had to have a tonsillectomy, which required several journeys to Ogden, Utah, where my parents went when major health problems arose. Dad drove Mamma and me to Granger, fifty miles east of the ranch, where we caught a train on the Union Pacific Railroad. After the first visit I was sent home with a list of foods to improve my anemic blood so that I wouldn't hemorrhage to death during the surgery, the fate of one of Mamma's cousins. I felt very privileged when foods such as brains, liver, and Jell-O were prepared especially for me. The tonsillectomy was a difficult experience with complications. But during the trauma of the surgery, I felt secure in Mamma's constant presence and undivided attention.

Not all of Mamma's cures and practices were successful or benign and some, learned from her mother, were shockingly archaic. An example was shaving the heads of four-year-old children, boys and girls, to ensure the growth of beautiful heads of hair as they matured. I was told that Barbara accepted this shearing as an adventure; she decided she'd be a boy and wore overalls until her hair grew. Socially shy by nature, I became neurotically afraid of strangers and would hide when visitors came to the house. I continued this behavior until I entered school with a scant head of hair, but the shyness lingered on, or perhaps always existed and was merely exacerbated by the shearing.

I have considered how this practice could have originated and suspect it came out of necessity in the crowded stone huts of our ancestors, in an attempt to rid children's thick tangled hair of lice. My response taught Mamma one thing: Each child is different and responds differently to the same circumstances. DJ, a tiny and lovely child, spared herself and my mother the ordeal of tampering with her doll-like Shirley Temple image. Although it took me years, I have forgiven my mother's transgression since it grew out of ignorance rather than malice. She believed that a woman's crowning glory was her hair. When our hair grew long, she put it up in rags—strips of sheet which she wrapped firmly around strands of hair into tight little bundles that felt like sleeping on pieces of wood. If we complained when she removed the rags and brushed our hair around her finger into ringlets, she explained that if we wanted to be beautiful, we had to suffer. For whatever reason, as an adult I have a thick, unruly head of hair.

During my early years, women other than Mamma were important to me. They were similar to my mother in background and demeanor but different enough to be other than she was. Their similarities were comforting; their otherness gave me a hint of the world at large. I still remember the way they looked at me whenever we met, always with interest, sincere affection and approval for this little person worthy of their attention and friendship and thought.

As a result, I was very close to Anna, my mother's dearest friend, and to Aunt Jennie, Mamma's sister. As I grew, their approving gaze never seemed to change. Anna had a cheery disposition and indefatigable impulse to serve others. Her pastries were heavenly. One of my memories of early childhood was a birthday cake she baked when I was three. After Anna's first husband died, she married Joe Dona, our favorite ranch hand. Anna and Joe returned to live in Italy late in life. After his death, I visited her several times, sometimes with Mamma.

Independent and assertive Aunt Jennie was an anomaly among women in our family. As a young woman, she divorced her abusive husband and set out on her own to make a living as a wait-ress in Ogden, Utah. She married Uncle Max and together they fashioned dignified and secure lives for themselves. Although childless, she showed her love to nieces and nephews as she had to me. I was able to be of some help to her during the last years of her life. I appreciated the positive regard these childless women showed for me during my childhood and tried to return the kind-ness in their old age.

In these early formative years Miss Beyda was an appropriate transition from my mother, while Rae and her family provided a preview into privilege and status. Stella Petrie came into my life with still another variant on womanhood. Educated and gra-cious, she was the wife of Pete Petrie, one of the owners of the Opal Mercantile and Hotel. She managed the latter. Childless, she showed sincere interest in our family and offered to keep us daughters when our parents were called away from home on busi-ness. Staying with her at the hotel was one of the delights of my childhood.

The Opal Mercantile, the only store in the small shipping center where I went to elementary school, occupied most of the first floor of a two-story brick building. To the rear of the build-ing an entrance opened onto the hotel lobby, which was deco-rated with mounted heads of buffalo, moose and elk. A staircase led to hotel rooms that occupied the entire second floor. Through French doors beyond the lobby were the Petrie's kitchen and par-lor; a suite of rooms upstairs, consisting of a sitting room, bath-room and bedroom, completed their living quarters. An equal and respected member in managing the hotel and home was the young housekeeper, Lena Borino, who replicated Mrs. Petrie's kindness to us and attention to details.

The ambience of the hotel was enchanting. We had our own bedroom and separate beds with ironed sheets and white bedspreads. Free to wander in and out of the rooms that were unoccupied, I favored a south-facing room where sunshine played on immaculate bedding and polished mahogany furniture.

The small parlor next to the hotel lobby contained many objects of art. One especially captured my fancy—a lovely, pink-hued marble angel sitting on a seashell and displayed in a niche about my height. Eye to eye with the sculpture, I ran my fingers over the satiny marble, marveling at how something so beautiful and flawless could be carved out of a piece of stone.

From the stairs I could reach a bison horn hung from a huge mounted head. When blown into, the horn made a loud trumpeting noise, strangely animal-like, as if it were calling again from the dead. The sound fascinated me and, one Saturday morning, I sat on the stairs and blew the horn repeatedly until the clerks in the Mercantile next door, apparently driven to distraction, beseeched Stella to take it from me. She explained gently that the sound was disturbing customers and clerks in the store next door and asked me to please hang the horn back on the bison head. I was dismayed that the sound so compelling to me disturbed others. This episode was a lesson in the limits of personal boundaries that can be so easily and unknowingly violated, especially by noise.

After dinner when weather permitted, Mrs. Petrie allowed us the unimagined delight of playing "No Bears out Tonight" in the lumberyard with the Opal children. She seemed to have none of the reservations held by Mamma who feared we might get lost or hurt if we played out after dark. We ran helter-skelter chasing each other among the stacks of boards and came back covered with sawdust and ready for a good night's rest.

Sundays were special when the Petries drove us to the Victory Theatre in Kemmerer for Shirley Temple or Walt Disney movies. In the evening when we returned, Stella and Lena served hot chocolate and deviled ham sandwiches on a big wooden tray with a brightly colored rooster at its center, which we feathered with olives and pickles secured with toothpicks.

Mrs. Petrie, always gracious and amiable, provided an example of a lifestyle where aesthetics were not as organically and pragmatically grounded as they were on the ranch. She brought amenities into our lives, without any utilitarian function whatsoever, merely to enhance the quality and pleasure of living. Each visit with Stella Petrie was a window into still another world.

The Opal Mercantile, where we waited for our parents after school each day, was an educational experience in its own right. One large room accommodated all human and ranching needs from groceries to harnesses. As one entered, the grocery counter was on the right with glass-fronted bins of candy and dried beans sold in bulk; behind it on shelves were patent medicines. The meat counter was at the rear. In the center aisle were sundries such as reading glasses, wallets and Chamberlain lotion, whose fragrance I preferred among all others I sniffed. On the left side of the huge room was a ladder on a rail that could be pushed to the appropriate spot to access boxes of shoes and Levis, overalls and woolen jackets stacked to the ceiling. Guns in cabinets and saddles hanging from hooks were at the back, and beyond at the very rear of the store was the post office with its brass-trimmed mailboxes for each of the patrons. One could also buy ranch supplies—grain, feed pellets, hay, straw, coal oil and coal for heating and cooking stoves—stored down the road in a big warehouse. Every need of family or ranch could be purchased in the one-roomed Opal Mercantile, the shopping mall of those days.

As we awaited our parents, Barbara and I were allowed to

wander around to our hearts' content. I preferred, however, to sit on the warm radiator in front of the big glass window at the front of the store where I could watch for my parents and observe people coming and going. I'd eavesdrop on conversations of shoppers with jovial Finn Petrie, who wrote an award-winning column in the weekly *Kemmerer Gazette*. With more than my share of curiosity about the adult world, I listened wide-eyed to discourse on community and world events: Great floods in the Ohio and Mississippi valleys were devastating people and property. A suspect named Bruno Hauptmann, proclaiming his innocence to the end, had been sentenced to death in the kidnapping and murder of little Charles Lindbergh, Jr., who was found buried near his home. Much to the chagrin of my father, President Roosevelt was elected once again. At a gas station near Kemmerer, Sparky Dawson bludgeoned her husband to death with the handle of a gas pump. I gave much thought to how this woman could have contrived and carried out such a terrible deed. Did she sneak up behind him and hit him on the head?

Although from an early age I had a rudimentary sense of right and wrong, my childish mind attempted to unravel the constant reminder by Mamma to be good. As with most children, the first moral voice I heard was my mother's, a circumstance that, some psychologists insist, sets men and women forever against the voices of women no matter what they are saying. Women may not be any more ethical than men, but the unwritten societal plan for most women, set in place by their biology, is to care for, protect and guide their young children. Reprimands and warnings come with that territory. As a result, the sound of our mothers' voices follows us throughout our lives.

When I was a young child, my family did not attend church regularly. My parents, however, were professed Catholics and Mamma tried to follow minimal precepts of the church. The spring I reached the age of seven, she decided it was time for Barbara and me to have our First Communion. She drove us over muddy, unpaved roads to Saint Patrick's church in Kemmerer to consult the priest.

Father O'Connor—later in life he became a monsignor—gave Mamma a little brown paper book called the *Baltimore Catechism* and the responsibility for instructing us. The booklet contained a series of questions with answers we were to memorize. Little of what I repeated gave me true insight into Catholic doctrine. To the contrary, it seemed to further mystify the meanings of life, death and afterlife. Nonetheless, I was convinced that the key to heaven was locked in that little booklet and I took Mamma's instruction seriously.

It is challenging for an adult, let alone a child, to cognitively understand the Holy Trinity, three beings in one God. Or to fathom how Jesus could die, rise up from the dead, ascend into heaven and in three days come back to earth to instruct others. The symbolic and deeper meanings of these mysteries set apart from ordinary experience were not elucidated. All such teachings were to be accepted through faith. I was puzzled as to how to acquire this faith and was concerned that I might never reach heaven if I failed.

As the big day approached for my First Communion, I became more and more anxious about failing the test and being banished forever to purgatory, or, Lord help me, to hell. Barbara received her First Communion with me and, in her usual confident manner, was unperturbed by it all. On the Saturday preceding the big day, we went to town to have our hair styled and set, make our first confession and practice marching into the church with the other children. Our white communion dresses, veils and shoes, purchased earlier, added to the mystique of this important occasion.

On that Saturday afternoon, the comforting ambience of the little church, with subdued light pouring from its lovely stained glass windows, stood in contrast to the dark confessional at the rear of the church. When my turn came, I clip-clopped down the isle, opened the door, closed it behind me and knelt. My trips to the cellar hadn't prepared me for this kind of darkness. A door on a little screened window slid open. Behind it I could barely discern the figure of the priest.

"Bless me Father for I have sinned," was my opening supplication. Although I have no idea what I conceived as sin or what I confessed, I remember emerging greatly relieved to have been forgiven. I said my penance and on the drive back to the ranch came down with a splitting headache. Too sick to eat that night, I went to bed without supper and complied with mandatory fasting. The next morning in my white frilly dress and veil, pale and wan, I lined up with the other children and with lighted candles marched into the church. After the beginning of Mass, the priest paused to question communicants and blessed me by passing me by. It's almost over, I thought—then the girl next to me set her veil on fire and I promptly fainted.

Watchful matrons extricated us from a mass of burning candles and singed veils and hair, and whisked us out of the church. With the fire extinguished and spirits restored, I entered the church in a somewhat otherworldly daze. On wobbly legs, I walked to the rail and, after receiving communion, was flooded with a sense of relief and wellbeing. If I just kept at it, perhaps I'd get to heaven after all.

Through my early years I was grounded psychologically in the activities and topography of the ranch. But nothing was more important to my socialization than school, which presented new challenges and new knowledge, the mastery of learning concepts and skills, and provided, via an organized classroom, a built-in social structure into which I could fit. With wide-eyed amazement, I watched the maneuverings of my peers, so self-confident and assured.

During the Depression, the mines began to shut down. School District Number Two had to cut back and closed the Opal School. Students were bussed to Diamondville, a mining town twelve miles from the ranch, where I entered the fourth grade in the Burgoon School. Named after its rotund principal, the school consolidated students from the surrounding mining camps, ranches and railroad stops into grades one through nine. Elmer, a mechanically gifted high school graduate who lived in Opal, had spent the summer building a school bus out of wood, tin and salvaged automobile parts. He painted it red and was hired as the bus driver. Starting at Opal, with stops along the way for ranch and railroad children, he dropped us off at the Burgoon School and went on to deliver the older students a mile away at Kemmerer High School, which was in School District Number One. Each afternoon Elmer repeated the process in reverse, driving the seventeen miles back to Opal to deliver children home.

Debarking from the bus, I greeted cheerful Mr. Burgoon, who met us each morning, and I then headed for the classroom that housed the third and fourth grades. The bell rang and we quickly took our seats at desks screwed to the floor in straight rows. Miss Eastman stood tall and straight and dignified at the head of the class. The lesson plan for the day and week, as well as the dresses she wore, seemed immutable. Very different from the gentle and imaginative Anna Beyda, my teacher during my first three years of schooling at the Opal School, Marie Eastman was as precise and predictable as the pendulum in the big clock on the wall. Her goal was to bring all students to proficiency in reading, writing and arithmetic. We colored between the lines on mimeographed paper.

Miss Eastman spiced up the daily routine with activities that pitted us against one another, our abilities or disabilities laid bare for all to see. At the blackboard, working individually or in teams, we raced against each other to develop speed and accuracy in mathematics. As my skills grew, I looked forward to these contests. Taking turns reading out loud also revealed our proficiency or incompetence to the entire class. The person who out-spelled everyone in written and oral tests would compete in district and county spell-offs and might even go to state and national meets. I was, and remain, a phonetic speller and knew beyond doubt that Shirley would be the undisputed champion in our school. Working toward certificates in penmanship in my own time, I was convinced I could never achieve the accuracy of Marguerite, who precisely replicated the Palmer Method of Penmanship. Nonetheless, I enjoyed tracing the regimented loops and up and down movements, executed over and over with the entire arm, as well as the prescribed, graded exercises, some written with pen and ink. But bringing a paper to perfection and passing Miss Eastman's scrutiny was not easy. Within this closely structured classroom, I assumed an underachiever niche: I dreamed of excelling but set my expectations comfortably below my abilities.

Recess presented more challenging problems where a competitive spirit flourished unchecked. Whether in jump-the-rope, hopscotch, jacks, playing basketball in the old dance hall or walking the high, rickety wooden fences that swayed and frightened me, the object of endeavor was to be number one. The most serious of these activities was softball. Teachers rarely supervised the games except before an upcoming competition with the Frontier School, our prime rival.

During school and afterwards on the school grounds, town children assertively established a hierarchy of positions for catchers and base players. Without the advantage of this after-school cohort, I was always placed somewhere in left field, metaphorically and literally, thankful to be there, and hoping desperately no fly balls came my way. The position of pitcher was the only one contested and Rosie and Minnie literally fought for it and, in one instance, one of them ended up with a black eye. As we practiced and played other schools, as was the norm, winning was always the point of the game rather than giving everyone a chance to play or just having fun.

At home on the ranch I tried my best to hone my skills by bouncing a ball off the porch roof and catching it, which did little to increase my eye-hand coordination. Nevertheless, participating in sports, even in minor positions, was the delight of my pre-puberty days, as well as the context for my fantasies that revolved around making home runs and being a star. Thrown into this competitive mix with aggressive, tough children, I learned to skirt conflict without forming allegiances.

When we advanced to a new room in the fifth and sixth grades, Mr. Edwin Hampton, my first male teacher, was the main course of study. Somewhat of a sissy by local standards, he was handsome, clean-shaven, and neat, with thick, straight hair combed back and had a warm and caring demeanor and a scent of Old

Spice—the perfect teacher for pre-puberty girls. He came with us onto the playground at recess where we gathered admiringly around him.

For Christmas he gave us each a picture painted on a cross-section of a tree limb, done by his artist mother. A tiny cabin in the woods with smoke coming out of the chimney and a light in its window is pictured in a snowy landscape. An ice-covered stream meanders in the foreground and shimmers in a colorful sunset. This idyllic scene, abounding in images of contentment, brought me aesthetic pleasure as well as a sense of ownership. To this day it sits on a bookshelf with a coyote skull and other memorabilia I've gathered through the years.

According to the French philosopher Gaston Bachelard, our human attachment to home, represented by a cabin in the woods with a light in its window, touches a chord in our heart held in common with others. That shared meaning may have led Paul and me to build our cabin in the Hoback Basin. I must admit to feeling my heartstrings plucked each time I return after dark and see a light I had forgotten to turn off, shining serenely from the cabin window.

A field trip in the spring to Fort Bridger was probably my first great educational travel adventure. Here Jim Bridger had lived with his Indian wife, and pioneers, traveling west to Utah or California, stopped to rest and take shelter. A picture of us gathered around Mr. Hampton on this field trip reveals our love for our caring teacher. I am wearing high riding boots and jodhpurs, popular at that time among young women, and probably bought at great sacrifice for Barbara and me by our mother who wanted us to be in fashion. Our school dresses, although inexpensive, always seemed elegant compared to the girls with WPA sack dresses made from thick, printed cotton chicken-feed and flour sacks, from which my mother made dish towels.

These were the years of the Great Depression. Franklin Delano Roosevelt with his New Deal initiated changes that provided relief for the unemployed and assistance for bankrupt ranchers and farmers. The Work Project Administration (WPA) involved jobless men in projects to improve communities and their resources; they built an outhouse for us on the ranch. The Civilian Conservation Corps (CCC) placed male youth in conservation work on forests and degraded land. The Federal Land Bank provided loans for farmers and ranchers like my father, to sustain them through the economic crash exacerbated by a prolonged and severe drought. Each week boxes of food were distributed to families on Relief, including crates of oranges, which I eyed with envy, when schoolmates brought them to school each day.

The plummeting prices for sheep and wool and the persistent drought placed our ranch in constant jeopardy of foreclosure and set my folks scraping as they fell deeper into debt. One of the governmental solutions, initiated to solve the problems of drought and over-grazing during the Roosevelt era, irked my father. The government paid ranchers to reduce their herds by mandating the killing of a designated number of sheep. None of these animals were to be given away since that would have kept people from buying meat in stores and further impacting the failing economy.

As I recall, the government paid my father three or four dollars per head for sheep he had bought at about five times that price just before the great market crash at the end of the Hoover years. Dad, who did not see the sense in this plan, invited everyone he knew to come to dress out sheep to take home after the mass slaughter had been carried out and properly supervised. The ranch was teeming with men carrying off a supply of mutton in their cars. We hauled the leftover carcasses to a hillside where their bleached skeletons stood as a testament to the chaos of the

Great Depression. Later when we contributed to the war effort, we gathered the bones from the hillside and sold them to the government to make fertilizer.

In an ironic way, this reiterated the plight of the bison in the settlement of the West, which were slaughtered to solve the so-called Indian Problem and intended to rob native people of the source of their subsistence. Bleached bones of thousands of bison were later gathered and shipped by railroad to cities where they were made into fertilizer, which would be shipped back to improve production on the land the bison once roamed.

At times, we daughters would be asked to get cleaned up in anticipation of visits to certain Italian families who had money to loan—a successful merchant, a man who had made a fortune (and saved it) during the Alaska gold rush and a distributor of beer and liquor. We sat quietly listening to the talk that ended with a handshake. Dad handed over a check that paid the interest and some principal on the previous loan, and received another loan for the coming year.

At other times we waited expectantly for a visit from Mr. Baer, the traveling representative of the Wyoming Production Credit Association. Somehow Dad didn't connect this part of Roosevelt's recovery plan with the government control that he so adamantly opposed. Mr. Baer had a non-threatening way about him as he visited with my parents and audited my mother's financial records. Mamma set before him operating expenses from the previous year and estimated income for the coming year from projected sales of wool and lambs. From these figures, he negotiated the amount of the loan approved for the coming year. Kind and friendly and genuinely interested in my parents, Mr. Baer showed faith in their ability to work through their debts and pay back loans and interest each year. But he expected accountability and a strong case for the use of new funds. Undoubtedly props in the case, we children were expected to sit quietly and politely through these money-borrowing sessions as the transactions proceeded. Although unaware of the details of these meetings, we listened attentively, sensing the gravity of the situation.

This financial documentation tested Mamma far beyond her accounting skills. For weeks preceding the meeting, during every spare moment, she would sit at a card table doing the books. Often following such meetings with Mr. Baer, she would be stricken for days with skull bursting migraines and vomiting until she drew up nothing but bile. In her room with blinds drawn, I stood on tiptoes peering over the high brass bed (in which I now sleep), at the stricken woman lying with a cool cloth across her brow.

"How are you feeling, Mamma?" I would whisper with concern.

She would respond as best she could and ask if I'd dip the cloth in the cool vinegar water and apply it to her forehead. Dad administered to her and, with Barbara's help, he took over the cooking during these times while I hovered nearby to do Mamma's bidding. This often included instruction to prepare *panada*, an Italian remedy: a mixture of water, bread, and butter simmered together until it became a bland thick soup, guaranteed to settle the sickest of stomachs. The poignant scene emerges with absolute clarity as I recall my concern for my mother lying stricken helplessly in pain. Her suffering through this once-a-year ordeal was relieved when my parents finally consulted a professional accountant who instructed Mamma in simple bookkeeping procedures.

Complicated gender relationships and tragedies of various kinds intruded on my innocence. It was whispered that one of the older girls in my sixth grade class was pregnant. I watched her stomach grow under her sack dress but couldn't imagine how such a thing could happen. She did not return to school the next year and I still wonder about the fate of this hapless child mother.

My mother once asked me if I understood about men and women and did I want to ask her anything. "I know all about that," I said dismissively, although I hadn't the faintest clue. I had certainly seen enough copulation in the barnyard, but I couldn't extrapolate this to what transpired between a man and a woman. As I grew, so did my curiosity and misconceptions.

A schoolmate with nephritis died one summer, and the father of a classmate committed suicide. These events touched me deeply as did the circumstances faced by many of my classmates. One in particular, a motherless girl, who lived with a less than admirable father. She was not clean or well groomed, and when she took me to her house for lunch one day I was dismayed by the conditions under which she lived. She was frightened of her father and my heart still goes out to this poor waif who bore the scars of abuse.

The sense of belonging to a group became very important to me at this age and, although I'm not sure they saw me as such, I adopted various girls as my friends. Some took me to their homes during lunch break. I remember Tena Annala, Shirley's mother, and the aroma of fresh-baked bread and Finnish coffee brewing in her warm and welcoming kitchen. Peggy Flatterer, the postmistress and Margaret Verne's mother, invited me to stay over. In their home I first tasted delicious Scottish scones dusted with powdered sugar. However, I found rhubarb sauce, which I had never tasted before, impossible to swallow. Seeing my difficulty, Peggy assured me I didn't have to eat it. I was embarrassed and felt it terribly rude and wasteful to refuse to eat what one was served. But, try as I might, my throat would not cooperate. As previously noted, since then I have acquired a taste and appreciation for this sturdy, cold-weather plant.

After a hard day at school, Barbara and I boarded the yellow school bus, which by this time had replaced our first homemade version. A little building about the size of an outhouse was erected at the bus stop to shelter us as we waited for the bus each day. When the weather allowed, we walked the two-mile stretch home to the ranch. Arriving there we always found a simmering pot of soup, and Barbara and I served ourselves a bowl to which we added slices of fresh *tuma* cheese and homemade bread.

While we ate, we listened to radio serials, "Jack Armstrong the All-American Boy" and "Little Orphan Annie," whose adventures and mysteries we followed religiously. With the official badges, purchased with Wheaties box tops, we deciphered the daily coded messages, which provided clues to the coming adventures for Jack, the hero. On days when we walked home from the school bus stop but wanted a ride, we blew the whistle purchased with Ovaltine lids, which brought Punjab to Annie's rescue. But neither our parents nor a faithful genie seemed to receive our message.

These programs inspired my cohort of girlfriends at school to create our own serial adventures, coded messages and a secret society. We gathered old jewelry and buttons from our mothers and buried them in a matchbox under the porch of the abandoned Mountain States' Trading Company store. At recess, we would run to the old building, about a block from the school, and crawl under the porch, periodically retrieving our treasure and convincing ourselves that there was a ghost that haunted the premises and appeared from time to time. Fellow conspirators in this contrived adventure, none of us would admit that we had made it all up. Without television, videos or computer games, we created our own serial adventures.

The Burgoon School ushered me into a new awareness of self in a community of others, very different from the idyllic sand table days at the Opal School where we were little plants being tended. Weekly readers brought current events beyond our horizons into scrutiny. Competition increased and rewards were meted out disproportionately to teachers' pets, highlighting the entitlement of some students based on the standing of their parents.

From my earliest school days, I had a keen sense of the local social class structure, as replicated in the schools—a rather complicated hierarchy that was, however, not impenetrable. The unequal allotment of awards and privilege were not entirely divorced from the ability and gifts of the children. Children of English-speaking educated parents were naturally more prepared to excel in situations similar to their home environments. Schools , then as now, are an extension of the home and follow the trends of society. Yet many of the children at the head of the class were bright and serious sons and daughters of immigrant parents. With few exceptions, parents from this diverse mix believed in the advantages of education and were very supportive of their children's schooling. Eight years of education were mandated by the school districts, but most parents expected their children to graduate from high school.

Wealth, education, ethnicity and gender set the boundaries of entitlement established with the founding of this country. The West, with natural resources free for the taking, opened the way for wealthy investors. Destitute laborers from foreign countries and failed farmers from the East were recruited to extract those resources. The hierarchy of privilege was reflected in the placement and quality of company houses, repeated in mining and railroad communities, and replicated, to a certain extent, in the schools.

Societal expectations for young girls were quite different from those for boys. Women were expected to marry and be mothers and housewives. Single women worked as nurses, secretaries, waitresses, schoolteachers and housekeepers. A cadre of prostitutes resided at the infamous Southern Hotel, which continued its thriving business until the 1960s, when city fathers closed it.

The playground was the most egalitarian environment. Here, parental status or privilege carried no sway over individual assertiveness and prowess. My schooling may have introduced me to exclusion and social stratification, but also to the fact that ability and self-determination leveled the playing field. Class reunions have shown that despite humble beginnings for some of us, we all have achieved middle class prosperity. We have a strong feeling of commonality and little distinction in terms of class, race, or ethnicity; our clothes are tailored from the same humble cloth and they fit us equally well. It's enough to make one believe in the American Dream.

Aunt Jennie (right) at Jim's Cafe (late 1920s)

Aunt Jennie

*Florence and Barbara,
First Communion (1934)*

School bus station

DJ, 1935

Fifth grade class on field trip to Fort Bridger.
Florence second from left.
(Mr. Hampton, insert right)

· 5 ·

Turning

On forays to and from Jackson Hole for groceries, I drive the switchbacks in Hoback Canyon very slowly. Without impatient summer tourists tailgating me I can take my time and enjoy the equinox ambiance. The colors in the canyon are much more vivid than in Hoback Basin where most of the leaves have fallen. Anglers in meditative poses stand knee-deep in the cold, clear waters of the Hoback River surrounded by golden cottonwoods, yellow-green willows and crimson-leaved bushes, all capped by a brilliant blue sky.

Autumns come in many colors. The array of maple, redtwig dogwood and chokecherry bushes brings red to the canyons. Under stress of frosts and in order to survive the winter, plants send chlorophyll and starches from their leafy shoots into their roots for storage. Leaves are left with pigments that are no longer needed. Colors after a long, dry summer seem to me more vivid, whereas an early, hard frost can turn the leaves a disappointing brown. But a cold storm with high winds in any year can send the leaves flying and cut short the glory. This year, for whatever reason, leaves are lustrous as if lit from within. The peak in fall colors, like rainbows and sunsets, lasts only a fleeting moment so I slow down and take it in.

By the autumnal equinox, along with other "bluebirds," I am usually preparing for the move south to my home in Salt Lake City. But this year I'll stay through the winter. Grandson Jason, a student in radiation technology at Saint John's Hospital in Jackson, will be available should I need help. Although I have passed many winters in Wyoming, I have yet to spend one in the Hoback Basin. I anticipate the experience with interest but also some dread of the mythic winters that residents talk about.

But that's in the future, and I'm here now in this season that instills deep appreciation, both aesthetic and spiritual. Below the embrace of the high mountains, the textured mosaic of sun-drenched conifers and aspens magnifies my spirit and makes me thankful. These summer quarter days, when the cycle of growth is ending, somehow fill my heart with hope. Lingering memories of anticipation for the beginning of school may explain part of this proclivity. More importantly, it brings back the time when as a young college student I was given the chance to start over.

Yellow leaves were falling outside the window of a basement room lined with rows of empty cots. It was September of 1946, and the University of Wyoming faced an unexpected over-enrollment, so it set up temporary housing in the basement of Old Main, one of the first edifices built on campus, to accommodate veterans back from the war and dalliers like me. Apparently the university was succeeding in placing students in permanent housing, since

a woman, sitting across the room on her cot and smoking cigarettes, and I were the only ones left. I kept checking the bulletin
board in the hallway, and when my name finally appeared on a
list, I intended sharing the good news with her, but she had suddenly disappeared.

I packed quickly and loaded my luggage on a cart and headed across campus to Knight Hall, where I had been assigned. The
day was sunny and warm and golden. Happy to leave the overflow
quarters in Old Main, I felt as light as the falling leaves drifting
under trees and along the sidewalks. It had been a hard summer,
but things were looking up.

As I pushed the cart across campus, I thought of the ranch
where shipping of the lambs would be in full swing. By then Dad
would have culled the dries, ewes that had not raised lambs, from
the herd. If I were there I'd be bedding down these old biddies in
the sagebrush foothills near the ranch each evening. Two things,
according to Dad, were anathema when herding sheep: losing
them or running them, which would make them lose weight.
Come shipping time, he would recruit me to trail the culled ewes
to Opal and caution me to go slowly to allow the sheep to eat
their way over the five-mile trek to the railroad pens. Dad would
be waiting there when I arrived and we'd allow the sheep to slake
their thirst at the watering troughs before driving them into a cor-
ral where they'd spend the night without food or drink. Every
extra pound they retained in their stomachs would count next
morning when they would be weighed before shipping. To replace these culls, Dad would supplement the breeding herd with
some of our own prime ewe lambs and additional mature ewes
that he'd purchase.

At Knight Hall I waited in line and was finally issued a key and as-signed a room. When I arrived I was surprised to find the woman from Old Main there unpacking her things.

"It looks as if we are going to be roommates," she said with a smile.

"So it seems," I replied without enthusiasm. Long before the no smoking bans, I had just spent the previous two years with roommates who smoked and, as a non-smoker, I was not particu-larly thrilled with the prospect of another.

Tall and poised with a direct gaze and a quick smile, she openly related her life story as we unpacked and arranged our belongings. Dorothy Tupper (Dottie or Dot if I preferred) had been discharged from the Army Nurse Corps and had just re-turned from Southeast Asia, where she had served during the war. First sent to Manila, she was evacuated with the soldiers when, in 1942, the war with Japan was not going well and our soldiers were in retreat.

She went on to explain that this was her second attempt to earn a degree from the University of Wyoming. Coming from a family dry farm on the Nebraska/Wyoming border, she had first enrolled as a high school graduate with a major in elementary education. Unmotivated, unhappy and overweight, she dropped out and entered the School of Nursing at Creighton University in Omaha, Nebraska. She loved nursing, lost weight, gained con-fidence, and, upon graduation, joined the Army. Now with the G. I. Bill she was pursuing a degree in zoology, which included pre-medicine requirements. Her long-term goal was to enter Co-lumbia University for a graduate degree to qualify her to teach nursing at a university. She did not elaborate on the horrors and suffering of war she had undoubtedly witnessed.

Rushing off to an appointment I had made with the Dean of Women, I avoided giving her any details about me other than that I was also a junior majoring in zoology and from a ranching family. With a last name like Bertagnolli, it was obvious that I was Italian. I was hesitant about revealing much more to this woman who was to be my roommate. She was a chain smoker and quite old, twenty-seven to my nineteen years. My biases told me we wouldn't be together for long.

Dr. Gallagher, the Dean of Women, looked like she had just stepped out of a movie. Tall, statuesque, and stern, she epitomized higher education authority and scared me half to death. She invited me to sit down, leafed through my folder, and then asked me what was on my mind. Tied up with guilt and worry, I blurted out my concerns: "I failed to make my grades at the University of California, and I want very much to succeed here. I'm going to study hard and am determined to do well, but I want my records kept absolutely confidential."

She reviewed my folder once more and then set it aside. Her demeanor softened but her look was direct and sincere. She assured me that I had nothing to be ashamed of and that all student records were held strictly in confidence. She clarified that all of my transferred credits were accepted and I was a junior in good standing and welcomed at the University of Wyoming. As we parted she reiterated that she had every reason to believe I would be successful and invited me to make an appointment with her whenever I had a concern. I left the office feeling that I had found a friend. This was a new beginning for me and I was determined to make necessary changes and become a conscientious student. With luck, I wouldn't have to see her again.

Two weeks later, I found a note from Dean Gallagher in my mailbox asking me to call her. Concerned, I responded immediately. She said she had received a rather strange call that day from my father, who was in town and wanted my bank account number. The Dean said she had not given it to him and thought I should know that he was staying at a hotel whose address she gave me.

Puzzled, I headed downtown. The walk, which I took often to Mass, always against a strong wind laden with pollution from coal-fired train engines, was difficult, especially when a cinder lodged in my eye. But it gave me time to sort through the various scenarios that would bring my father to Laramie and have him staying at a hotel in the red-light district. By the time I reached the hotel, I had pretty much sorted through the possibilities.

Looking around the lobby, I recognized a man asleep in a leather lounge chair. I walked over and kicked his foot. Startled, he jumped awake.

"Vincent, what is the big idea calling the Dean of Women and telling her you're my father?"

"I was out of money and needed to get those people up there on the ball."

"Where are the sheep, Vincent?"

"I don't know, I guess on their way to Green River."

Vincent was quite hung over and reeking of liquor as I escorted him into the café. I bought him breakfast accompanied with several cups of strong coffee. I then marched him to the ticket agent, to whom I explained Vincent's grave plight. The agent booked him on the next train, which arrived shortly. As he boarded the train, I handed him five dollars with the warning:

"You had better catch up with those sheep, Vincent, see that they're watered and fed, and arrive with them in Opal, or you're a dead duck."

I made another appointment to see Dean Gallagher to explain that the person that called was our sheepherder, not my father. She seemed thoroughly amused by the circumstances, quite different from the usual coed troubles she sorted through. I thanked her once more for her help and went back to my studies.

Since there was no telephone on the ranch, I wrote a letter to my parents telling them what had transpired. In about two weeks I received a letter from my mother. Vincent had arrived home with the ewes, which Dad had purchased in Nebraska to replenish the herd. They arrived in good condition and Vincent made no mention of the hiatus in his travels in Laramie. However, Mamma said, he soon quit and had gone to town to follow the usual life of a sheepherder—to buy new clothes and then spend his accumulated salary on drink and women. Broke and satiated he'd soon be looking for another sheepherding job to see him through the winter.

Despite the economic and social turmoil of the Great Depression my first six years of primary school were filled with the excitement of new discoveries and intellectual growth. I suppose I now idealize and romanticize those early years, but I sincerely carry forward positive feelings from those times. This was not the case with the next eight years, from junior high school until I entered the University of Wyoming as a junior. Adolescent angst and the cloud of war undoubtedly exacerbated the tumult of the years from 1938-46. Even before the declaration of war with the bombing of Pearl Harbor, the United States was up to its ears in the European conflict, supplying arms and assistance to the allies to stem German advances.

Moving into the seventh grade at the Burgoon School was a challenging transition. Although we remained in the same classroom throughout the day, three teachers took turns teaching us the different subjects. The teachers were as diverse as night and day and adapting to them and their idiosyncrasies was as much of an education as the subjects they taught.

Miss Sweet, a misnomer, raged in anger when we failed to grasp her explanations. However, I learned the rudiments of grammar by passing her tests on rules for tenses, grammar, spelling and punctuation, while constructing hundreds of diagrammed sentences to learn the parts of speech. She was passionate about the King's English and literature and one summer traveled to the United Kingdom. Returning with grand tales of the places she had visited, she assigned us passages to memorize from *The Rime of the Ancient Mariner* and *The Lady of the Lake*. Her frequent scolding about our errors or failures approached cataclysmic proportions, often ending in fits of coughing. She died early in life of cancer of the throat.

Mr. Barnett, a tall and lanky Ichabod Crane type, was full of jokes and humor. He taught us mathematics without much expectation that we would master the concepts but seemed to thoroughly enjoy teaching. Mr. Kelly, relaxed about personal cleanliness, was difficult to tolerate within a yard or two but he taught geography and agriculture and Wyoming history, all interesting to me. The games in the playground changed from fox and geese to being chased and teased by boys.

National Assemblies, traveling programs presented to grade schools during those Diamondville days, were thrilling and mind-expanding. At one on snakes, I fearlessly volunteered to stand before the entire school audience with a boa constrictor draped around my skinny neck. I proudly narrated this adventure to my mother after school and showed her the piece of snakeskin given me for my bravery. She seemed more puzzled than pleased by this fearless act, perhaps because she had more ladylike aspirations for me. I encountered this same quizzical expression many times during my life when my mother seemed thoroughly bewildered by my proclivities.

As I was entering the eighth grade, DJ entered the first. From the moment of her birth she was a very petite and adorable child, so tiny that Mamma determined to give her another year of growth before starting her in school. Unfortunately, the extra year made little difference and she could barely climb the steps into the school bus.

Armistice Day celebrations with speeches by veterans of World War I infused me with patriotism and pride in our country. Politics entered the school when, during elections, we were excused for free movies paid for by political parties. The logistics of supervising and being responsible for DJ on our mile-long walks to the Victory Theatre in Kemmerer, along with catching the bus afterward, were considerable. Even more worrisome were the notes from boys who wanted to sit next to me at the movies.

Besides these special trials there were also opportunities; hints of things to come. A special course in first-aid conducted by the county nurse in the Slovensky Dome, an old dance hall also used by the school as a basketball court, was especially exciting. A challenging learning experience from those Burgoon School days, it awakened my innate leanings to help others.

The sun, low in the southern sky, flooded through the kitchen windows and set the geraniums on the windowsill on fire. Mamma and I were cleaning up after Sunday dinner when the announcement came over the radio: The Japanese had attacked

Pearl Harbor. It was December 7, 1941. Our official declaration of war against Japan was followed by Germany's declaration of war against us. Although we had been providing the allies with supplies, this clarified our position unequivocally and caught us in a web of war that circled the globe. Several of our cousins had already been drafted on both sides of the Atlantic and our concern for relatives in Italy grew as their home territory became a battlefield. My immediate concern was for cousin Alex, who was among the first young men to be drafted into the army. He, the oldest grandson of Uncle Richard, with his younger brother Paul, had spent Christmas with us for years.

The declaration of war became another area of my concern in a school year full of new challenges. My parents had always been bothered by the poor conditions of the Burgoon School. A frame building with oiled wooden floors, it was clearly a fire hazard. Although it had plumbed water for drinking fountains, there were no indoor lavatories and the outhouses were poorly maintained and unsanitary. To add to my parents' concerns, they questioned the safety of the schoolyard, a portion of which had caved into an old mine shaft, leaving a crater.

Burgoon School in Diamondville and several other schools in nearby mining camps were in School District Number Two. Only a mile away, Kemmerer was in School District Number One, where the brick school buildings and modern lavatories were immaculately clean. Dad was a taxpayer in both school districts and he joined a few parents who decided that the only way to improve the Burgoon School was to consolidate the districts. At a referendum in the spring the Diamondville community unanimously rejected the proposal. Since Dad paid taxes in both districts, the next fall he decided that DJ and I should go to the school of his choosing. So he instructed me to stay on the bus with the high school students going to Kemmerer. There I was to register DJ in the Kemmerer Elementary School and myself in Kemmerer Junior High School. So in the ninth grade, at the end of which I would have graduated from the Diamondville School with my classmates, I entered a new school as a total stranger.

In 1942, the year I entered high school, we moved to Kemmerer for the school year and lived in the house where I had been born. During that year, Dad, accompanied by Mamma, had gone to Ogden for surgery for a benign bone tumor on his right arm. Through some surgical error, the doctor severed a nerve that left Dad with a crippled right hand. The doctor who performed the operation died, or I presume Dad would have sued him. Dad and Mom went on to the Mayo Clinic where the doctors corrected the problem with muscle transplants, which required considerable time and therapy to re-educate Dad in the use his hand.

Over their long absence, DJ stayed with family friends, Barbara was away at college and I stayed at the house in Kemmerer with Uncle Richard. He had always complained of a sick stomach and now this malady worsened. I worried about him but didn't know what to do other than to make him chicken soup. After the folks returned, they encouraged him to go to Ogden where he, too, had relatives and could receive medical attention. Uncle Richard did so but never recovered and in a few months succumbed to what may have been cancer. At about the same time, Grandpa Louis also died of cancer, followed in less that a year by Grandma Teresa. So in a short time, in 1943, the elders of my family left this world. None of them were really what we would consider old by today's norms. Uncle Richard was seventy and my grandparents only in their sixties. This was before the development of antibiotics and other medical treatments used today, which extend the lives of the elderly.

The war continued and our armed forces faced many defeats and progress was hard fought. Hometown boys were losing their lives. Patriotism grew into propaganda. Everyone was expected to give their all to the winning of the war. In rallies to sell war bonds at the local theatre, I was a reluctant Dorothy Lamar with a sarong held in place with scotch tape. As the boys went off to war, we girls were inducted into the home guard and learned to march in formation to commands. This may have been an embryonic form of homeland security in preparation for a possible invasion, which was very unlikely. More likely it may have been devised to give girls a sense of participation, as were the letters we were asked to write to service men from our home town to build their morale.

Like Joe, most of the men whom Dad had hired to do ranch work went back to the coal mines, which had stepped up production for the war. Consequently, we daughters had to take over the ranch work in the summers, including digging ditches. Food, gas and tires were rationed and the government asked us to collect old tires and scrap metal for recycling and bones needed for fertilizer.

Dad followed international news assiduously on the radio since one of the war fronts was in Italy, the home of his relatives. He opposed our going to war and insisted steadfastly that the Germans were good people and incapable of the atrocities claimed. Dad was not a Fascist and was very much against Mussolini, who had taken over Austrian Tyrol (Dad's birth place) after World War I, and had tried to Italianize it. Dad voted as a staunch Republican, was very much against Roosevelt and his New Deal and was conservative and isolationist, somewhat like the Libertarians of modern times. He made money during the Hoover administration and struggled to keep the ranch during the Roosevelt era. His orientation to politics was personal and measured in dollars and cents.

My attitude to school continued to deteriorate throughout high school. War became my major preoccupation, but I was also caught up in extra-curricular activities—homecoming, prom dances, dating, going steady, cheerleading, admiring the young Frank Sinatra, and the rest of it. I genuinely enjoyed girls' intramural basketball and volleyball games, although there was no organized athletic program for girls. A stereotypical air-head, I worried about being asked to a prom by a boy I disliked while waiting for an invitation from one I preferred. Even in my under-achiever mode, I slipped by with better than average grades, making it into the National Honor Society without expending much energy, and, concomitantly, without using the opportunity to expand my knowledge.

Consistent with my experience at Opal School, I was never selected for a leading part in a high school play but had hopes of making a splash with a minor role. In one, after walking on stage on cue, the leading actor inadvertently skipped several lines— the ones to which I was to respond—and I walked back off stage without saying a word. With that, my hopes of being discovered by a movie scout faded.

One exception to my lackluster high school vita was an essay written on a subject I took seriously. In the spring of my senior year, the Veterans of Foreign Wars sponsored a contest with the theme, "What it Means to Be an American." Miss Hocker, the speech teacher, was to choose a boy and a girl to present their speeches to the community. A recent confrontation with Miss Hocker, who acted somewhat as a counselor in the school, led me to believe she did not see me worthy of this honor.

She had asked me to drop by her room one afternoon after school and lectured me firmly about my lack of commitment to my studies. But more than my grades, she said she was concerned about my moral character and expressed how shocked she had been to learn that I had been drinking during an out-of-town basketball tournament. I admitted that the first criticism was justified but denied the second vehemently, demanding she tell me who had informed her of my purported transgression. Soon after this encounter, I asked my father to accompany me to the home of the woman Miss Hocker claimed was her informant, and I asserted before her and my father that the rumor she had started was absolutely false.

As a teen-age girl sensitive to my public image, I felt greatly wronged by this false accusation that blemished my all-important reputation. Like most adolescent girls, boys were very much on my mind. Since pre-puberty days, sexuality and spirituality had been ambiguous areas that caused me much tension. I had become a devout Catholic, strictly following the mandates of the Church. When I became interested in a boy, I first assumed a hard-to-get role like the ones played by Doris Day in the movies. Under popular demand and in accord with the norms of the day, I had several steady boyfriends, all of whom were very fine young men. I appreciated the attention and admired boys very much but formulated rules of conduct that satisfied my own conscience. I did not want to be seen as either wild, boy crazy or loose and definitely did not want to "get into trouble." At a time when I dearly needed the mentorship of a mature and understanding woman, Miss Hocker's attack was devastating.

The night before my speech was due, having procrastinated as usual, I set my alarm for the wee hours of the next morning. Half asleep, I sat in my bed with a notepad and seriously considered the theme: What it means to be an American. The theme raised a more personal question for me: What does it mean for a girl to be an American in a world where boys are asked to sacrifice their lives? At this time we were living in Kemmerer during the school year and I began writing about the common wonders and blessings of this small, ordinary town, which I observed as I walked to school each day. Still in a somewhat contemplative mood when I delivered the speech that day, I was astounded when I looked up to see hard-hearted Miss Hocker wipe away tears. Perhaps in partial compensation for her misguided questioning of my character, she selected me as one of the two winners to deliver our speeches to enthusiastic citizens' groups. This was my first gratifying experience of writing personal narrative.

No one was more surprised than my teachers when my scores on college placement tests were among the highest in my class. I had been tracked in a non-college bound program with classes in shorthand and sewing and no advanced college preparatory classes. When our scores were posted, a classmate, whose sister was attending the University of California at Berkeley, suggested that I apply there. I was accepted but was unprepared for navigating its academic rigor.

"You're lost, aren't you?" I was standing at an exit from the university campus when a handsome man carrying a huge camera asked the question. Dressed in a skirt I had made, a white blouse, hose and high-heeled shoes, I assumed that I blended with the crowd and no one would recognize my confusion. That he had seen through my cover and quickly assessed my predicament caught me off guard and I admitted that, yes, I was lost. I had walked to campus that day from my cousin's house where I was staying until a dorm room opened for me. After a long morning of orientation and registration, I was on my way home when I ended up at an unfamiliar gate to the university. The man offered to show me the way back to the proper entrance, giving me a tour of the campus and taking pictures along the way.

In a week or so a package arrived in the mail with the pictures he had taken and a return address for the San Francisco Chronicle. Although I don't remember his name and never saw him again, I still have the pictures he sent that remind me of his unusual sensitivity, and kindness and honesty. Atypical of any male I had ever met, this absolute stranger, in a fleeting moment, introduced me to the possibilities of genuine friendships with men.

It was September of 1944 when I had left home by train for the University of California at Berkeley with my wardrobe, most of which I had sewn that summer, and belongings packed in a steamer trunk. The next two years on journeys to and from California, I rode trains brimming with servicemen heading for deployment or returning from the Pacific. The train ride, for a naïve seventeen-year-old who had never been beyond northern Utah, was an education in itself. Unaware of the challenges ahead, I stepped off the train into California, a lush wonderland in stark contrast to the arid steppe of Wyoming.

With deep sadness, I said good-bye to high school friends in the service as they stopped by on their way to the Pacific war. Meanwhile, radicals on campus recruited students into the Communist Party and rumors spread throughout campus about the clandestine operations in the cyclotron on the hill. I hiked there one day to look at it from a distance, trying to imagine the secrets guarded behind the high electrical fences.

In April of 1945 I was at the amphitheatre, standing in line at the break of dawn. I wasn't about to miss an event I had awaited since the beginning of the war. The first meeting of the United Nations was taking place in San Francisco and leading delegates had been invited to a convocation at the University of California. Seated in the front row of the amphitheatre, I was awestruck by the dignity and stature of the representatives: Anthony Eden of the United Kingdom, General Jan Smuts of South Africa, France's General Charles De Gaulle and our own white-haired Secretary of State, Edward Stettinius.

A highlight in my days at the university, this meeting gave me hope that peace would come to the world. But that summer, at home and working in the hay fields, I was appalled to hear that our country had dropped nuclear bombs on Hiroshima and Nagasaki. By fall, when I returned to the university for my sophomore year, Japan had surrendered.

War had overshadowed my first year at the university. Our girls' dorms entertained returning service men still in their fatigues and the wounded, many amputees, who had endured unbelievable miseries fighting in the Pacific. Scarred from the war, many were still wearing their combat boots, which I admired. The following summer in Wyoming, back on the ranch, a package arrived from one of the soldiers. Home and discharged, he had sent me his boots.

During those war years, the smell of death hung over the world. For countries that had lost the war and were involved in fighting and protecting their homelands, losses of soldier and civilian lives were staggering. Although actual numbers will never be known, estimated military and civilian deaths include six to eight million Germans, two to three million Japanese and twenty-six million Russians in their long struggle, both as aggressors and allies. Countries like Poland that had been battlegrounds lost seventeen percent of their total population. The United Kingdom had about 300,000 war casualties and the United States, about 400,000. Over 200,000 civilians were killed in the two atomic bombs dropped on Japan. About sixty to seventy million lives were lost throughout the world. And added to that, European Holocaust victims are estimated at about six million. These vast numbers of casualties are incomprehensible, as are the reasons nations would engage in such mayhem.

I followed the post-war developments avidly, and for the first time in my life had serious disagreements with my father. Although I admitted that we had been propagandized throughout the war, I insisted on the truth of the Holocaust. He was unconvinced until ten years later when he and my mother went to Europe to reunite with relatives. There he learned the truth about the death camps. When Dad returned from that journey, he admitted to me that the tales of horror were true, although he, like the rest of us, was perplexed as to how such evilness could have transpired unchecked.

Throughout my first two years of college, I was very interested in courses such as geography, inorganic and organic chemistry and physiology. But I remained undisciplined in classes I did not like, such as the 'English' course, where the professor insisted that *Walden* was not about nature. I skipped Spanish classes because I didn't like the teacher. Miss Hocker had been wrong in her assessment of my morals, but she was absolutely right in her criticism of my poor attitude and study habits. I carried arrogance into those first years of college as a cover-up for my insecurities and closed-mindedness. Since I had no failing grades, I was in denial of the consequences of being down in grade points and, at the end of each semester, fully expected to bring them up with my final exams.

On the ranch that summer, when I received notice that I had not made my grades and could not return to Cal, I was bereft and cried and kept to my room. My parents were bewildered, not knowing what I had done wrong or what they might do to help. I finally decided to dig myself out of the hole of my own making and sent off applications to Northwestern University at Chicago, the University of Colorado and the University of Wyoming. When I received acceptances from all, I had a serious talk with myself. The war had brought my parents out of debt for the first time since the Depression and they would have sent me wherever I chose. But after considering how I had failed to take advantage of a wonderful opportunity at the University of California at Berkeley, I decided to stay close to home and attend the University of Wyoming, where tuition and travel expenses were much more reasonable.

It wasn't long before I shared my dark past with Dottie, my new roommate at the University of Wyoming. We discussed our academic histories and decided our main problem had been lack of motivation. With the same majors and similar academic records, we pledged to help each other adhere to a study schedule. The only thing I disliked about this new friend was her smoking, and I regularly begged her to quit. But in every other way, with a big heart and a generous spirit, a bright and active mind and an incomparable sense of humor, she was a godsend. We studied hard and proudly made the Dean's honor roll every quarter. An important contributing factor to our success was the exceptional teaching of Floyd Clark, professor of zoology, and George Baxter, his laboratory assistant at the time.

Dottie also felt it her duty to take me under her wing and teach me the essential knowledge needed by a young woman in the cruel world. We planned a weekend in Denver at the Brown Palace Hotel with the explicit purpose of measuring my capacity to drink alcohol—a vital bit of information she thought I needed to know. It was all very scientific. She bought a fifth of whiskey and we measured our capacities, shot for shot, and documented our responses. As I recall, I exceeded her limit. However, the morning after, my hangover felt terminal and may have saved me from alcoholism since to this day the odor of whiskey nauseates me.

The summer after our junior year, Dottie and I attended the University of Wyoming's science camp in the Snowy Range, where we enrolled in aquatic and terrestrial zoology. I received a working scholarship and was on the job each morning with the crew at 4:30 A.M., setting tables, helping the cook, serving students and professors, and, finally, up to my elbows in soapy water, washing the dishes in deep sinks. Along with cleaning the dining room, these chores were repeated with each meal. For this I was given free housing, meals and tuition.

The science camp was administered in collaboration with Dartmouth and Vassar Colleges, and, while serving these students their meals, I acted the part of a wild Wyoming cowgirl. I caught the eye of a handsome geology student from Dartmouth. Against the rules, we would sneak out of the camp during weekdays to Centennial for a beer. The best description of me that summer was sleep-deprived. My folks were disappointed when I did not come home at the beginning of the summer but were pleased when I finally arrived in time for haying. I had thoroughly enjoyed the field courses and now see that a degree in wildlife biology, one not encouraged for women at that time, would have been an appropriate major for me.

The next fall, my senior year in college, Dottie moved to an apartment near the hospital where she worked while she finished her degree. I pledged the Kappa Kappa Gamma sorority and was appointed scholarship chairman, of all things. Intramural sports competitions between the girls' dorms were a constant delight and I made the university's women's basketball and volleyball teams. The sorority enhanced my social life and through my sisters' efforts I was chosen homecoming attendant and inter-fraternity queen. I dated many fine young men, but fell in love with only one, who was dealing with a lost love. In the somewhat closed society of a sorority, I learned a bit more about class structure and entitlement, but also something about manners and social behavior that makes for a more gracious approach to life.

During that memorable equinox in 1946, two extraordinary women, Dean Gallagher and Dorothy Tupper, came into my life. Their mentorship and understanding, coming as it did on the cusp of my adulthood, made all the difference in my future development. They modeled independent and successful women and gave me courage to continue in college and earn my first degree.

On a cold day in February, half a century later, I drove Dottie through one of the worst blizzards I can remember from Laramie over a high wind-swept pass to Cheyenne for her radiation treatment. She had called to tell me she was dying of lung cancer and wondered if I could visit. I had driven to Laramie to be with her. While there she asked me to drive her to her radiation treatment. Knowing full well that the procedure would do little to allay her illness, I could not deny her wish to continue her struggle against death. We survived the hazardous journey but she succumbed about a week later.

Our friendship had continued unaltered throughout our adult lives until her death, when she was in her seventies. She had become a beloved professor and dean of the School of Nursing at the University of Wyoming and had mentored many nursing students, just as she had me. Her good work and generous spirit are carried forward to this day with an endowed scholarship fund for prospective nurses. Throughout her career, she never forgot me and always showed great concern for my welfare and interest in my children. And I shall never forget her. She came into my life at a critical time and helped me forge a new path.

(1939)

*Autumn in the Hoback Basin
(photo by Susan Marsh)*

High school Junior Prom, Florence on left (1943)

Leaving for UC at Berkeley (1944)

(1945)

With dorm mates (1945)

Bertagnolli family (1946)

With Dottie Tupper (right), field studies, University of Wyoming (1947)

With sorority sister Jackie Martinez Ferrall (right) (1948)

Homecoming royalty 1947

(1947)

Homecoming, University of Wyoming (1947)

· 6 ·

Bearing

It's October. Rain is falling as I pack my car with down sleeping bag, winter, clothes, snacks—and bear spray. Since Paul's death I have been consolidating his archives and editing his unfinished books. My latest project has been to review his audiotapes and notes on bears. My head is swirling with his words and voice. I need grounding; I need to see real bears.

Katherine (Kat) and Bernie Krause are in Yellowstone Park where he will be recording bugling elk and they have invited me to join them. It's the time of year when elk, bison, moose and wolves come down out of the high mountains to winter in geyser country. Bears are concentrating on eating to build fat for hibernation, which will soon begin. Except for a few stalwart animal watchers, tourists should be scarce and animals numerous.

I first met Kat and Bernie several days after Paul died when they stopped by to see me. We sat in my garden at the old house in Salt Lake City and talked. As was the case with many people who had come to know Paul through his books, they regretted not having met him. Hearing of Paul's terminal illness, Bernie, author, musician and well-known recorder of natural soundscapes, had sent Paul some of his recordings. Paul listened to them during the last peaceful days of his life and thus had met Bernie indirectly through his recordings. Since that first meeting, Bernie, Kat and I have enjoyed many special times together.

I've been anticipating this meeting with them but, as I lock the cabin and drive down the road, a dark cloud over the Hoback Basin descends on me. I suddenly feel old and alone. I miss Paul and our journeys together. The Tetons are cloaked in mist as I proceed along their base. In Yellowstone Park the saturated mauves and crimsons of berry bushes and shrubs are interspersed with white and charred tree trunks, memorials to the great fire of 1988. Descending the multicolored terraces at Mammoth, I maneuver the hairpin curves cautiously, wary of the ease with which I could miss one. Ignoring the dark gorge below, I steer the car carefully over the high bridge that crosses the Yellowstone River.

Bernie and Kat are waiting for me at Soda Butte in Lamar Valley. I park my car and join them in the warmth of their van and friendship. We drive back down the road past a group of wolf-watchers, take a road up the mountain to the south, park the car and hike a trail, pock-marked with wolf and bear scat, overturned rocks and diggings. On the crest of a ridge, under a Douglas-fir sheltering playful Canada jays, we scan the Grand Canyon of the Yellowstone below. Seeing no bears or wolves, we head back.

Darkness descends as we reach my car and I follow my friends to Cooke City, past bugling bull elk and their harems. After a hearty meal and good conversation in a tiny café, we drive to the motel and say goodnight. My room is cold. I turn up the heat, spread my sleeping bag over the covers, crawl in and soon fall sound asleep. I dream:

Bernie, Kat and I are attending a lecture on bears. The speaker walks in with a huge bundle wrapped in a bearskin and places it on a table. He explains that instead of lecturing on bears he has decided it would be more useful if we ate the bear he has just killed and roasted. He sets out the roasted meat and places the motley bear hide to the side. We gather around and begin eating, picking up the pieces of meat with our fingers. We eat on and on and on, never seeming to get our fill of the delicious, tender, sweet, succulent meat.

Embedded in the meat I keep finding bones, big beautiful bones, smooth as ivory and luminescent as pearl: A long bone that seems to be an usik, a penis bone; another that is wishbone-shaped but thicker and looks somewhat like a butterfly; a lovely spiral-shaped disc; and one shaped like a ladder. As I pluck them out, I try to categorize the bones according to function, but none seems to fit.

Suddenly, like a door slamming shut, my stomach cannot hold another morsel. The speaker, sensing our satiation, announces that we may now leave and take with us anything that remains.

"Anything?" I ask.

"Yes, anything," he replies.

Since no one else seems interested in them, I bundle the bones in my arms and wrap the bearskin around me. They infuse me with a sense of security and well-being.

I awaken in a sweat and crawl out of my sleeping bag and turn down the heat. This is not the first time I've dreamed about bears. A bear dream preceded my meeting with Paul, and I have had several since his death. As the dream fades, the taste of bear meat lingers. I have actually eaten bear meat twice, the first time as a child.

One summer day Dad had just returned after a visit to the sheep herds on our forest allotment in the Wyoming Range and was reporting back to Mamma. She was working in the kitchen, preparing for visiting relatives from Utah who were expected the next day. Dad related how Dominick, the camp jack, was treed by a bear that had been killing sheep. After the bear finally went away, Dominick climbed down, retrieved his gun from camp, tracked the bear down and killed it. As my father talked, he unwrapped a huge roast, not a leg of lamb as Mamma anticipated, but leg of bear. She was dubious about cooking it. Although her mother had taught her the fine art of cooking, she had never prepared bear roast. Dad assured her that it would be very good, but suggested they not tell the relatives what they were eating until after the meal. He cautioned, "Tilda, roast it a long time."

The next afternoon sitting at the big round table in the breezy dining room used only on hot summer days, I ate slowly, rolling each tender morsel of bear meat on my tongue as I listened to the conversations, anticipating the unfolding drama. When everyone had finished and was thanking my mother for the delicious meal, one of them asked as an afterthought, "By the way, Tillie, what kind of meat was that?"

"Bear."

"BEAR??"

After a long silent pause, animated conversation followed as they discussed bears and the sheepherder, bears in general and the experience of eating a bear. It was obvious to me, even as a child, that this was no ordinary event, but one with deeply felt prohibitions.

The next bear meal came about fifty years later in 1985, the year I met Paul and we became partners. In late summer I accompanied a friend, Walter Prothero, a professional hunter and outdoor writer, who had invited me on a journey he had planned on the Sheenjek River in the Arctic National Wildlife Refuge. We had first met when he was a participant in a writing workshop I offered with Edward Abbey in Arches National Park. Paul disapproved of this journey with Walt, but I wouldn't sacrifice my chance to see the National Arctic Wildlife Refuge. Reconciled, Paul gave me a copy of his latest book in press and wished me well.

Roger, the bush pilot, landed us on a sand bar on the upper Sheenjek River. We cached rafts and floating supplies and food stored in a fifty-gallon drum, which Walt sprayed with oven cleaner to deter bears. The iron drum, not the usual luggage, had attracted the curiosity of travelers when I boarded the plane in Salt Lake City. Instructed by Walt, I had filled it with dehydrated meals for thirty days on the river.

With the drum safely hidden in willows, we hoisted our backpacks and headed for the Brooks Range. In the high mountains after a hard hike, Walt killed a mountain sheep. Sheep steaks broiled on an open fire complemented our backpacking meals and we stayed on for about a week, exploring the high country of the Brooks Range. Silhouetted on the horizon or roaming the high slopes around our camp, grizzlies presented a fascinating and fearful sight. I read and re-read Paul's 1985 book, *The Sacred Paw: The Bear in Nature, Myth, and Literature*, during the long, twilight evenings as I tried to rationalize my fear of bears and clarify my feelings about Paul.

Off the mountain and back at our cache, we met Walt's hunting friend, who had just flown in. Now we began floating the Sheenjek River. Each evening we camped along the riverbank and each day hiked into the countryside. One evening after a solo hike, Walt walked into camp and came toward me with something in his hand.

"Here," he said, "give this to your friend." In my hand he placed a bear's bloody penis.

The next day, along with helping Walt salt and prepare the bear skin, I boiled the penis and removed and cleaned the *usik*, the penis bone that I would have prepared as a pendant for Paul when I returned to Fairbanks. These bones are prized and kept as mementos by native hunters. That evening we cooked some of the bear meat. Although it was delicious, I had some difficulty swallowing the first morsels. After reading Paul's book I had gained some understanding of the prohibition expressed long ago by my relatives. Beyond rejection of a food strange to the palate, my response stemmed from something deeper. I felt I was eating one of our kind.

Historically, the Cult of the Bear had arisen simultaneously among many northern peoples around the globe. In the heart of winter when food was short, they rejoiced upon discovering the den of a hibernating bear. They killed the bear and, with a great feast, honored it and its bestowal of life-giving nourishment. But the one we ate was killed merely for sport, not to fend off starvation.

The next morning Kat and I quietly follow Bernie as he records bugling elk. Bernie, a scholar of bioacoustics, has introduced the idea of studying habitats by analyzing aural niches within a common soundscape. He is concerned that in the park, even far from the road, the noise of traffic can be heard in the background. One of his purposes on this trip is to meet with park officials to make a case for reducing the noise intrusion by cars in summer and snowmobiles in winter. His claim is that such extraneous noises upset the biological rhythm of animals, especially those such as elk, frogs and birds, whose territories are marked and breeding directed by vocalizations. Unnatural sounds also corrupt the experience of tourists who come to the park to observe wild animals in their native habitats. And some animals, such as owls, are dependent on silence in order to hear the sounds of prey species, the source of their food and sustenance.

In late afternoon we join other animal watchers and are rewarded with sightings of grizzly and black bears and a wolf pack feeding on a dead moose across the Lamar River. Following a good dinner and conversation, I sleep soundly and dreamlessly.

The next morning I reluctantly say good-bye to Bernie and Kat—our visit has been too short. I head back to the cabin, stopping for every moving creature, and enjoy more bear sightings: a mother black bear and two cubs along the roadside that seem focused solely on berry eating, and a grizzly mother and her cub moving across a ridge, overturning rocks, grazing on moths and digging for roots. A huge lone male grizzly, snacking along the roadside grows impatient with being watched by hordes of tourists and suddenly lunges across the highway directly in front of my car, then vanishes into the forest.

Rested and pensive upon my return to the cabin, I think back on the journeys with Paul, planned around his research on the bear. I had hoped that time spent watching bears would firm my resolve to edit his final notes into a book on bears. Now I know I'm not up to the task. Nonetheless, after reviewing Paul's files, the bear now means much more to me. As with those following the Bear Cult, it has illuminated my own life cycle.

The meaning of the verb "to bear," Paul said, "conforms to... three general meanings: to carry or transmit; to give birth; and to hold to a course". I carried my children in my belly and on my hip and now must help them bear the trials of their lives. Although an older woman, I still give birth to new ideas, to new ways of seeing and acting, and must support others to do the same. Most importantly, nothing is more important than holding fast to a course not always clear. But we must approach first steps with confidence that they are necessary if the journey is to continue. The mother bear is a model disciplinarian, sometimes cuffing the cubs, sometimes leading them to food and, at times, licking them into shape, always steadfast in her determination to protect them as they grow toward independence. She is a mother I try to emulate.

At sunrise, lowing cattle and barking dogs awaken me. I dress quickly and go downstairs to investigate. The sagebrush flats beyond my fence are teeming with cows, cowboys, cowgirls, cutting horses and cow dogs. Sitting at breakfast at my parent's old dining room table watching the saga unfold, I am starkly reminded that this is cow country. It's roundup time.

The roundup is a seasonal family affair. The crew, some old, some young, men in high-crowned white Stetson hats with slouchy brims, and women with long braids, are dressed for the occasion and seem in high spirits. They've been in the saddle since before dawn gathering cattle that have been drifting down out of the forest. With lassos draped over saddle horns and yellow slickers tied on behind, they work the cattle, aided by their well-trained, hard-working cow dogs. The cowboys and cowgirls ride beautiful cutting horses that respond to the slightest nudge or weight shift of the riders. Their movements in the saddle and their horse's responses are grace notes in this autumn symphony.

Now settled in a rocker on the porch with a cup of tea, I continue to watch the process. Riders on the periphery of the herd keep the cattle in a tight group while others work through the herd, cutting out cows and calves with like brands and segregating them off to the side. Most of the cattle belong to the Pape Ranches, near Daniel, about twenty-five miles away. Their cows are herded into a holding pasture, a pie-shaped wedge of fenced forestland along the east side of Clark Butte that adjoins my property. They'll graze there until they can be trucked home.

With the cutting completed, the roundup crew calls it a day. Some load their horses into trailers that are lined up along the road and drive off. Others herd their cattle down the roads to nearby ranches. Tom Filkins, chief range rider hired by the Hoback Cattleman's Association to look after the cattle on their summer range, rides with his crew back up the Upper Hoback Road to the cow camp, their headquarters.

At midnight, I awaken to unfamiliar sounds and odors. I get up and go to the window to investigate. The yard is filled with munching, mooing, huffing cows nudging and pushing each other. Some of the hundreds that were left in the holding pasture overnight have broken through my fence. In Wyoming, it's up to landowners to keep fences repaired. I try to do so but each year the cattle break through to my greener pastures. With the pick of several acres of unmown grass, they apparently prefer to crowd around my unfenced cabin. I throw a warm jacket over my pajamas and stand on the porch and yip and holler. The cows look at me unperturbed and placidly chew their cuds. They won't budge. Defeated, I heat a cup of milk and go back to bed as the scent of manure drifts through the window.

This morning the cows are still bedded down around the cabin. Just as I am about to call the Cow Camp for help, a galloping crew comes riding in. In a few minutes, they round up the cattle, drive them through the gate into the holding-pasture, and then push the herd around Clark Butte to the highway. From the loft I watch the procession move down the highway, past the post office and around the curve to the corrals. There they'll be loaded into trucks and hauled to the mowed hay fields where they'll pasture until the snow falls, after which they will eat the bailed hay set before them each day.

It's time for grocery shopping and today, for a change, I drive to Pinedale about thirty-five miles to the east. At this time of year this stretch of road is a testament to the importance of cattle ranching. Even before the forests are closed to grazing in the fall, nudged by frosts and occasional snowy weather, the cattle begin drifting down from the hundreds of miles of mountain pastures where they summer. Range riders urge them the final miles to designated roundup locations for cattle associations, which are organized around ranches clustered in particular forest drainages. During roundup, each rancher's cattle are separated and then herded or trucked to the home ranch where they'll winter. Along the highway, I pass a familiar location that reminds me of what I refer to as "The Last Roundup."

In the summer of 1953, Bob Krall, my then husband, and I decided to try ranching. We moved from Kemmerer to a ranch about fifty miles east of my present cabin to one near Boulder, Wyoming, a small community on the New Fork River in the foothills of the Wind River Mountains. How and why we got there is a rather complicated segment of my family history.

I first met Bob the summer of 1948 just after I had graduated from the University of Wyoming with a major in zoology and a minor in chemistry. That spring during my last semester in college, I had been considering various post-graduate options. My first choices would have been to pursue advanced degrees in zoology or go on to medical school, but both would have demanded a long-term commitment, as well as some financial assistance from my parents. At the time, Dad was was facing financial problems. Tirelessly entrepreneurial and riding on the prosperity after World War II that had erased his debts, he had ignored my mother's objections and invested in a phosphate mine that failed. At the same time, Mamma was experiencing a difficult pre-menopausal pregnancy and DJ was still in high school. As a result, none of them were able to attend my college graduation.

Their absence was a great sadness to me because I considered completing a degree a great accomplishment, especially after rectifying a poor beginning. But it also clarified my position in the family. I was now on my own and could not expect any financial help from my parents.

This was a time when the United States had been experiencing increasingly severe infantile paralysis (poliomyelitis) epidemics. They occurred primarily in the summer and affected mostly young children, although some adults contracted the crippling disease. President Franklin Delano Roosevelt had been crippled by polio before becoming president. During his campaign he tried to hide the braces he wore on his legs by always being photographed standing up. The National Society of Infantile Paralysis offered generous scholarships to college graduates for training in physical therapy. My Kappa Sorority roommate, Jacquie Martinez, suggested I apply for one of these. I received one and was subsequently accepted for training at the Mayo Clinic in Rochester, Minnesota.

The summer after graduation from the University of Wyoming, I returned to the ranch to care for my mother, who had been hospitalized for delivery. The child, a little boy, Matthew Paul, was stillborn. I stayed with Mamma continuously until she was released and we took her home to the ranch where DJ had taken over the ranch chores during Mamma's ordeal. When I think of my mother's sad experience coupled with the financial problems facing her and Dad at the time, I am amazed at the strength she exhibited in such adversity.

That summer I was invited to a picnic in Kemmerer where I met Bob Krall. He was a decorated war veteran who had served with distinction as an officer in the infantry during World II. He had led his company through the first bloody invasions of Italy, with enormous loss of life. The Germans captured him in the battle of Monte Casino and imprisoned him in Poland, where he suffered inhumane conditions for over a year. During a forced march of the prisoners by the Germans as they were retreating, Bob and some of his cohorts escaped and were sheltered by peasants. After several months of wandering he arrived at Odessa, USSR (now Ukraine) and boarded a British ship back to Allied forces. Most of the soldiers who had not escaped died on that death march by the Germans. Bob was a handsome, mature man about nine years my senior. We dated the rest of the summer and corresponded during my training.

In late summer of 1948, I headed for physical therapy training at the Mayo Clinic. During that year we were confronted with patients with every variety of crippling disease, from the crowds of polio victims to those in post-operative rehabilitation. The doctors and supervisors were dedicated, competent and rigorous in their training. Applying the knowledge we had gained to the skill needed to treat patients was challenging and rewarding. Ann

Logan Baird, or Slim, as we called her, was my constant companion during this experience and remains a friend to this day.

Upon certification, I wanted to join an emergency team that flew throughout the country treating patients in polio epidemics. But this worried Mamma, and I complied with her pleas to find employment closer to home. I secured a position in Salt Lake City with the Society for Crippled Children and Adults and worked mostly with children crippled by polio and cerebral palsy. I thrived in the position and grew to love my little patients and their eternal optimism in the face of huge challenges. But I have often speculated on how differently my adult life might have unfolded if I had followed my whim to fly with a team, rather than to take my mother's advice.

I continued dating Bob when home on visits while I worked as a physical therapist in Salt Lake City. War with Korea was declared in June of 1950 and that summer Bob, in the reserve, was recalled to active duty. He had grave misgivings about going back to war. Knowing the extent of Bob's previous war experiences, I felt great empathy for him and this influenced my decision to marry him before he had to report for duty. I had ambivalent feelings about the marriage and consulted a priest who assured me that doubt was a natural part of this experience and with prayer and commitment I would make a good wife. Reassured that my doubts would disappear, I hurriedly sent out wedding invitations, bought the gown and planned the wedding. It took place on a beautiful autumn day in September of 1950, followed by a reception at the ranch. Although the wedding day was idyllic, I had an ominous feeling that I may have made a bad decision.

As an army wife, I accompanied Bob to Fort Breckinridge in Kentucky and then to Fort Benning, Georgia, where I found work in Saint Anthony's hospital. When he received his overseas orders in June of 1951, we returned to Wyoming. As I saw Bob off at the railroad station in Kemmerer, I was convinced he wouldn't return. My parents invited me to stay with them on the ranch and in November Kathryn Ann was born. When Bob finally returned the following year, he was a decidedly different person. The Korean War was no minor skirmish. Forty thousand U.S. soldiers lost their lives and men like Bob who lived through it bore the scars of yet another war.

Bob returned to his position as a civil engineer for the State of Wyoming Highway Department and we bought a home in Kemmerer, where we both had grown up and attended schools. We settled into a typical middle class existence in this small town and began raising our children. Bob enjoyed his work and fishing and hunting on time off but was not overly ambitious about changing our circumstances. Although enthralled with the children, whom I was determined to bring into this world as the Lord ordained, I was bored with housework and life in the small town. As I later learned, I was also suffering from post-partum depression and was repressing the reality of an unhappy marriage.

After the end of World War II, Dad had turned to cattle ranching and opened a garage in town with a Studebaker dealership. He was doing well financially until he invested in a misrepresented phosphate venture that led to his financial ruin. In the end he had to mortgage the family ranch to meet his debts. Filing for bankruptcy was not an acceptable alternative in those days, at least not for Dad. He chose to pay off his debt. The bank that was holding his loans and had seen him through the harrowing seas of the Great Depression had faith in his ranching ability and made him an offer: His debt would be transferred to a ranch that was being foreclosed. The agreement was that Dad would bring the ranch to productivity and then sell it to pay off his mortgage.

Beside himself with worry and remorse, Dad visited me frequently at my home in Kemmerer during the winter of 1953, the year my second child, Matthew, was born. Dad, twelve years older than Mamma and in danger of losing the ranch, was worried about what would happen to her when he was gone. He was then in his early sixties. Considering the stress he was under, I was seriously concerned about his physical and emotional health.

When Dad proposed that Bob and I run the ranch, located near Boulder, Wyoming at the foot of the Wind River Mountains, I was thrilled with the prospect. Dad suggested that if things went well, we might keep the ranch and have a new life. Bob, not a rancher at heart, was not particularly inclined to make such a drastic change in his life. I had always longed to return to ranching and also felt a deep commitment to help my parents out of their financial morass. Against his better judgment, Bob finally agreed to give ranching a try. We rented our home in Kemmerer, and went off in 1953 with our two small children, Kathryn Ann, eighteen months old, and Matthew, six months of age, to a ranch with cattle-grazing rights on the Upper Green River.

That fall, Bob drove to the roundup site each day to join other ranchers as they separated their cattle from the drift herd. Like others without adjoining ranches, we rented a pasture for our cattle until the roundup was completed and we could drive the entire herd down the highway to the ranch, twenty-two miles away.

I suggested to Bob that in order to save money, he and I could drive our cattle home ourselves instead of hiring extra help. We could take the children to the Hams Fork Ranch where Mamma would tend them for a few days. I would ride Ginger, given to me years before by my friend Rae Roberson when her family sold their Opal ranch. He agreed reluctantly.

We knew very little about the logistics of a cattle drive down the highway with over a hundred cows plus their calves. Bob, upon advice from our friend and neighbor, Floyd Bowsman, had arranged pasture about mid-way. We planned to complete the drive in two days.

We loaded the horses in the trailer and left the ranch before sunrise. By daybreak we were well on our way driving the cows down the highway. We had forgotten to notify the sheriff that we'd be passing through Pinedale and arrived at the height of busy morning traffic along with school buses and people on the way to work. We created a chaotic traffic stopper that required state patrolmen and the sheriff to untangle.

By noon we had reached the halfway point and pasture that Bob had arranged. Amazed at how far we had come in such a short time, I convinced Bob that we should just keep going and get the cows home. A few miles beyond the pasture, the calves began tiring and lying down on the highway with the cows standing steadfastly beside them. It took constant yelling and prodding to get them to the ranch. The sun had set when we finally opened the gate and drove them into the hay meadows.

Since we'd expected to be home by noon, I hadn't packed a lunch. I was exhausted and spent as we rode our horses to the barn. As I dismounted, I collapsed. Bob helped me to the house, put me on the couch, piled blankets on top of me and went back to unsaddle and feed the horses. When he returned, he built a fire in the big pot-bellied stove and brought me a hot drink and something to eat. Unable to move, I spent the night on the couch. Henceforth, I went back to cooking and left the roundup to those more knowledgeable about cattle drives. Similar to my first expe-

rience with drinking whiskey, this ordeal ended horseback riding
for me.

Up before sunrise to build a fire in the heating stove, I am stopped
in my tracks by a coyote howling just off the porch. I slide the
atrium door open slowly; the animal is answered by whimpering
and snarling nearby and howls from across the Basin.

The most common predators of this region, coyotes are
heavily hunted and carry the enmity of ranchers. Interesting
and tenacious carnivores, they are programmed by evolution to
respond quickly to movement; they jump high into the air and
pounce on small prey scurrying through the grass or shrubs. They
live primarily on mice, Uinta ground squirrels and rabbits, but, at
this time of year, their scat, which I examine on my hikes, shows
the remains of seeds, vegetable matter and insect carapaces as
well. They also feed on carrion but in the spring may kill newborn
fawns or sickly pronghorns, elk moose and deer, as well as lambs
and calves. In late summer, the adults hunt and feed their young
on staging grounds where they fight over the pickings with a lot
of howling and yipping. By this time of year they are hunting in
packs.

On my evening walks in Clark Draw, I look forward to coyote encounters, although a lone curious coyote that once followed
me home, barking from time to time, left me uneasy. It brought
to mind another memorable encounter with a coyote when son
Matt was about sixteen. He invited me to hike with him from the
Hams Fork River over Commisary Ridge into Fontenelle Basin.
After hiking over the top following this vigorous teen-ager, I was
footsore. I found a log beside a little creek near a beaver dam with

a ready supply of wood. I built a little fire and sat on a log nearby where I could soak my throbbing feet in the cold water. After sitting there for some time enjoying the warmth of the fire and the cool water, I glanced across the stream. There, directly across the tiny stream, was a coyote staring at me, the red light from the fire reflected in her eyes. Romping and playing in the field behind her were two young pups. We stared at each other until she finally turned and with her pups headed into the forest.

On another late evening walk, years later when Paul was still alive, the full moon was rising when I found myself surrounded by howling coyotes. A few days later while out walking, I noticed a flock of ravens circling down by a water hole. I investigated and found the carcasses of five coyotes. They had been skinned and their pink flesh was the source of raven interest. Shaken, I came back to the cabin and asked Paul to come with me. We cut off the coyotes' heads, which I took to a taxidermist. All but two were riddled with bullets. I had the two perfect skulls prepared. One I gave to a friend. The other is on a shelf in my bookcase with other *objets trouves.*

At times I take down and examine this perfect skull, ivory colored and smooth as satin. The intricacies of the skull amaze me with their complexity: the little openings, where nerves and blood vessels entered or left the brain and depressions and tubercles, fissures and protuberances, where muscles or tendons were attached. Foramen for nerves from eyes and ears are visible but the nerves for the sense of smell are not. They are deeply imbedded in the long snout, with its honeycombed sinuses, an elaborate system serving an animal dominated and driven by scent. The jaws, now unhinged, sport a perfect set of pearly white teeth, indicating that this was a young animal, with long canines for biting, ripping flesh and threatening others in territorial displays.

The skull is a relic of a real animal, a tenacious and adapted product of evolution, guided by its highly developed sense of smell. The coyote, along with the cougar, pronghorn, mule deer and wolverine, evolved on the North American continent; its genes are perfectly tuned to the land of its genesis. European skull mounts of a pronghorn and a mule deer, prepared by my son Matt, hang on my walls in the cabin. I must admit to deriving as much pleasure from looking at them, as I do at a painting. What interests me about these bony remains is what they explicitly reveal about the life orientation and behavior of the animal.

Since childhood, I have watched the coyote defy extermination. On the ranch each spring, Joe, the government trapper, set his traps and destroyed pups in dens. In the 1940s, cyanide bombs and poisoned bait almost decimated the wily coyote along with ranch dogs, golden eagles and other carrion eaters. But somehow the coyote survived. The use of such poisons is now closely controlled because of its devastating effect on the total ecosystem.

Coyotes are classified as varmints in Wyoming and can be hunted and killed at any time. I accept selective killing where damage to newborn livestock is clearly a problem. But indiscriminate trapping or shooting coyotes for sport is an atavism of earlier, less-informed days and unjustified when one considers their place in the balance of nature on the steppe. As Will Stolzenburg has shown in his book *Where the Wild Things Were*, top carnivores are necessary for healthy ecosystems since over-population of herbivores, unchecked by predators, can devastate pristine environments.

Last week a warm front moved in and rain fell throughout the night. In the morning the Hoback Basin was shrouded in fog. As I stood on the porch with my steaming mug of tea, out of the mist came mournful howls. Goose bumps rose on my body. Wolves! Knowing what happens to coyotes in this country, I tell no one. During the past summer on my walks I had often found what I presumed to be wolf scats, filled with moose hair and bones, but had never seen or heard one here before.

At an "End of the Year Roundup Party" given for the residents of the Hoback Basin by Joe Ricketts, the owner of the huge and opulent Jackson Fork Ranch, I venture a question to a game warden: "Have you had any sightings of wolves in the Basin?" He confirms that recently a small pack of three was spotted. I take this as good news yet am cautious to rejoice. A wandering pack of wolves will undoubtedly face the same fate as coyotes when ranchers, hunters, trappers or recreational predator hunters learn of their presence.

Controversy has continued for years over the hunting of wolves that were introduced into Yellowstone National Park. Within the miles of wilderness afforded by the park and adjacent national forests, their population has stabilized and is in balance with the elk and buffalo, upon which their survival depends. As a consequence of the reduction in the numbers of ungulates, ecologists agree the ecosystem is much more diverse and healthy.

The problem is that wolves require a large territory and many of them have roamed outside Yellowstone into Grand Teton National Park and into bordering territories of Montana, Idaho and Wyoming. Controversy with the game managers has arisen among ranchers and hunters about their proliferation. Hunters and outfitters want the wild elk, deer, pronghorns, moose and bighorn sheep protected against excessive predation from wolves.

Debate over policies for management of wolves in Wyoming and surrounding states will continue as state and federal agencies and ranchers try to formulate satisfactory policies.

I am not an animal rights advocate but believe that wild animals should be allowed to live out their natural life cycles whenever possible. Neither am I an animal welfare activist but I believe that animals should never be mistreated or harmed willfully. I am not a hunter or fisher but I believe in fair chase and ethical hunts and catch limits set by state wildlife agencies. I do not own a pet but understand the close relationships that develop between humans and their kept animals. I believe, however, that pets, like all animals, should be treated in accordance with their own biological requirements and not kept to satisfy the unfulfilled needs of their owners. I believe that life is precious, but when death is inevitable, no creature, including humans, should be kept alive by extraordinary and unnatural means.

Wolves that survive predator hunters' bullets, following their instincts, will kill old and ailing animals on the wintering grounds. In spring, after raising their pups, they will follow the elk herds back into the mountains and, living on the easily killed calves and weak or sickly cows, will continue to cull the herd. My hope is that in years to come, as snow gathers in the high mountains, I will once more hear the wolves. Until that time I'll anticipate their long, heart-aching calls.

Mammoth Hot Springs   *Flo and the Tetons (2006)*

Slim and Flo in physical therapy training (1948)

Yellowstone River

Dead coyote

· 7 ·

The Orrery

From the opening overture of sunrise, through the mellow interludes of midday, to the finale when the curtain drops and all is quiet and black, shadow and light across this majestic basin landscape are operatic in their intensity. Each change affords ample opportunity for contemplation. This morning, however, I'm not interested in contemplation. The sky is absolutely clear, and I anticipate a perfect day. Snow is building in the high mountains and this may be my last long hike in the foothills. I pack a lunch along with my usual hiking provisions and head out. My goal today is to identify the watershed of archaic Sometimes Creek.

I start hiking where the foothills taper off at the curve in the Upper Hoback River Road and follow an old trail along the crest of the ridge that separates Clark Draw from the Upper Hoback. I don't expect to see many birds and animals since migratory instincts have carried them away, but four pronghorns—a doe with her twins, now almost as tall as their mother, and a yearling— bring me a pleasant surprise. I've watched this foursome since the fawns were born in the spring. I noticed a restless doe wandering around in the sagebrush at the edge of the meadow one morning and got out my binoculars. I saw the first and then the second fawn drop to the ground. The mother stands during birthing, and the jolt to the ground aids the fawns with their first breath. Amazing little creatures, they immediately try to get up and, after repeatedly being knocked off their wobbly legs by the hefty licking by their mothers to clean off birthing fluids, they finally find their balance on terra firma.

This doe and her brood stayed apart from the herd through most of the summer. But I expected that by now they would have joined the others on their annual fall migration along a route followed by their species for over six thousand years. From here they'll travel over one hundred miles to the lower Green River Basin where strong winds scour the snow from the sagebrush steppe of their wintering grounds. For some reason the doe and her offspring are lagging. Eight big eyes stare at me for a moment and then, with the characteristic alarm call from the doe that sounds almost like a cough, they run ahead and disappear over a knoll.

Mule deer, who have exchanged their lovely tawny coats for the gray of winter, have also stayed a bit longer. Some mornings I watch them sail effortlessly over the fence on their way back from Clark Butte where they have spent the night. They cautiously make their way across the meadow to the concealment of the willows along the Hoback River where they go for water and to spend the day. A little gang of whitetail deer surprised me the other morning as they milled around the cabin. Not common in this area, they are smaller than mule deer. They flash their large flat tails like white flags as they run. Before long the deer will also have migrated to their winter grounds to the south.

As I work my way along the crest of the ridge, I notice extensive diggings on the hillside. I'm not sure whether they are the work of badgers, foxes or coyotes, all of which will remain here throughout the winter. Down below on my left and to the south, the Upper Hoback River, a textbook braided stream, outlined with leafless willows, shines silvery in the morning light as it meanders across the meadows, outlined leafless willows. Small drainages formed over the years run into Clark Draw on my right. The ridgeline I'm walking gains in altitude as it trends west and then makes a large arc to the north to meet Monument Ridge. Beyond, the Hoback Range forms a snowy white backdrop.

As the elevation increases, clones of aspen run up the gullies to the ridge top. Through bare white trunks and branches underlain with golden leaves, I see the forest allotment fence that borders Horse Pasture Draw. Down below, horses are grazing near the cow camp, summer headquarters for Tom Filkins and the range riders of the Hoback Cattlemen's Association.

The forest at the head of a draw on the south side of this ridge must have formed most of the watershed for Sometimes Creek. After this morning of reconnoitering, I can now visualize the extent of its drainage area. By my rough calculations, it covered about twenty-five square miles of forest and sagebrush steppe. Except in years of drought, I suspect the run-off from this watershed, together with water from springs in the meadow, supported some irrigation early in the year, a sustained trickle of water for most of the summer and increased flow in the fall when cool weather slows evaporation.

I skirt patches of snow and find a seat on a fallen log in a patch of sunshine to eat my lunch. Juvenile bluebirds, enticed by late-hatching insects, linger in this peaceful ambience. Rousing myself, I continue my hike, angling down off the mountain. To my surprise, the four pronghorns appear ahead of me and then disappear over a ridge in a flash. Apparently they've been following me surreptitiously. As I scan the ridge with my binoculars I can see they have stopped on the other side and are still watching me; their eyes and ears, held upright, are barely visible over the rise. I've been told that if one waves a white flag, these curious creatures will walk up to you. I'm wearing an old white cotton safari hat, and, standing very still, I nod my head back and forth. They begin walking toward me, coming into the open and plain sight. I take one step and off they streak with their white rumps flashing. On with our hide and seek game. When I reach my starting point near my fence, they are grazing just about where I joined them this morning. I thank them for their company and head for the cabin.

As I approach, two ravens fly low to check out my compost heap. Vocalizing as they fly by, they appear deep in conversation. I mimic their calls to which they seem to reply, in truth, a self-centered justification for hearing the sound of my own voice. The tap, tap, tap of the sturdy bills of a migrating flock of flickers, intent on drilling holes in my cedar cabin, draw my attention as I approach. I smack my walking stick against the walls and yell and they explode off the roof and settle along the ditch bank where they forage for ants. After a cold drink and hot shower, I prepare dinner. Bone tired after a very enjoyable day, I head to bed early.

Autumn quarter days arrive at the end of October, and Halloween. Here I do not expect trick-or-treaters. After the first year when I bought goodies and turned on all of the porch lights but had no visitors, I learned that the Bondurant Community Council sponsors a party for the children so there is no need to drive them to remote parts of the basin to seek treats. I can't imagine what I was thinking—unless it was the joy of meeting expectant kitty faces, princesses with crowns askew, ugly witches, Superman, Batman and Dracula with blood dripping from his fangs, masking the real purpose of the visit: to fill with treats the pillow cases and baskets held out expectantly.

What I was thinking was probably along the same lines of northern hemisphere pagan agrarians. They undoubtedly felt uneasy at this seasonal boundary after the harvest, when life and death intermingle and the urge to celebrate hit them. At such times witches, guarded by their black cats, took flight, and bonfires or candles placed in squashes carved with eerie faces waylaid death. From a less historical or mythological perspective, I was facing another birthday. In childhood, it was always celebrated on Halloween, a sort of two-for-one deal.

My mother, acknowledging my birthday properly, enhanced the Halloween party at Opal School with special treats. Whether or not Miss Beyda was taunting death or winter I do not know, but we celebrated properly. Taking a bite of an apple floating in a washtub of water or hung from a string was a feat I could never master but nothing spoiled the fun. I was invariably a witch in my black dress.

Although I've never been able to trace the source of my anxiety, Halloween was always a bit stressful for me as I raised my children. Perhaps it was not the event but the fact that, indeed, I was getting older. In a huge box in the basement I stored old masks and costumes for various spooky characters: an ugly witch with a pointed hat and my black pilgrim dress, a hobo with raggedy overalls and shirt and hat, a green alligator, a monster, a black Mammy in a red bandana dress and a savage Indian with tomahawk (I regret that at this time, when we still had minstrel shows at the school, I was unaware of stereotypes). Matthew, Lisi and Bobby were satisfied with this array of accoutrements but Kathryn Ann had used them before and made requests that stretched my limitations. A horse? A Viking? Good Lord!

Since parents have taken upon themselves to occupy their children and redirect the instinctual drive to become a little wild at this time of year, treats have become the name of the game. Although the steady line of costumed children exclaim "Trick or Treat," the pranks have vanished. This was not so in the Burgoon School in Diamondville, Wyoming in 1935. The day after Halloween I listened with awe to the bad boys bragging about their exploits of waxing windows and overturning outhouses. Although these misdeeds fascinated me, I realized I could never commit such acts. It was wrong; but more to the point, I was not that brave.

I disagree with the amateur meteorologists in the Post Office who say: "Looks like winter is on its way." Actually, it seems to have arrived. Since the end of October, snow on the mountains has been accumulating. Days are cool and night temperatures keep inching down. Snow is sticking. The last storm put an end to any bare spots on the mountains that had appeared from time to time on sunny days. As sunset arrives earlier each day, I become a giant. My shadow extends all the way down the road to the willows.

With each snowstorm, domestic animals seem disoriented. Cows pace along fence lines, following each other in single file, dreaming of hay handouts, I suppose. Horses stand together with their rumps to the wind, and, finally, in unison start pawing through snow to find buried grasses to feed on. Wild animals are more adept. Buffalo push the snow aside with their heads. Moose browse on exposed twigs of willows and other bushes. Elk, deer and pronghorn migrate to winter grounds swept clean of snow by wind.

The road to my cabin is snowed in but, because of the expense, I won't have it plowed. It joins a long driveway, which is kept open by neighbors, David and Tracy, who work in Jackson. I park my car in daughter Lisi's yard about a quarter of a mile away—she lives here only in the summer and returns to her home in New York by mid-August. Her cabin is just off the Upper Hoback River Road, which is plowed daily by the county.

I bought a snow blower last summer as I formulated this winter plan. Still, I worry about the logistics that will involve snowshoeing to my car, keeping the parking area cleared, driving to Jackson for groceries through the Hoback Canyon (where avalanches are common) and then, upon returning, hauling food to my cabin on a toboggan. I question whether I'm tough enough, mentally and physically, to withstand the winter solitude and maneuver the complications of being snowbound. Yet I remain determined to give it a try. Although finally rejecting the idea, I reconsider running into Pinedale while the road is still open to sign up for satellite television, which might help numb my brain to the threats.

Unlike me, unperturbed by doubts, bears are now denned and slumbering away. I envy their biology and wish like them I could crawl into a winter den and curl up in somnolent bliss free from worries, not even the birthing of cubs, until trickling water and the smell of growth and expanding roots awaken me to new possibilities.

Before sunrise, I check the thermometer on the porch that hovers near zero. Still in my pajamas, robe and warm slippers, I rush back into the cabin to light a fire. With the suggestion from a long-time resident, I've learned how to set it quickly. I sprinkle a scoop of fire-starter—prepared by mixing kerosene with ashes stored in a lidded metal container—over kindling and touch it with a lighted match. The wood bursts into a roaring blaze and after I add more wood to the flame I move to the atrium doors.

A pinkish glow on the Hoback Range draws me away from the fire's warmth to witness the day breaking dramatically on the landscape. Before the sun rises above the horizon to the east, its rays flood the snowy Hobacks to the west and then slip slowly down the slopes of Monument Ridge, at the same time illuminating the Gros Ventres Mountains to the north. When the sun finally breaks over the East Rim, pale, cold light floods the cabin and surrounding meadow. The angle of radiation at this time of year is only about twenty degrees and does not carry much warmth.

The transition during autumn quarter days brings highly variable weather patterns. The dynamic microclimate of the basin, with its own idiosyncrasies, provides additional astonishing variations. Weather forecasts and maps on the internet, which I sometimes consult to get a notion of high- and low-pressure air masses moving over the West, are often less reliable than just looking out the window.

No two sunrises are the same. At times the sky overhead is a clear, pale blue with the entire mountainous horizon obliterated by clouds that form over the peaks like a heavy, grey scruff of hair around a man's bald pate. As the sun rises, the clouds turn from gray to pink and then to yellow. Shafts of light shoot upward, outlining the clouds in brilliant gold. As heat is generated, the clouds disappear and the sun shines brightly.

Cloudy days present different scenarios. Following rain or snow the previous day or night, the basin is often enveloped in a great, gray blanket of fog, which, if we're lucky, burns off by midday. Although it may not be snowing in the Hoback Basin, white curtains of snow showers frequently hide the mountains. On overcast days, clouds may suddenly change to white puffs tinged with pink.

On clear days, the sun in its low arc shines through the south-facing clerestory windows and helps warm the cabin until late afternoon. On cloudy or windy days I keep the fire burning since the cabin is more difficult to heat. The daily movement of the sun, although barely discernible, carries with it explicit cause and effect of the yearly cycle of changing seasons. In quite a different way, the moon is a daily calendar. Startled by its rapid changes, and showered with celestial sensations, I have no doubt that time is passing and feel an emotional and spiritual connection to the cosmos and the great unknown.

More than we are aware, we are endowed with energy levels and moods determined by the increasing ratio of darkness to light. Confined to dwelling in one place with externally imposed schedules, we fail to acknowledge our innate responses to these seasonal variations. Ritual has always been a powerful bonding and centering force to relieve the tension for humans at seasonal transitions. Spiritual communities or retreat centers, no matter the religious orientation, prescribe individual and communal prayer or meditation at similar times of day. Routine and ritual enhance meditation as well as contemplation. An imposed schedule reduces the effort needed by the devotees to make daily decisions and gives them the opportunity to concentrate on their inner life.

When not constrained with society's daily plan, I follow a winter schedule that satisfies the needs of body and spirit. I awaken and rise each morning before the sun is up, light a fire in the wood stove and witness the sunrise. Following this I read by the warmth of the fire as I enjoy a cup of tea and an English biscuit. When the cabin warms, I move to my desk and my computer where I survey the news and weather report for the day, answer e-mail and write until early afternoon, taking a break for breakfast along the way. After lunch, I take a long walk, work in the yard and chop kindling and fill the wood basket. I prepare a good dinner and after clean-up, telephone friends and family and then spend more time by the fire reading until bedtime.

Traditional prayers are not a part of my day, although I do have daily conversations with the powers-that-be as I go about my activities. Out of long-standing habit, I've been known to call on help from the Lord when I'm in a predicament. When not concentrating on a particular logistical problem or writing project, my thoughts run the gamut of concerns that most people share: the welfare of family and friends, plans for the future, politics and societal dilemmas, the environment, finances and self-improvement. When seasonal changes draw me back to vivid memories of Paul, Mamma or Dad that flood me with longing for them, I dwell in those memories momentarily, breath deep and then move on to the present.

Through November and into December, the days become increasingly wintry. The snow sifts downs steadily and as it builds, the temperature continues to drop below zero each night. As a result the snow is crusty and solid enough to walk on. My daily jaunts these days are on snowshoes.

As the winter solstice approaches, I become more preoccupied with that precise point along the horizon when the sun pauses momentarily on its movement south and begins inching northward once more. The slow descent into darkness commenced six months ago on the summer solstice in June. Now, at the end of December, I anticipate the day when the sun will start shining a little longer and arc a little higher overhead.

With this seasonal change, my spirits rebound with the optimism of a young child. I feel it in body and soul, biologically and spiritually, and want to acknowledge this astronomical event. Whether public or private, in saturnalias, joyous holidays or quiet meditation, northern dwellers at this time of year have paid homage to our bright star that infuses the cold, hibernating landscape with light and new life. Even in the blossoming moments of the summer solstice, I anticipate this moment. Now I'm ready for more light.

I've described the transitional time of the winter, when I find new purpose in life, as if I were the center of the universe—clearly a Copernican regression. Never mind that I know that the earth's tilted axis and revolution in its orbit around the sun create the illusion of movement of sun and moon and stellar bodies across the sky.

To overcome our earth-centeredness, Miss Beyda enthralled us with an orrery, one of those solar-system models that, with the turning of a knob, sent earth and moon and all the planets whirling in their orbits around the big shiny brass sun at the center. When I first began teaching general science, I retrieved such a model from a dusty storeroom and, with the addition of handouts, created a game that made each student an actor in the great solar system drama. I contrived an excellent teaching unit that explained perfectly how our solar system works, a lesson that these kids would comprehend—and remember! But despite my efforts and multi-sensory approach, the looks of stubborn disagreement in the eyes of the pubescent earthlings made it very clear that they would not deny what they saw each day with their own two eyes: The sun rose in the east, moved across the sky, and set in the west. It moved around the earth, not the opposite. They were earthbound. And so am I.

As I follow the course of the sun each day and the phases of the moon each night and make my calculations, I ignore our planet's path around the sun and our dance with sister moon. I concentrate on where these two magnificent stellar bodies rise into view and slip out of sight. And as the sun inches south along the horizon, I imagine the great shimmering arc above me from solstice to solstice with dark voids on either end, where sunlight is never direct.

I anticipate the first day of winter with particular interest this year. I will spend the holidays with daughter Kathryn Ann and her family on the West Coast and plan on leaving the cabin the day after the solstice. I don't want to miss the sunrise or sunset I have been awaiting since the summer solstice when I began recording the progression of the sun across the horizon. That the winter solstice almost coincides with a full moon makes it all the more thrilling.

As the solstice approaches, my sleep becomes sporadic. I prowl the cabin like an old cat, moving from window to window, watching Venus and then Orion rise, and the moon as it grows toward fullness. At times I step out on the porch in the cold, cutting air to witness the unbelievable brilliance of the night sky.

One night, I am awakened by light and think it is morning. At the window I see the long shadow of the cabin splayed across the snowy yard and meadow. I check the clock. A shadow of the cabin to the east at three in the morning? How can this be? I pull on tights, throw on a robe, step into my sheepskin slippers and hurry downstairs and out onto the west porch. The moon, a huge globe glowing in the cobalt sky, is about to set behind the Hobacks. It seems within reach and illuminates the winter landscape with yellow light so bright that the cabin casts a shadow.

At the beginning of this year at the cabin I sketched a line drawing of the east and west horizons to record the rising and setting sun through the seasons and quarter days. I allow a day on either side for cloudy or stormy weather but as the winter solstice approaches, I fear my goal may not be met. For over a week, clouds have obliterated sunrises and sunsets. Often, predawn has been absolutely clear, but by sunrise when the air above the mountains has reached the dew point, a bank of clouds forms on mountaintops and obliterates the skyline.

At last the winter solstice arrives. At sunset last evening, I watched patiently as the sun approached the horizon. Clouds formed and dissipated and formed again and then, miraculously, parted momentarily as the sun set at the southwest end of the Hoback Range. At the same time a near-full moon rose over the East Rim. On this clear, cold morning, the sun and moon have exchanged places. The moon sets in the west as the sun rises in the east where Elk Ridge tapers off. Along a short section of the South Rim between those points, the sun ventures no farther south.

Why such interest in this project? I cannot say with certainty, but it may be to take hold of time. In a blink of an eye I have moved from child to crone. From where I stand, time stretches away from me into the past, a seamless expanse where one day is indistinguishable from the next. Like a huge reversed pendulum swinging back and forth over me, the course of the sun when contemplated in its entirety gives me a sense of the span of one year, although from day to day, the movement is barely discernible.

Not so for the moon. The changes in the moon are obvious and tell me day-to-day that time is passing. Its phases, repeated about every twenty-nine days, have been a timepiece worldwide for diverse people with differing cosmologies. Still there is much I don't know about its changing position in the sky and apparent size. This winter I have developed a healthier respect for astromers and astrologers and their understanding of the relative movement of stars, planets and their moons.

The inertia that binds me to this place, along with the logistics, makes it hard for me to leave the cabin, but I'm finally packed. I pull on my boots, lace into my snowshoes, load the bright blue toboggan with luggage and Christmas gifts, and head for the car. It takes two trips. When I arrive at the car after the first haul, I realize that I am missing three essential items. I make a second trip to retrieve my coat and purse where they fell off the toboggan and the keys to car and cabin, which I left dangling in the lock of the cabin door! I make the second run amidst much self-incriminating muttering about getting my senility in check if I expect to drive safely over three hundred miles of winter roads to catch the plane. The attraction that binds me to this place may exacerbate my forgetfulness and carelessness, which subvert my best-laid plans.

Fortunately the skies are clear and the highways free of snow. In Kemmerer I stop briefly at the cemetery. Christmas wreaths I ordered earlier from the Petals and Treasures Shop are bright spots amidst snow and gravestones. Paul and my parents are buried near each other. Each time I visit their graves, I think of my last hours with each of them.

In the spring of 1965 Dad stopped by to check on the duplex he had built across the street from my home. He mentioned he was satisfied that, with its additional income each month, Mamma would be able to manage financially after his death. A few days later, his heart stopped while they were watching "I Love Lucy," his favorite television show. Almost thirty years later, Mamma, surrounded by family, slowly eased into her last moments as I assured her it was all right for her to go. Paul, attended by our daughters and me, left this world when the wind blew in the open window as he took his last breath. Each of these last moments with them is fixed in my mind and reassures me of the natural release and peace that death brings to the dying.

Back in my car, I stop by son Matt's cozy little home to leave gifts under his brightly decorated tree. After working graveyard shift the night before as an electrician, he is fast asleep. By sunset, I am safe in Salt Lake City in the old house that has been my home since 1972. It holds fond memories for me and is where I raised Matthew, Lisi and Bobby to young adulthood and made a home for Kathryn Ann and her two children, Meredith and Jason, when Kathryn entered medical school. I watch the moon rise round and full over my neighbor's house. The city lights sparkle and the familiar sounds finally lull me to sleep.

The next evening, after a short and uneventful flight, I am with Kathryn Ann and her family enjoying the precious gift of their company. That is not to say there are not little upheavals now and then, remnants of tender spots touched unknowingly. The ability of my children to pass over my missteps always astounds me. But grandchildren are a bit more resistant to my compulsive inclination to give advice—and should be. I have too much insider information but am really clueless about the challenges they face. But we are honest with each other and have learned not to hold grudges. The week is spent browsing in bookstores, walking on the beach, going to movies, playing cards in the evenings and eating special meals we've prepared.

For as long as I can remember, holidays have been special celebrations shared with family. On the ranch, Mamma worked tirelessly to make Christmas a festive occasion. During the Great Depression, it must have also been a tense time for her since she had to dip into operating expenses. She planned gifts well in advance for us as well as relatives in Italy. Early in November she would begin baking fruitcakes that she wrapped in wine-soaked cloths and stored in her walk-in closet. In order for them to arrive in Italy by Christmas they had to be shipped six weeks in advance. Included in the huge box that she prepared for Italian relatives, in addition to several cakes, were clothes (over-alls, wool socks, and gloves for the men; nylon hose and sweaters for the women), coffee, medications (aspirin and ointments), nuts and hard candy. The huge packages had to be wrapped in canvas and stitched together into a sturdy canvas covering since they would cross the ocean by boat.

Mamma ordered our Christmas gifts from the Montgomery Ward and Sears catalogues. When the packages arrived, she announced that she was storing them under her big brass bed and that we were not to get into them. I figured that there was no harm in looking and would lie on the floor under her bed staring at the boxes. Once when a doll's tiny shoe protruded from one, I did not touch it, but tried to imagine what the rest of the doll might look like. When I entered the seventh grade and was too old to play with dolls, I was given my last. Beverly, a beautiful baby doll, sat on my bed, playing her part in my socialization as a future mother.

When we were young children, Dad would take us on a glorious sleigh ride each Christmas. He would tie our sleds together and, on a galloping horse, pull us through the fields and down to the pasture on a breath-taking course with frequent over-turns and new starts and much squealing with delight.

From the time our cousins Paul and Alex arrived, each day was filled with fun and games. Their mother, Uncle Richard's daughter Lizzie, had died when they were young boys. Since then they had attended a private boarding school. Both were older than I, and spent most Christmases with us from elementary through high school.

We shoveled snow from a stretch of the river and spent hours skating. Dad enhanced our efforts by flooding the river so that it would freeze into a smooth sheen. When tired and cold after playing outdoors, we'd come into the house to begin a round of Monopoly at a card table set up in the front room by the Christmas tree. We alternated the game with stints at a complicated jigsaw puzzle. After dinner we played into the night, stopping occasionally to snack on fruitcake, cookies, nuts and roasted chestnuts set out by Mamma. We were allowed the luxury of sleeping late each morning.

This relationship with surrogate brothers continued through childhood and adolescence. Alex was one of the first soldiers drafted in 1940 before World War II had begun. Paul received an agricultural deferment in order to help his father run their sheep company. Since they were the same age, Paul and Barbara were close friends. But after she had left home for college, Paul continued to drop by the ranch on his way to check on the sheep outfit. A sense of ethics led him to give me advice on studying, boyfriends and going to college; we discussed the meaning of life in general and ours in particular. We corresponded regularly until we both married and had families of our own. In my mind's eye I see him on one of his last visits to the ranch, a handsome, auburn-headed, articulate young man dressed in a fawn-colored buckskin shirt.

Paul was one of the important young men in my early life. Like beloved Mr. Hampton, my upper elementary school teacher who helped me with the transition to adolescence, Paul, like a big brother, helped me bridge the gap to young adulthood. But no man was more important in my life or the lives of my mother and sisters than our father. He was the constant shining sun at the center of our orrery who set us on our independent orbits but always, even after his death, circling around him.

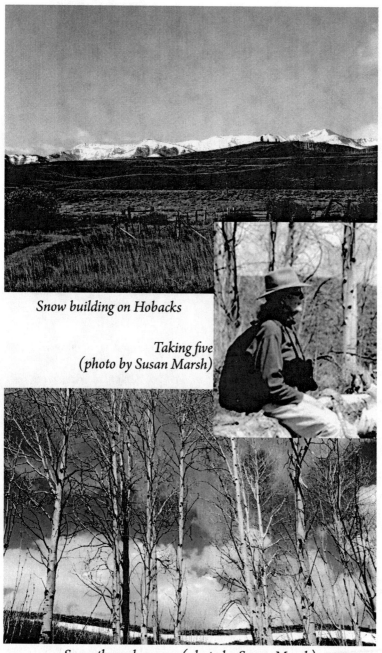

Snow building on Hobacks

Taking five
(photo by Susan Marsh)

Snow through aspens (photo by Susan Marsh)

Kathryn Ann, Matthew, Lisi, and Bobby (1963)

· 8 ·

Winter's Hero

After a deep sleep in a feather bed, I am standing on a balcony at the Albergo Aurora in Tret, Italy, my father's birthplace. Whenever I visit this village, I feel his presence and see his likeness in our relatives. Down below, in a bright blue Tyrolean apron, Gusterle, my father's nephew and my first cousin, is working in the gardens bordered with red geraniums in bright ceramic pots. Beyond, the Dolomites rise to meet the sky. With the help of daughter Lisi, an able driver on tortuous Alpine roads, I've escorted my sisters here to this village. This is DJ's first visit. Barbara has visited before, as have I, the first time with my mother in 1981. Although Italian relatives and I grow older, the Aurora and the towering mountains remain immutable.

Gusterle is a multi-talented, hard-working man, who has transformed the rustic rock house where my father was born into a *pensione* with immaculate tiled floors, white walls and beautifully crafted wooden doors. Besides being a skilled worker, he is a folklorist's dream. In the little tavern after a day's work, he recites regional poetry that describes the history and inventiveness of the Tyrolean people. In the garden or at the dinner table after a good meal, he often bursts into song.

From the balcony I can see the little village of Tret and, about a mile in the distance, Saint Felice, another small settlement. The two villages, only a stone's throw apart, were a part of the Austrian Tyrol, yet German-speaking Saint Felice and Romance-speaking Tret were 'miles apart' in language and culture. *The Hidden Frontier*, a fascinating ethnography of these two villages, written by John Cole and Eric Wolf, provides a detailed history of the ecology and ethnicity of these two villages.

The two small settlements are very similar with their clustered huts and barns of rock and hand-hewn pillars. Surrounded by a few acres, the tillable land is cultivated to provide fodder for kept animals and vegetables for the family. During the last three centuries, the boundary separating these two villages and their countries has moved north and south between them several times. Yet, ignoring the political reality of their proximity and common geography, they have remained surprisingly separate and culturally unique.

Until recently, the inhabitants did not intermarry, but lived peacefully apart while maintaining different clans, practices and languages, German, in Saint Felice, and Nones, in Tret. Nones is a variant of Romansch, an Indo-European dialect spoken in Switzerland as well as in this part of Northern Italy. Long-standing cultural barriers are being bridged in modern times as young couples marry. Teresa, one of Gusterle's daughters, has married a man from Saint Felice, where they now live and raise their families.

Because of Gusterle's fastidious management, he, his wife Maria and three of their adult children and families have established their homes on the few acres of arable land. Dorotea manages the albergo, son, Luca, a small dairy and Joanna works outside the village. They occupy the original homestead settled by my ancestors for hundreds and, possibly, thousands of years. Since the first local jurisdiction in Tret, documented in 1280, wood gathering and pasturing have been carefully regulated. As a result, the present Alpine ecosystem surrounding its acreage is healthy and sustaining.

When my father was born at the end of the nineteenth century, land-use was regulated but the population was not; the villagers over-stepped the land base. In one century after 1300, the population increased by fifty percent. The potato, introduced in 1700, provided meager sustenance but insured the survival of still more children, and the population kept growing at an unprecedented rate.

The village road winds past the Aurora, turns in front of a water fountain, where some of the villagers still draw water, and heads up a slight incline to Santa Anna's Catholic Church. On a cold day in January in 1895, two little boys, four years old and dressed in ankle-length infant dresses, peered in bewilderment from behind a hand-hewn door in this very building at a procession bearing a coffin up the cobble road to the church. The church bell was tolling, calling the villagers to a Mass for the passing of my fraternal grandmother, Barbara Maninfior Bertagnolli, born thirty-nine years before. Weakened through the birthing of twelve children—four of whom had died at birth or as infants—she had died of pneumonia. The bewildered little boys peering at the procession were Matteo, my father, and Alphonso, his cousin, who were about the same age and had grown up together.

Only one blurred photograph of Grandmother Barbara exists. Yet I see her likeness in the faces and personalities of some of my kin, including sister DJ and cousin Rosetta, who show common traits that bear no resemblance to Grandfather Francesco, whose pictures I have studied. I imagine Grandmother Barbara as a diminutive little woman, with large hazel eyes and curly black hair, inventive and spontaneous and with a quick reply and laugh. Her body was interred in the cemetery on the north flank of the church with countless other ancestors who had passed their lives in this little village across hundreds of years.

I can imagine the desolation felt by Grandfather Francesco and his children with the passing of this young wife and mother. Like many poor peasant women in her situation, she must have been the glue that held the family together. Upon Grandmother's death, seven children, ranging from sixteen years to six months of age, sat around that table. By that time the oldest son, Joe, had left home for America. At four, Dad was second to the youngest, Anna, about six months of age. Dominica (Aunt Minica) was sixteen and became Dad's surrogate mother and caregiver. Gusto, Dad's big brother, was his guardian. Aunt Minica, for reasons now clear, was very dear to my father and like a grandmother to me.

Dad's family was not just poor; it suffered abject poverty. Around our own table on the ranch, looking at the substantial meal set before us, Dad often recalled family meals of childhood where there was never enough food and Grandfather Francesco insisted that he wasn't hungry in order to leave more food for the children.

One short-term solution to the problem was to send young children away from home to work in the winter. They were paid primarily with board and room and a few cents a day. This arrangement removed the burden from the family of one more mouth to feed. My father, at the age of about nine, was sent off to Saint Felice. Although the situation was not ideal—he had to sleep with the grandfather who died in his sleep one night—Dad's stronger memory from those days was that it was the only time during his childhood when he had enough to eat. Remembering this, Dad always looked kindly upon Germanic people.

Marrying outside the village was another viable route out of poverty. One of Dad's sisters, Barbara, followed this course and some of her family moved to Switzerland, where my cousin Rosetta and her family now live. The exodus continued as men and women married outside of Tret or left for urban areas where menial jobs were available. Immigration to other countries, such as the United States and Argentina, where laborers were in demand to help fuel the Industrial Revolution, was the primary solution chosen by Grandfather Francisco's children as well as by many in Tyrol. Between 1880 and 1920, immigration of the Tyrolese peaked, leaving Dad's generation of men decimated.

Uncle Richard, the first of the immigrants from this family to come to the United States, settled in Rock Springs, Wyoming in the late 1800s. Aunt Minica and her husband joined him there and later her sister Fortunata (Aunt Tuna) and her husband arrived. The two youngest, unmarried brothers, Vigilio and Matteo, cast dice to determine who would remain in Italy to fulfill the family's obligation to enlist one son in the military and who would go to America. As it turned out, Matteo, my father, won the toss and came to America in 1918, accompanied by an older brother, Francesco, and his cousin and childhood friend, Alphonso. Vigilio enlisted in the army and was killed as World War I drew to a close. Guilt always plagued Dad with this sad twist of fate.

Alphonso, Phons to us, settled in Rock Springs and became a sheep rancher and prominent businessman and sheriff. He and his wife, Mary, were my parents' dearest friends and, during my childhood, our families spent many holidays together. When Bob and I lived on the Boulder ranch, Phons, on his way to supervise his sheep ranch on the Big Sandy River, would stop by to visit me. On one of these visits he described my grandmother's funeral scene.

As was the case with many immigrants to America, Dad identified strongly with his birthplace. That identification did not merely refer to country but to village, geographical location and province. He was born on January 2, 1891, in Tret, which means mountain meadow. Besides being a Trettner, he was also Nones, since his village is located in a place called the Val di Non (the valley that isn't) and Nones is the dialect spoken. The entire region at the time of my father's birth was known as the Austrian Tyrol, a segment of the Federated Republic of Austria. And Tret to this day is in the province of Trento. Thus my father was also Tyrolian, an Austrian and a Trentino. In conversations among Italians on the ranch, whenever they referred to acquaintances, they identified them by village or province as well as by name.

As a child, tales of the Old Country intrigued me. When at school I was asked to designate my nationality, Dad insisted that I should specify Austrian, rather than Italian. He had left his homeland an Austrian, and he remained one; he refused to acknowledge the political changes in power and boundaries that occurred after World War I.

On my first visit to Tret with my mother in 1981, my cousins and I hiked to the summit of Monte Luca. Cows and sheep, communally pastured by villagers, were grazing on meadows on the forested mountainside. The trail passed lush meadows and huts of animal tenders and long barns where in summer animals were milked and managed cooperatively and cheeses made, as they had been for years. On up the mountain, the trail wound around hairpin curves, some marked as echo stops, where my cousins yodeled and I listened to their voices repeated by the high mountain walls. We climbed to the cross on the summit where we signed our names in a registry. On the way down, exhausted with trying to keep up with my agile and sturdy relatives, my legs gave way and I tumbled off the trail and was impaled in azalea bushes, from which I was extracted with much hilarity on the part of my rescuers.

One day Mamma and I rode with the family on a hayrack, then towed by Gusterle's shiny tractor but once pulled by oxen. We rode into the high lush meadows where a section of land was allocated to them by the local jurisdiction for harvesting grasses and flowers for winter fodder. Gusterle had mowed the hay with his tractor, but in the past, it was cut by hand with scythes. I joined the women and, with large wooden rakes, we turned the hay to help it cure in the summer sun. Cousin Elena and Mamma served a delicious noontime meal of polenta and veal stew cooked over an open fire, accompanied with garden lettuce, wine and apples and cheese for dessert. Following the meal the family visited and rested on blankets, after which we loaded the hayrack with the sweet-smelling hay and climbed aboard for the ride back to the pensione.

After that day spent with relatives, I understood why each summer, while we hayed the upper meadow, Dad would ask Mamma to bring a polenta dinner into the field to keep alive this tradition. She served this delicious meal with lettuce from our garden and lemonade, accompanied with lemon meringue pie for dessert, one of her summer specialties when there was a surplus of eggs. After the wonderful meal, we would rest in sweet-smelling clover along the ditch before getting back to work.

On the journey with my sisters we rode the Mendola, a tram that carried us down to Bolzano in the valley below. There we toured the museum dedicated to Ötze, the Ice Man, whose remains have been dated to about 5,000 years ago. He was plucked from a melting glacier in the mountains above Tret. Some of his DNA has been matched with residents of a nearby village, and I like to think that I might also harbor some fragment of this hunter-gatherer's genes. Replicas and dioramas show how well equipped Ötze was to survive on his own. His clothing from head to toe, including his shoes, was sewn from a variety of animal pelts. Longbow and arrows were skillfully crafted. He carried antibiotic herbs as well as the scars of battle; an arrow had penetrated his back and may have caused his death.

From the balcony of the Albergo Aurora, I can see a gorge beyond the barn where I walked last night and followed the swift flowing stream to a waterfall. Streams such as this have cut deep clefts in the ancient limestone and divided the Val di Non into isolated segments that finger up into forested lands and mountain peaks, and drain downward toward the west. Rushing from glacial snowfields high above, these streams coalesce in the fertile lowlands into the Adige River that flows east to Venice and thence into the Adriatic Sea.

Because of the segmented topography, peasants in this area have maintained independent provincial lives on the edge of society as incursions from the south and north passed them by. From 200 B.C. to the Middle Ages, invaders ranging from Etruscans to Romans traveled through the region via the Brenner Pass to Europe. Germanic speaking peoples periodically migrated south through the area, and Christians, intent on converting the pagans, followed on the heels of the Roman decline.

I scheduled a day for us sisters to visit a sanctuary dedicated to Saint Romedio, a monk who rode into this country on a donkey. The story told is that after a bear killed his donkey, Saint Romedio tamed it. He and the bear lived peacefully in a cave in a cul-de-sac where the present chapel has been built. Here, the bones of saint and bear are venerated. A stairwell leading to a high balcony is adorned with pictures and icons in remembrance of answered prayers, interventions and miraculous cures performed by Saint Romedio. To honor the brown bear, one is held in a pen adjoining the sanctuary.

Tret, Dad's village, was first mentioned as a settlement in thirteenth century documents. This is not to say that humans have not lived in the Val di Non for thousands of years before recorded time. Prehistoric Paleolithic hunters and gatherers ranged from low fertile valleys to the uplands with the seasons. Neolithic foragers followed and utilized the copper and silver from these parts. In the interglacial periods, hunters and gatherers, like Ötze, continued to subsist. When the glaciers permanently receded, agriculturists took over the fertile valley bottoms.

Isolated pockets of indigenous foragers continued living more or less permanently on small homesteads on marginal land higher in the mountains where they developed methods of mixed agriculture and animal keeping. I suspect that these were my ancestors. Invaders from the north and south passed through the Val di Non to the Brenner Pass, some claiming and ruling the territory. The peasants of the region conformed their behaviors to the changing mandates of occupying entities but maintained their independent lifestyles by living isolated lives apart from mainstream society.

When I asked Dad about our ancestors, he said they were English bandits who rode in on horses. This was probably a peasant interpretation of the history of the region that had been invaded repeatedly by Celts. The Hallstatt, a Celtic or Alpine race, who were horsemen and occupied Austria during the first Iron Age, from about 1500 to 500 B.C., may have been the source of my father's violet, and my somewhat paler blue eyes.

In 1909, cousins Matteo and Alphonso Bertagnolli, both eighteen years of age, accompanied by Dad's older brother, Franco, boarded a ship for the United States. Aunt Minica who resided in Rock Springs, Wyoming, had sent Dad money for his fare. On Ellis Island, they were de-loused and transferred to a train headed for Wyoming. Dad recounted how upon boarding he was given salami and cheese and a round loaf of bread, which he promptly dropped. It rolled down the aisle and he ran to retrieve it, knowing that it had to sustain him on the long, cross-country train ride.

Upon arriving in Rock Springs, Dad began working on the railroad. He lived with Aunt Minica and her family and gave her his pay each month, most of which she sent back to their father and family in Italy. Dad, filled with impatience and longing for independence, yet constantly aware of the needs of his beloved family in Italy, kept looking for a way to improve his life.

Work on the railroad did not go well for him. In his early twenties, he was short, only five feet six inches tall, but very strong. By his account, the foreman, a tall burly man, constantly bullied him each morning by pulling his cap down against his nose and making it bleed. He was not one to tolerate such treatment and his resentment built; yet he was too small to go to battle directly with the man. One day after such an episode, when the foreman turned away, Dad picked up a board, hit him over the head, and ran off. "Did you kill him?" I asked in dismay when Dad told me the story. "I don't know. I didn't wait to see. I got out of town and got a job herding sheep for the LaBarge Livestock Company out on the Green River," he replied with a twinkle in his blue eyes.

Dad herded sheep for about a decade and worked his way up to foreman with earned shares in the company. During these years he consistently sent money back to his family in Italy. In the summer of 1919, he and Mamma met and fell in love. As they were preparing to marry, the head of the sheep company told Dad they would no longer need his help. They wanted an unencumbered foreman who could give all of his attention to running the sheep outfit; a married man wouldn't do. So at the time of his marriage in 1921, Dad found himself without employment and his shares in the company withheld. In his own words, he said he had been double-crossed, a phrase I heard often as he recounted the times he had been cheated or swindled. In those days in the frontier mining and railroad towns, law enforcement was poor and transgressions were common but difficult to prove. Several times, Dad meted out his own kind of justice with his fists.

Prohibition may have been the law of the time, but seeing a way out of his financial dilemma, Dad started to bootleg. Distilling grappa must have been a skill he carried with him from his homeland. He and a cohort of friends and relatives, including my mother's brothers, set up stills on the familiar Wyoming steppe. Like other bootleggers, he paid informers who held respectable positions in Kemmerer, who themselves were informed by federal agents, who were also paid off. When a raid was in the offing, Dad was notified. At such times, he and his partners dismantled and hid the stills and dumped the whiskey so that no trace of the operation remained. After examining photos from that time, I now understand why Joe Abram, Louis Concinni, and Joe Dona, who appear frequently in the pictures, were frequent boarders on the ranch. They were not only friends and comrades but also partners during those dangerous, illicit bootlegging days.

Although Dad was never arrested, he was in constant danger of being discovered as he hauled truckloads of barrels of the *White Mule* in the middle of the night over hundreds of miles to buyers. He was making money and borrowed more to finance the purchase of the Diamond Bakery in the mining camp of Diamondville. It was used as a cover for the large quantities of sugar, grain and yeast used in bootlegging. Later he built an automotive garage and two brick bungalows in Kemmerer. My sister Barbara was born in 1923 and the family moved into one of the houses where I was born in 1926. Dad bought a beautiful Cadillac that year and invested in an olive orchard in California.

Things were going well and in 1927, with his pockets full of cash, Dad decided to go back to his homeland, which after World War I had become a part of Italy. It had been almost twenty years since he had seen his father or visited his older brother, Gusto, his loving guardian and protector through the destitution of their earlier years. Dad left Mamma with two young daughters—Barbara, then three, and me, six months of age—to visit Gusto and his family of seven children, all of whom lived with their aged father, Francesco, in the family home in Tret.

During this visit, Dad fell seriously ill with gastroenteritis. Close to death, he was nursed back to health by a cousin and didn't return to the United States for six months. I suspect that the illness was only part of the problem. Seeing his father, aged and ailing, knowing that he might never see him again and feeling the pull to the homeland that he loved, he may have been sick at heart as well. My mother, a worrier by nature, must have been overjoyed upon his return. But this man, who suddenly came rushing back into our lives, undoubtedly frightened me, at the age when children manifest a "strange person syndrome." As I grew into childhood, this fear grew into admiration and there was no one I wanted to be with more than my father.

I preferred working at Dad's side, with the added advantage that it excused me from housework. I relished accompanying him with supplies to the summer range, which reminded him of his homeland and drew up stories from his past. One memorable summer day, we hiked up Fall Creek, a beautiful stream with magenta and yellow monkeyflowers adorning its banks. Dad left me under a huge Douglas-fir while he rode his horse to the sheep camp high in the mountains to check on the herd. He had given me precise instructions not to leave the spot and, in case of rain, to stand under the tree. It began to rain and when Dad returned he was dismayed to find me drenched. I had done what he said, but instead of standing close to the trunk I stood under the dripline of the branches. At times like this, Dad seemed totally baffled by my total lack of common sense. As he slowly learned that my cognitive development and experience lagged considerably behind his own, Dad's instructions became more explicit.

Following his instructions precisely one day when I was a teenager, I helped him accomplish a rather remarkable feat. By this time, Dad had added some cattle to the livestock on the ranch and we were riding out to check on them where they ranged on Bureau of Land Management (BLM) land adjoining our ranch. A herd of wild horses grazed in the area and, whenever riding for pleasure, my sisters and I always marveled at the beautiful stallion that ran at the head of a harem of mares. On this particular day,

Dad and I were able to get very close to the wild horses, and he suggested we try to run-in the stallion. As we cut the horse out of the herd, Dad instructed me, riding bareback as I always did, to take the lead as he followed behind. I still can't imagine how we did it, but we succeeded in running the stallion into our corrals. My memory of the event is of riding like the wind in the lead and feeling elated afterwards for our amazing accomplishment.

Dad named the stallion Cowboy. He was a beautiful animal with the conformity of a mustang and a spirit that never left him. Dad hired a man to break him for riding. When my parents sold the ranch, Dad kept Cowboy in a pasture nearby. One fall when a man borrowed him for hunting, he escaped and went back to his home on the open range.

Bertagnolli family, Matteo top row, second from left (c. 1902)

Gusto and Matteo (c. 1899)   *Dad (Matteo) (1918)*

*Matt and Matilda, wedding
(1921)*

*Barbara, Mamma, and Florence
(1927)*

Diamond Bakery (1923)

Albergo Aurora, Tret, Val di Non, Italy

Bertagnolli cousins on Monte Luca, Italy

Dad, Anna and Joe Dona, Louis Concinni (1960)

Dad with catch (1961)

· 9 ·

White Out

Into the heart of January the weather here at the cabin becomes increasingly threatening. We've just experienced a major snowstorm with several days of powder snow steadily sifting down. The pearl-gray sky holds no promise that the onslaught is easing. The spigot that stands at three feet in the yard has disappeared, as has the burn barrel, which I must burrow down to like a fox after a rodent. Snowfall is even with the deck, which needs shoveling. I have work to do.

The storm builds in momentum. Judging from the amount I've shoveled from the deck, I calculate a foot of new snow has fallen during the night. I reconsider the depth when I step off the deck and sink up to my hips in fluffy powder the consistency of goose down. I decide I'd best postpone cabin chores and clear the parking area before my car is buried.

The snowshoe path across the field, previously packed by my treks to the car, is completely obliterated. "Getting back on track" holds new meaning for me this morning. Deep, new-fallen snow obliterates the packed trail, and I step off and flounder as I struggle to lift one snow-laden snowshoe while mired deep with the other. My tracks across the meadow are a jumble of crosshatched prints interspersed with pits. Finally I reach my gate and the lane that my neighbor David has plowed, and I snowshoe effortlessly down to Lisi's yard.

I congratulate myself that upon leaving the car last time, I encased the snow blower and the plug-in on the electric cord, run from Lisi's cabin, in a blue plastic tarp held in place by bungee cords. I now plug the cord into the block heater, installed last summer, to warm the car engine. I begin plowing and the snow flies out in a huge cloud, settling on me, an abominable snowperson. I clear the space behind the car, start the car and back it into the plowed area. Leaving the motor running, I repeat the process and then re-park the car. With that, I take a break in the warm car and restore my energy with a granola bar and a good drink of water.

About three hours into this snow-blowing saga, I've accomplished my goal. Out of water and hungry, I head back down the lane to the cabin. Although it has snowed at least six inches since this morning, I can still retrace my faint tracks along the packed trail across the meadow and manage to avoid the previous pitfalls.

It's afternoon when I finally get home. After a long drink of water I stoke the fire, heat a fajita left from last night's supper and wash it down with one last bottle of ginger beer I find in the pantry. I put a chicken in the oven and get back to cabin chores: shoveling the decks, chopping kindling and bringing in a good supply of wood. As I finish my work, the wind picks up. Huge plumes spurt off the roof and mix with snow driven east parallel to the ground. The storm and high winds continue through the afternoon. I suspect that by now my car and snow blower are once more completely buried.

At sunset the wind continues howling and the electricity fails. I light candles, take the chicken out of the electric oven, put a lid on it and set it on top of the wood stove to continue cooking. By now the wind is gale force and blowing so hard I'm fearful it might take the roof with it. Another fear that creeps into my mind is that the wind might pick up the wood stacked on the west porch and slam it into the atrium doors, breaking the glass. The thought fills me with panic! What would I possibly do in the dark in such a catastrophe? Why did I ever decide to stay here alone all winter? I take several deep breaths and vow that next winter I won't be anywhere near the Hoback Basin.

After dinner, to assuage my fears, I call my sons and daughters on opposite coasts. The dial tone hums when I pick up the phone, assuring me that at least the phone lines aren't down. Matt tells me the wind has taken roofs off in Kemmerer. In Flagstaff, Arizona, where all is calm, Bobby advises me to stay put until the storm blows over. Never saying I told you so, Lisi gives me sympathy but some stern advice: "Flo, do not leave the cabin under any circumstances until the storm subsides!" I reach Kathryn Ann at the L.A. Airport, on her way back from a meeting. I tell her that I am worried that in this wind, the roof of the cabin might be ripped off and that, like Dorothy, I'll go flying off to the Land of OZ. "Philosophy Rose," she says, "you are not going to Oz. YOU ARE IN OZ! Where you'll be going is to Kansas."

After about two hours the lights come on and I eat a late dinner of baked chicken, rice and salad. As the wind continues to howl, I sit by the stove reading until I doze off and then rouse myself and go to bed. Too tired to worry about the howling wind that continues unabated, I pull the covers up and turn my life over to Mother Nature, who has been in charge all along.

Flashing lights on the cabin walls awaken me. It's three A.M.! The snowplow is out clearing the Upper Hoback Road. I stand at the window with my binoculars and watch the sinister-looking monster with lights flashing and snow spurting. Then I return to bed and a sound sleep.

Next morning, I cannot see through the windows and step out on the porch to assess the aftermath of the storm. The cabin looks like a gingerbread house that has been completely frosted. The air is clear and calm and the sun shines brightly, but the landscape, completely reworked by wind and snow, seems unfamiliar. I write in the morning and then spend several hours straightening up around the cabin, shoveling the porches again, chopping kindling and once more locating the burn barrel.

"Looks like an eastern blizzard," Dad said as he stamped the snow from his boots on the porch and then stepped into the kitchen. The coal stove stood next to the door for easy access at times like this. He opened the oven door, placed his gloves inside to thaw, moved one of the lids of the stove to the side and rubbed his hands together over the glowing coals. Throughout this ritual, he shared with Mamma the ordeal he was encountering in that snowy netherworld.

In western Wyoming, winter storms usually come out of the northwest. They begin gradually, last about three days and then taper off, leaving behind several inches or, at times, feet of snow. Stormy days are often followed by clear cold weather. But occasionally a mass of air over the Rockies becomes stationary and diverts storms from the west northward into Canada where, super-cooled by frigid Arctic air, they flow south into Wyoming and the Great Plains and then westward into the Rockies, replacing an air mass that is slightly warmer and less dense. This scenario produces high winds, frigid temperatures, blizzard conditions and drifting snow for several days. Such storms are called eastern blizzards and are dreaded by ranchers as they slam full force against the Rockies.

My father's temperament—part fury, part persistence—was like winter weather: He carried the dread of eastern blizzards deep in his soul. During his sheepherding days, he was the camp jack, the man who cooked the meals, kept the sheep camp and commissary wagon clean and organized, and moved them from time to time to new locations with good grazing for the herds. He was also in charge of feeding and wrangling the horses.

One day, heading out on foot to find the hobbled horses that had wandered off, he was caught in a sudden blinding eastern blizzard. Lost and disoriented, he wandered around for about three days, the duration of the storm, knowing that if he rested he would freeze to death. When the storm finally cleared, he found his way back to camp. The terror of those days was always on his mind when an eastern blizzard moved in.

Although weather is always highly variable in the Rockies, one constant is the wind, whose blasts can make it feel twenty to thirty degrees colder than the actual air temperature. To protect us from the wind chill, Dad had built a tall windbreak for the house out of slabs, the first cut of logs that he hauled from sawmills in the forests where they were given away or burned. In the summer, Mamma planted a small kitchen garden for her herbs in this protected area, which was more convenient than the larger garden, planted farther from the house. The windbreak was contiguous with a line of buildings that extended across the west side of the entire yard from north to south.

In order from the slab windbreak, the buildings in this little compound were: plant house, cellar, double-garage and bunk, ice and meat houses, all built of railroad ties. The adjoining coal and woodshed and the chicken coop were constructed of slabs. Dad built all of these structures for utility rather than aesthetics. Other than a small harness room built by him, the blacksmith shop, tool shed, smoke house, corrals, barns and a huge hay barn were older structures built of logs or stone by the original homesteaders.

The plant house was not a place where we grew green things but rather the building that housed a 32-Volt Delco diesel generator that produced electricity stored in huge transparent batteries on a shelf. From time to time the batteries were replenished with distilled water Dad obtained by melting snow. Two white balls rose or fell with the charge in the batteries, which were also connected to a wind charger that stood on a high tower in the yard. When the charger whirred and whined in a strong wind, the batteries bubbled and gurgled with the surge of power, sending the white balls floating to the top of the liquid and providing ample electricity for brightly glowing lights. We attempted to gauge our use of electricity to wind power, which unlike diesel fuel, was free but unreliable. On windless days when one or both white balls descended in the battery, the lights dimmed and we often turned them off and lit gas lanterns to conserve battery power for pumping water and to avoid running the generator. Rural electrification to the ranch was not available until after I had left for college.

Built close to the ranch house, the plant house was the center of many activities, especially during winter months. The cement floor had a drain and could be washed down after each project. It housed the water well and a coal cooking stove for heating water and keeping the pipes from freezing. It also served as a milk house where we separated the milk into cream, churned into butter, and skim milk, which was fed to calves, lambs and pigs. In the spring, when the cows with newly born calves were fresh and milk was plentiful, Mamma made cheeses in the plant house.

Joe used the plant house as a washhouse and kept his shaving equipment on a shelf above the water taps and basin. One summer, Barbara tamed a crow, which she called Popo. When the plant house door was left open, it would perch on the shelf and push Joe's shaving materials off to the floor. One day Popo disappeared and we suspected that Joe had killed him. Uncle Richard, always neat and well groomed, also used the plant house as his bathhouse. He'd build a fire in the coal range and heat the room and a washtub of water for a bath. He resented Joe's slovenly habits especially when Mamma had to remind him to bathe and change so that she could wash his dirty clothes.

On washday, Mamma turned the plant house into a laundry room where she washed clothes in a ringer washing machine with two tubs for rinsing. Before the advent of clothes driers, she had to hang the clothes on a line in the yard where in winter they froze solid and battered around in the wind. Mamma said that when the clothes were frozen, they were half dry. If the weather warmed above freezing, they would eventually dry. If not, which was the usual case, we carried them into the house and draped them over racks and chairs next to the big coal heater in the front room to finish drying. When frozen, the bib overalls worn by the men could stand on their own.

The ice and meat house remained cool all summer. Like the cellar, it was well insulated. In winter after the river was frozen solid, Dad cut huge blocks of ice and stored them in half of the building in sawdust, which he had hauled from the sawmills in the summer. The ice lasted throughout the year, and, in the summer, it cooled the building where quarters of beef, muttons or lambs were hung in a screened-in portion to protect the meat from flies. We had no electric refrigerator or freezers in those days so the ice was used to cool our icebox. And each Sunday in summer, Mamma prepared a creamy mixture, which Uncle Richard cooled with chipped ice and churned into ice cream.

In winter the compound of fence and buildings on the windward side of the house and yard acted as a snow fence as well as windbreak, and a huge drift built up behind it along its entire length. The chicken coop at the end of the line of buildings was lower and was often completely buried in snow. We had to use a ladder to get down to feed the chickens, give them warm water and milk and gather their eggs. A light bulb burned in the daytime to keep them laying. Otherwise in the darkness and cold, they would descend into lethargy, stop laying and roost most of the time.

As the huge snowdrift grew, a strip of ground along the back of the buildings remained snow free and formed a long dark tunnel. Like an ice cave, it reeked of danger. My explorations through this tunnel were always accompanied with a fluttering heart and clutching claustrophobic fear. Yet I was drawn to this dangerous labyrinth. The drifts consolidated behind the buildings and I could hop across to the roofs to survey the ranch enclosure below. These first glimmerings of the fears and thrills of adventuring were previews of experiences later in life during my hiking and backpacking days.

Here in the basin, a predictable sequence of weather events typically follows a major blizzard. Skiers and snowmobile aficionados call the days after a storm blue bird days when skies are clear and it is exceptionally cold. Temperatures often plummet to -30°F or lower during the night. I hope we won't see the record low of -60°F that people speak of in these parts.

Not evident on a cloudy day, wind-driven snow seen in the sunshine resembles textured surfaces of sand dunes or the fine riffled silt on the bottom of a slow moving river. After a storm the wind sets to work reconsolidating the snow: contours are rounded off, jagged clefts are created, and new drifts appear in the wake of some slightly elevated object. Ripples, ridges, windrows and fissures appear as well as huge drifts and cirque-like depressions where the day before all was homogeneous and level. Wells form around the bases of trees and bushes and around buildings. Drifts build on the summit of Monument Ridge and plumes of driven snow form enormous cornices on the peaks of the Gros Ventres that will last into summer. After a day and night of this reshaping, and with the temperature plummeting under clear skies, the surface freezes solid and I can once more walk on the snow without sinking.

Each day, with the slightest change in sunlight or shadow, I am constantly brought up short by a new and magical scene. When it is foggy or the sky is overcast or the landscape obliterated by a white-out, familiar places appear unfamiliar, surreal, threatening. Familiarity engenders comfort; strangeness, unease. Slightly varying degrees of light, when observed in the context of this white world, influence different states of mind. On clear days I head out with a devil-may-care attitude; on cloudy or foggy days I proceed cautiously, always aware of directions and landmarks and my own tracks to lead me home.

On the weekend, grandson Jason drove out to help me plow out my car, which was completely buried by the storm. Today I make a run to town for groceries. Returning in late afternoon, pulling the toboggan filled with groceries back to the cabin, I am greeted by a bejeweled fairyland. The landscape is shot through with tiny sparkling lights in subtle opalescent blends of lavender, violet, carmine, coral, tangerine, and turquoise against pearl white. Wondering how such a thing could be, I get down on my knees to examine the source of this luminous wonder. Myriads of glassy, cup-shaped crystals, some as much as half an inch in diameter, are scattered across the surface of the snow. These little concave, glassy crystals, called hoar frost, act as prisms. Light, repeatedly reflected at various angles, produces secondary hues, quite different from the primary colors we see in rainbows.

These extraordinary crystals grow on sunny, cold days when deep, new snow, penetrated by the sun's rays, sublimates and turns from a solid to water vapor, a gas. The water vapor is lighter than the air and rises upward through the snow to the surface, where it condenses and freezes, adding to the size of the crystals.

Dad was the first to rise on cold winter mornings. He kept us from sleeping in with a cacophony as he shook down and emptied the ashes, lighted a roaring fire in the coal range and restocked the fire in the heater in the front room, all of these activities punctuated with hefty sneezes. After brewing a pot of coffee, he carried the first cup of café latte to Mamma, still ensconced in her warm bed. He then set a scant cup of coffee out for himself, to which he added several teaspoons of sugar and a hefty shot of home-brewed grappa. This coffee royal gave him a robust start on his busy rounds of morning chores.

Down from the cold upstairs bedroom, I relished the warmth of the kitchen. On entering, I was expected to say good morning to Dad and any hired men present and to address each person by name. The fragrance of Dad's steaming brew drew me and he'd share a spoon or two with me.

By the time we had dressed by the heater in the front room, Dad had prepared breakfast, usually *smorn*, a kind of German pancake made with beaten eggs, milk and a small amount of flour, which he poured into melted butter heated in a huge cast-iron fry pan. When the batter browned on one side, he turned it, browned it on the other side and then chopped it into small pieces, slathered it with more butter and popped it into the oven until it was toasty brown. Served a bowl of smorn, we sprinkled it generously with sugar and ate heaping spoonfuls dipped in café latte.

Hardy breakfasts were important. Some mornings Mamma would make a kind of porridge cooked with sweetened milk and cream of wheat until thick, and served with melted, browned butter. On other mornings we had *pan de segala*, rye buns containing caraway seeds, spread with butter and jam and eaten with café latte. And, of course, there was home-cured bacon or ham and eggs, fried potatoes and heaps of pancakes. During certain times during the year when they were available, we had seasonal specialties, such as sautéed mushrooms, scrambled eggs and brains and mountain oysters, the testicles of lambs. Needless to say we went off to school with full tummies, and, with doses of coffee, were wide awake.

On my afternoon walks after a big snow, I have a sense of absolute freedom. I can snowshoe without concern over deep gullies, sagebrush or fences. On heading back, I find that my tracks meander like an animal's. In order to walk in a straight line I must focus continuously on a distant point, but with so much to see, I find it impossible.

A heavy snowfall worked by wind leaves an immaculate palette. Snow-free wells around the porch and the shed provide easy access to shelter for small mammals that remain active through the winter. Tracks running back and forth between the cabin and shed indicate a sizeable population of active little critters sharing my residence. I have previously identified skunk tracks; and with field guide in hand, I surmise I am also sharing my dwelling with a short-tailed weasel. Although I have seen it in the summer around the woodpile, I have yet to see it in its frosty-white, ermine coat once prized for robes by royalty. It feeds on mice, shrews and voles that also remain active, living on insects and larvae and seeds under the snow.

At first I was puzzled by the tracks of a snowshoe hare. Using its small forelegs for stability and leverage, it hops as we children used to when we played leapfrog. It brings its large hind feet forward and plants them on either side of its forelegs. As can be imagined, it leaves a unique track: two tiny, closely-spaced points in the snow bordered on either side by long diagonal depressions.

Small rodents forage on the surface until the snow gets deep. Although they seek safe harbor under the buildings they can also survive under a thick layer of snow that metamorphoses into crystalline depth hoar at its base, making it possible for them to move about in this subnivean world. Weasels and foxes, hearing the rummaging of these rodents under a heavy snow pack, can burrow down like augers and zap the little critters. Wondrous, circuitous tracks, like a scribble drawing of a child, show how foxes follow the sounds of the prey animals in their underworld domain.

Tracking through new-fallen snow on sunny days brings back memories of the chasing games of Fox and Geese and of gleefully running and falling in the snow. Covered from head to toe with the soft powdery stuff, we had to stand on the porch to be brushed off with a broom before we could gather around the warmth of a good fire to thaw our frosty fingers and toes. Paul, in his book *The Others: How Animals Made Us Human,* explains how such games of flight and pursuit, where children exchange roles of fox and goose, engage the growing child in a thrilling and somewhat frightening transition in identity and help build confidence in this shape-shifting world.

Today while out snowshoeing, I decide to explore a place I have noticed from a distance over several days, one that looks like an excavation of some sort on the south slope of Clark Butte. A trench leads to it from the top of the butte and then extends southward. Deep and wide, the trench is difficult to cross with snowshoes. Although I have not heard or seen a snowmobile, my first guess is that a driver may have experienced motor trouble and then walked back to the road for help, in the process making the trench.

I ease down into the deep trench and begin walking up the slope to where much digging has been done. It doesn't take long for me to change my suppositions. The bottom of the trench is thick with elk scat. Puzzled, I email David Petersen for an explanation. An author and experienced hunter of elk, he has been a loyal internet friend this winter. He confirms my observations and explains further what occurred. The huge, excavated area is called an elk crater, a good descriptor for the amount of disruption at the site that seems literally to have been blown apart, as elk dig down to feed on the tall wheat grass that grows near badger diggings. A large herd of several hundred elk had apparently moved in during the night, probably from a feeding ground in the Gros Ventres. After eating their fill of the wheat grass, they continued on to a new site, thus creating the trench.

At times the elk respond to an innate urge to move to their historic wintering grounds on the sagebrush grass steppe to the east in the Green River Basin. But ranches and fences and gas and oil exploration and extraction now block their way. The feeding grounds set up by the Wyoming Game and Fish Department are supposed to compensate for this loss of winter range. Occasionally, however, the urge to head east dominates and the elk raid haystacks along the way. Ranchers naturally protest loudly, and Wyoming Game and Fish personnel do their best to drive the elk back to their designated feeding grounds. The problem, of course, is that artificial feeding grounds do not mesh with elk instincts, which at times take over and set these magnificent animals roving in the middle of the night.

Getting us to the school bus, over a mile and a half of drifted snow on unplowed roads, was always a problem. Mamma, who had missed most of her eight years of education because of various family needs or bad weather, understood the importance of consistent school attendance. Both she and Dad did their best to drive us the five miles to the Opal School and, when it closed because of the Depression, to deliver us on time to meet the school bus. In winter, it was a constant challenge that required extreme commitment and often involved chaining up, shoveling, pushing and, occasionally, even after tremendous expenditure of effort, missing the bus.

Snow days, when schools were closed and parents notified, were unknown in those days. As I recall, schools were closed only once. A raging blizzard began after we had been delivered to the Burgoon School and blocked all roads for several days. Members of the community volunteered to take bus children into their homes until roads were re-opened. Since we had no telephone on the ranch and my parents were snowbound as well, the message that we were safe was delivered by the section foreman on the railroad that ran through our ranch. While my mother fretted over our safety, we spent an unprecedented vacation playing with other children.

One year Dad decided he'd solve the problem of getting us to the bus stop over snow-packed or blocked roads. He built a small one-horse snow sled that seated an adult and two or three children. Like a tiny sheep camp, it was covered in canvas to keep out the wind and snow. It had a window in front and, below it, a slit through which the reins were slipped to guide the horse. Dad hooked up old Blindy, a tame draft horse with one eye, and we embarked on our voyage with anticipation each morning. Like our contemporaries, the Princesses Elizabeth and Margaret, Barbara and I were royalty riding off in our carriage.

Light snow was falling one morning as we headed toward the bus stop. By the time we had reached the dug-out, where the road came up out of the river bottom and traversed a sagebrush terrace, it was snowing hard. On top of the bluff as we headed toward the highway, a blinding whiteout enveloped us and totally disoriented Dad. He could see nothing ahead or behind us; not the highway, the fence line or the road we were to follow. From his constant queries as to whether we were all right, Barbara and I sensed his concern.

Finally trusting in Blindy's homing instincts, Dad gave the old mare the reins, assured she would take us home. But with a shocking jolt, the sleigh suddenly overturned into a deep gully and old Blindy floundered in snow up to her belly. Dad crawled out and unhitched the horse and rescued us. He then pulled the sled to level ground. By the time he righted horse, sled and us children, the storm had begun to break and Dad could determine our location: About a half-mile east of the bus stop, we had overturned in a deep ravine along the highway. It was obvious there would be no school for us this day.

It was almost noon when we finally arrived back at the ranch, where Mamma was beside herself with worry. She and Dad sat us on chairs in front of the open oven door, rubbed our hands and feet with snow and gave us hot milk to drink. With his clever contraption, Dad had brought us close to disaster. The sled was parked and never used again except as a playhouse or a covered wagon for imaginary pioneer treks. Utterly confident in the ability of my father to get us home, I felt no fear during this adventure and was quite amazed and pleased with the special attention from our parents.

Whenever possible, I accompanied my father to check on our sheep herds and herders and to bring them supplies. The sheep wintered on the Carter Lease, which we called "the desert," on the BLM rangeland about five miles from our ranch. In the winter this meant riding on a horse-drawn hayrack whose wheels had been replaced with runners. Tucked into hay and covered with a good blanket, I nonetheless arrived home one evening with frostbitten toes. For years, whenever my feet were chilled in the winter, chilblains would swell my toes to scarlet, itchy, painful lumps. Such incidents did not quell my desire to accompany my father to the sheep, in whose management I had an intense interest.

Similar in bioregional characteristics to the high plateaus of Mongolia or Patagonia in Argentina, the Wyoming steppe is a perfect winter range for sheep. Not quite as omnivorous as goats, which eat almost anything, sheep nonetheless find forage in this ideal habitat. In the winter, winds clear the snow from the dried vegetation and drift it to the lee of tall sagebrush. Sheep differ from cattle in that they can eat snow as their source of water and dig through it to find plants. And their thick woolly coats are excellent insulation against the cold. These characteristics make them ideally suited for wintering on the steppe habitat of Wyoming.

The seasonal cycle of sheep ranching began in the fall after the herd had been culled of dry ewes. Healthy, good milk producers, especially those who had a record of birthing and raising twins or triplets, were selected for the herd. The sheep were also chosen for heavy wool production and, if possible, for bald faces—those with very short wool over their faces. Wool would grow over the eyes of those without this characteristic and would have to be shorn mid-winter to clear their vision.

Top-grade rams were released into the herds in December, timed so that ewes would begin lambing in early May. During the time of breeding and gestation, especially when the snow was deep, the herd's diet of desert plants was supplemented with hay from the ranch, together with pellets or corn. Thus the sagebrush ecosystem, which seems uninhabitable to humans, provides an ideal winter grazing habitat for what John Muir refered to as "fourfooted locusts."

Here at the cabin, after the invigorating activities of snowshoeing and chores and preparing my evening meal, I eat by candlelight. Although I know that days are getting longer, for the month of January the change in light is hardly discernible. Darkness descends quickly. With the dishes washed, I build a fire and sit reading for several hours before climbing the stairs to the loft and the warm comfort of flannel pajamas and sheets and down comfort-er. I leave one window open just a crack so that I can hear night sounds of coyotes and sometimes the mewing calls of cow elk across the meadow. Occasionally the lights of a car on the Upper Hoback River Road flash through the window, but for the most part all is dark and supremely quiet.

Winter in the Hoback Basin

Sheepherder and Dad

Dad's sled (1935)

Ranch house

· 10 ·

The Coming of Light

Candlemas, February 2, winter cross-quarter day. Since the winter solstice I've been under a cloak of darkness awaiting this day, midway to the spring equinox. Back at the cabin after a late afternoon walk, I light candles. As light builds, something in me stirs as it does in all creatures. Bears turn over or drowsily emerge from their winter sleep long enough to sniff the air and go back for a few more winks. Elk decide that its time to go elsewhere. Humans feel the need for celebration.

Long before human memory, creatures have responded to this inner calling. Original Northern Hemisphere human cultures marked this emergence with fire. Romans feasted and offered the sacrifice of goats and the young nobles, smeared with blood, struck women with goatskin whips called *februa* (from which February is derived) to ensure fertility. On the ranch in early February, we celebrated the coming of light with our own bloody sacrificial rite: we killed the pigs.

Usually diligent about getting us to school, our parents gave us the week off to participate in this grand event. After a summer of slopping the pigs—feeding them skim milk, scraps from the table, greens from the garden, and mash—the two weaned piglets that Dad bought in the spring had reached plump perfection. Uncle Matt Failoni, husband of Mamma's sister Mary, came to the ranch to help Dad with this project. He brought with him his two sons, my cousins Matt Jr. and Joe, and the paraphernalia for killing the pigs and processing their meat. Meanwhile Aunt Mary stayed on their Rock Creek Ranch to take care of things.

As our fathers set up their abattoir in the plant house, the front room became the children's domain where we enjoyed a week of unmitigated play, a wonderful respite from the darkness of winter. Chairs were lined up with desks for playing, of all things, school, the very thing from which we had been temporarily excused. Barbara, the oldest and self-appointed teacher, ruled us strictly, giving assignments one after another and tasks to perform to which we complied with absolute obedience. When bored with this, with blankets loaned by our willing mother, we set up a netherworld of tunnels and hidey-holes around the furniture. The games evolved during the construction as our imaginations improvised various adventurous scenarios. Through it we made periodic forays to see how our fathers were doing.

We weren't allowed to see the killing, when Dad dispatched each pig with a precisely aimed shot to the head with his pistol. Immediately following and subsequently, with frequent visits to the butchering site, we witnessed the complicated procedure unfold for each pig. If the piglet was a male, Dad cut out the testicles, braised them over the fire and cut them into pieces, which he shared with everyone present as the opening ceremony of butchering. They then hanged the pig by its hind legs, severed a vessel in its neck with a knife and collected the blood in a clean milk pail, which they handed to Mamma to store in the unheated dining room, which, closed off in winter, served as a walk-in cooler.

Dad and Uncle Matt repeatedly lowered the pig into a steel drum of boiling water heated over a pit with a roaring fire. After each dunking, they scraped the skin with large-bladed knives until the outer layer was free of hair and clean and white. They then gutted the pig and examined the entrails carefully. When sweetbreads, kidneys, liver and heart were determined free of parasites, Dad turned these over to Mamma who would store them in preparation for special meals served throughout the week. Next they cut off the pig's head and, after extracting the brain and tongue, relegated them all to Mamma to store in the cold dining room.

Dad and Uncle Matt then hauled the pigs to the plant house abattoir. They carved and sawed the pigs into various parts for hams, bacon, salt pork, chops and roasts. Scraps would be used for making pork and beans. They cut off and ground the fat, a portion of which they mixed with ground elk or beef and a variety of spices. They pressed the mixture into long casings for sausage and salami, tied off at appropriate lengths with white string. They reserved the remaining fat for rendering. Sometimes Mamma pickled the thoroughly cleaned and skinned pig's feet. At other times she boiled them with leftover scraps in the huge stock pot.

As time and room on her stove permitted, she simmered and rendered the fat. It melted to a light amber-colored liquid floating with little golden, crispy chunks we called chitlins. (In Southern states this name refers to rendered pigs' intestines.) Mamma strained the melted fat into empty Hills Brothers coffee cans, saved during the year for this purpose. In the cold dining room, the liquid solidified into smooth off-white lard. Afterward she lidded the cans and stored them in the cellar. With the lard, she made delicate pie pastries and deep-fried raised donuts, sprinkled with sugar, all of which were delicious, but unbeknownst to us, loaded with cholesterol. Handfuls of chitlins, stored in a large pan in the cool room, became snack food for the Italian boarders and children.

Butchering the two pigs took several days, during which Mamma prepared a variety of meals: kidney and heart stew served with polenta, fried liver with onions, brains and scrambled eggs, pork and beans, pork chops and roast pork. Mamma mixed the blood, which had been stored in the "cooler," with eggs, flour and spices and placed the mixture in a hot water bath to bake. She called it "blood pudding" and served the dark maroon wedges (about the consistency of quiche) as a side dish. She also prepared head cheese by simmering the pig's head in a huge pot for hours until the meat fell loose. She poured the strained and seasoned liquid from this brew over choice pieces of meat she reserved in a large, flat pan, which she placed in the dining room to cool. It jelled to the consistency of aspic and was served as an appetizer or a condiment with lunch. Tripe soup was made from the lining of the stomach that first had to undergo a long and careful cleansing procedure with lye.

The last step in this saga of pork processing took place in an old rock building with a sod roof, which may have been the first family dwelling on the ranch. Dad converted it to a smoke house where hams, bacon, and salt pork were soaked in brine or rubbed with various salt and spice mixtures, which he experimented with through the years. He had reserved some meat from an elk he had killed in the fall and with it made his version of prosciutto. After curing the array of sausages and meat, Dad hung them by strings from racks and smoked them by feeding a small fire with dampened wood chips. He smoked them for about ten days and then recruited us to help him carry the array of cured meats to the cellar where they were hung on beams and stored for use during the coming year.

The pigs, whose products lasted throughout the year, brought more variety to our diet than any other domestic creature raised on the ranch. They were relatively easy to raise in a pen with access to water and abundant vegetarian food and given no meat to eat.

Dad had carried with him from Italy the knowledge and habits of subsistence and frugal living on the land. And with Mamma's indefatigable dedication to gourmet cooking—she would have made an excellent consultant for Calvin W. Schwabe's recipe book, *Unmentionable Cuisine*—we partook of a series of delicious, although unusual, seasonal feasts.

We reserved all meat scraps and bones for sheep and ranch dogs. When Rae's parents left ranching, she gave me her horse Ginger and Frisky, her collie dog, who raised a litter of puppies for us each year. We played with the cuddly creatures until they were weaned and taken off to the sheep camps for training. I can still remember their distinctive musky and pungent odor.

I return to another cold February day when, as a grown woman, mother and teacher, I experienced the coming of light in a very private and introspective way. A blizzard was raging when I boarded the train early one morning and headed out of town. The throbbing, rhythmic rocking of the cars washed the tension from my body and suspended me in a meditative mood. Removed from the constant press of teaching and family, I suffered twinges of conscience for finding such pleasure in uninterrupted time away from my regular routine. I had packed sandwiches and a thermos of coffee, which I sipped from time to time, as I took my eyes from a book I was reading to stare out the window at the wind-driven snow shearing across the sagebrush.

I had followed Catholicism devoutly as a teen. In an idealistic frame of mind, typical of youth, I developed a plan for my life honed literally from Church doctrine. I avidly read the lives of saints and was enthralled with the book *The Robe*, a historical account of the crucifixion of Jesus, and the movie, "The Song of Bernadette," the story of a devoted nun, which romanticized the religious life. In the *Catholic Register*, the only periodical we received at home, I followed the latest news of Padre Pio, a stigmatic who bore the wounds of Christ and later was canonized. I listened avidly to the radio "Catholic Hour" hosted by Cardinal Fulton J. Sheen, a charismatic evangelist. Later, at the University of California, with the passion of today's fans for celebrities, I attended one of his talks in San Francisco. I joined the Newman Club, the Catholic students' organization, and volunteered to set out vestments each evening for Mass the next morning. I remember those moments alone in the lovely chapel as a special spiritual time of peace and contemplation.

After college, when in physical therapy training at the Mayo Clinic, I attended daily Mass and arranged for weekly instruction with a priest as I continued my search for faith. After completing my training in physical therapy, I seriously considered a religious vocation, but my attraction to the opposite sex as well as unequivocal objections from my father, deterred me. However, in spite of my father's attitude, I would have joined the Medical Mission Sisters if they had allowed women to volunteer for several years rather than a lifetime. In hindsight I realize that this would have been an ideal time for me to devote a few of my young adult years to a religious or secular organization, where I could have served others. The Peace Corps, which was instituted a decade later in 1961, would have been perfect for me. With no such options open, I revised my life plan and determined that my role would be that of a mother.

I had always loved little children and in both training and later as a therapist for the Society for Crippled Children and Adults in Salt Lake City I felt a natural bond to them. I looked forward to the experience of birthing and nurturing my own. Following the Catholic plan, I was determined that, when I married, I would never use birth control to time the birth of children but would accept them in their own time. Later as a mother, I felt unconditional love and devotion for my four small children, each born about a year apart. My prayers were always ones of supplication for patience and understanding and the blessing to raise these little ones to productive adults. My love for them knew no bounds as my love for my husband waned. With undiagnosed post-partum depression, my body and spirit began to falter. Fortunately, a fervent interest in nature and teaching began to replace my religiosity. Watching birds or hiking up a mountain lifted my spirit far more than kneeling before an altar.

Yet I continued to follow the mandates of my religion and herded my sleepy-eyed children to Mass and Holy Communion each day of Lent and on First Fridays. I served as president of the Altar Society, the organization of Catholic women, which was responsible for much more than overseeing the care of the priest's vestments, altar cloths and flowers. This group also organized religious instruction for children, provided support and food for families of deceased or ill parishioners and raised money for the church. Regular attendance at church became a duty to conformity. In my mid-thirties during the early 1960s when others throughout the country were celebrating their freedom, I felt shackled by the expectations of family, church and the social mores of a small town. Thanks to television and radio, I was not insulated from national and world events. Starting with the election of President John F. Kennedy my interest in politics and governance grew and, with the examples of Robert Kennedy and Martin Luther King, broadened to encompass the rights of all people, regardless of color or gender. The speeches and examples of these great men lifted my spirits; their deaths, coming one after the other, were devastating. I mourned the loss of each, but the tragedies increased my commitment to social equity issues.

Invited to take part in telecommunication education for scattered rural Wyoming science teachers, I was on a train on that particular February morning, heading for Sinclair, Wyoming, population about twenty. There Bell Telephone had set up a facility in an old hotel. I was to address teachers throughout the state on the topic of science fair projects, in which my students had demonstrated consistent success.

The next day, with tremulous voice over a telephone line and shaky writing on an overhead projector, I made a feeble attempt at multi-media education, transmitted to schools throughout the state. At a time before television or computers were used in the schools, this experiment would make good comedy compared to effective Power Point presentations in current distance education courses. Even so, the rudimentary program did facilitate two-way communication as I responded to questions posed by teachers from remote schools. Although inspired and passionate about inquiry, which I had learned paid off in terms of cognitive development and motivation in students, I was happy when the ordeal had ended and I could get back to the book I was reading.

I had started reading *The Phenomenon of Man* by Pierre Teilhard de Chardin as the train left the station in Kemmerer. After arriving at my destination, I continued to read into the night. A gift from Nancy Peternal, a devout Catholic and fellow teacher, the book spoke to my deepest concerns. Teilhard's words provided a bridge between my restless soul searching for meaning and my affinity for the natural world. A French Jesuit priest and paleontologist who spent many years in China studying the remains of ancient man, Teilhard was a dilemma to his superiors. He remained faithful to his vows, but in his writing he proposed a new concept of *cosmogenesis*, in which all life and spirit on Planet Earth were conjoined with an evolving God. A scientist and paleontologist, Teilhard was trying to find a way to reconcile the genesis of spirit and matter.

The Catholic Church banned *The Phenomenon of Man* but, nearing his death, Teilhard gave his papers to a woman friend who published them for him posthumously. His book persuaded me that I was not a creature separated from the rest of existence but part of a greater whole that encompassed all life in our diverse earth community. This was the first among a series of intellectual and spiritual insights that came to me through books and people that would slowly change my perception of the meaning of a spiritual life on Planet Earth.

The theory of evolution had been avoided or just mentioned in passing in my undergraduate studies. Meanwhile Freud's pleasure principal and Skinner's idea of learning and behavior modification provided little help in my efforts to understand the interrelationship of spirit and matter. One day, as an undergraduate, I interrupted the ranting of a psychology professor. He insisted that there was no such thing as motherly love in animals and suggested that the attraction of the female to its young stemmed from the pleasure she derived from suckling them. When I raised my hand and asked, "What about chickens?" the point of his assertion was lost in laughter, including his own.

Teilhard's book was my first reading of anything other than the standard Catholic account of our cosmology. Now before me was the writing of a simultaneously scientific and religious man who legitimized my feelings. Discussions with Father John O'Connor, our tall, stern Irish priest, who stopped by our house for a visit from time to time, invariably veered toward this subject. He often warned me, "Florence, you're getting a bit close to heresy."

Despite this warning, I could not turn away from the idea that life and consciousness were undergoing constant transformation. Whether moving toward a higher state of perfection as Teilhard asserted, I could not say, but I was assured that the spiritual and material world were not unrelated, static and predetermined, but mysteriously intertwined and evolving together. What did this mean for the practice of my faith? More importantly, how would this change of mind and heart affect my life as wife, mother and teacher? The answer came in an unexpected and alarming way.

Strangely enough, or perhaps not so strangely, at the same time I was beginning to question and revise my spiritual and philosophical orientation to the world, my emotional and personal life began to unravel. The break came one evening as I was sitting at the dinner table with my family when I suddenly felt as if I were losing touch with the world and floating away. I told Bob that I was not feeling well, excused myself from the dinner table and asked him to please clear the table and get the children ready for bed. I went to my room and called my mother and asked her for help. Alarmed by my state, she came right over and called the doctor who injected me with a powerful sedative and then prescribed a tranquilizer.

The consensus of my family was that I had been working too hard and needed time off from teaching. Heeding their advice, at the end of the school year, I asked for a leave of absence from teaching. I was told that the school district did not grant leaves, so I was forced to resign. Without the stimulation of teaching and under the influence of tranquilizers (which I later learned were counter-indicated for depression), I developed panic attacks and struggled to overcome the persistent fear that I was losing my mind. Truth be known, I probably was. Returning to some normality was a struggle, comparable, I suspect, to that faced by destitute people who find themselves in situations for which they see no way out.

As events unfolded, a year away from teaching did not relieve my anxiety and told me that over-work was not the problem. In the spring I was considering applying again for a teaching position when I once more became pregnant. The district rules prohibited pregnant women from teaching. I miscarried at five months in late summer. This was my second miscarriage following the birth of my fourth child, Bobby. I carried the first fetus, which had been dead for some time, until the seventh month and realize now that it's remarkable that I didn't die of septicaemic poisoning. After the last miscarriage, I decided I'd done my share for motherhood and would never get pregnant again.

I again applied for a teaching position and the only available opening was for a home teacher for a severely challenged polio victim, a young girl who was quadriplegic and homebound. Her father was a worker on the railroad and they lived in a dismal house about five miles from town. While the frigid winds blew through the frame house that winter, we sat by the coal-heating stove trying to keep warm.

Along with tutoring her each day, I gave Sherri physical therapy to try to develop some strength in her seriously affected muscles. She was undoubtedly the most challenging patient and student I had ever encountered. Her mother, although faced with what seemed to me insurmountable hardships, approached each day with courage. Her constant chatter, which sometimes kept us from the lessons for the day, told me that she too was mediating her depressing situation as best she could. After working my way through a bleak year, in the spring I learned that there was an opening for a biology teacher. I applied for and was accepted for the position.

Having recovered sufficiently from my emotional problems to realize that I needed professional help, early that summer I made an appointment with a psychiatrist in Salt Lake City. Driving to the first meeting, I was filled with doubts and fear. In my small town, seeing a psychiatrist branded the person as crazy. It was an admission that, indeed, I had serious problems that I couldn't solve for myself. It didn't ease my state of mind when two women about my age committed suicide that spring, one of them a friend who had recommended her psychiatrist to me. At this time, doctors frequently over-prescribed tranquilizers, and antidepressant drugs were still in the experimental stages.

The psychiatrist didn't dwell on uncovering the antecedents of my anxieties; one session with me probably told him all he needed to know. His orientation was to explore alternatives that would improve my life, primarily through intellectual engagement. As I left his office one day, he handed me a book and remarked: "Ecology is a very interesting and developing field. You should look into it. "

The book, *The Forest and the Sea* by Marston Bates, was my first reading on ecology. Loren Eiseley's introduction to that book led me to his own book, *The Immense Journey*. Both books were tremendously inspiring and whetted my appetite for the study of ecology and natural science. With field guides in hand that summer on weekend hikes and camping trips with the family, I began identifying flowers and trees. On one of these forays, a strange full-bodied bird with a long decurved bill circled a mountain meadow, calling a plaintive "curlew." The long-billed curlew captured my heart and led me to Fred Bodsworth's *The Last of the Curlews* and to the thrills of bird watching.

Changing the course of my life has not been easy. It has constantly demanded that I question my assumptions. It requires that I evaluate and revise firmly held beliefs and values. It asks me to walk away from the expectations of others and to formulate my own meanings. It challenges me to be a pilgrim, following a burning desire in my heart, a promise always undefined and often unfulfilled. It assumes that I can be strong and courageous enough to face the vagaries and uncertainties of life with hope and optimism. I state these challenges in the present tense because they have continued during every step of my journey. Movement toward change raises questions that I must ask myself over and over: How *do* I change my mind? As I gain a new perspective, how can I remain true to others? How do I maintain my energy and fortify my faith when confronted with hardships, losses and failures? How do I respond to and serve loved ones while acknowledging my own needs for fulfillment? Changes in my life have not come to me with fanfare or great epiphanies. Like the building of light in midwinter, they develop gradually and indiscernibly until one day I find myself making my way through a more accepting and interesting landscape.

As February moves along, the days lengthen noticeably. The increase in daylight buoys my spirits as it did back in the days when, as a child, I decorated a shoebox with red and white crepe paper and gave careful consideration to the valentine for each classmate. And after the school party, I examined valentines, given to me by friends for whom I felt a special attraction, for hidden messages. The first manifestations of human love entered my child's heart and brought hints of a force that would take precedence as I grew older. It was on such a day and at an unlikely time in my life, when I was approaching sixty and considering retirement, when I found a new beginning.

Valentine's Day, 1985. I scanned the deplaning passengers as they streamed out of the gate. A tall man with gray hair and beard, glasses, a worn brown leather jacket and carrying a small, brown satchel and briefcase, strode by me with giant steps. I recognized him from pictures on his book covers. Running to catch up, I called "Paul Shepard?" He turned, looked at me with surprise, and said, "Oh, Flo, there you are."

This was my first direct encounter with Paul Shepard, although I had met him many times before through his writing. For years in my graduate seminars, I had required his provocative books. Those out of print, I ordered directly from him. Several weeks before, I had received a note from Paul, asking if I might meet him at the airport for lunch on February 15. He would be flying through on his way to a speaking engagement in Wyoming. I replied by asking if he could possibly come in a day early to be a guest speaker in my graduate seminar where we were reading his *Nature and Madness*. He agreed and here he was.

I drove him from the airport to my class, where students were waiting expectantly. Paul admitted that for many years he had been "haunted by ontogeny, a kind of necessary pattern of growth toward maturity" in which we humans are inextricably entwined in a dance with other living creatures. His theory was that children nurtured close to nature—first in early childhood by a loving mother and caregivers and through adolescent challenges outdoors with good role models— mature into discerning adults with an understanding of our biological and cultural connections to the earth as well as its ecological limits. Without this experience they retain immature (neotenic) characteristics into adulthood, and, as a result, society suffers. I was spellbound by Dr. Shepard's ideas and his eloquence.

I watched him and listened intently as he explained the ideal development of children raised close to the natural world. His words were familiar; his being was not: tall and lean with clear blue eyes that scanned the shifting terrain of thought as he spoke, he was a little stooped, perhaps from years spent writing at a desk. The colors of his old brown jacket and navy blue turtleneck were poorly matched as were his socks of different colors, but I was immediately drawn to him.

Paul had a habit of taking off his glasses and running his fingers through his hair as he searched for a way to reframe his thoughts. He was soft spoken and articulate, gentle and humble in demeanor. He listened attentively to questions but never responded to them directly. Instead he elaborated on them further, weaving them into a speculative tapestry to show the complexity of the problem uncovered. During the lecture, Paul's mind overflowed with multiple sources and examples. Like fairy tales with mythic origins, his ideas tapped our desires to make this world a better place for the children and filled us with hope, curiosity and the desire to initiate change. This first encounter with Paul Shepard was a very special moment, when life set before me undreamed-of alternatives. The image of him walking off that plane into my life that day has never left me.

Following the class, we dined with two other guests visiting me at the time: nature philosopher Dolores LaChapelle, my house guest and a previous acquaintance of Paul's, and Noreen Garman, a friend and colleague who would lecture in our department the next day. Paul explained that after his speaking engagement at a humanities symposium in Jackson, Wyoming, he would be leaving on a Fulbright lectureship in India and Australia. When he mentioned that he had just completed *The Sacred Paw*, a book on the bear, my companions asked me to tell him about my bear dream that I had previously related to them:

With a child in my arms, I was walking along a ridge crest with tundra falling away below. A man walked at my side. Two yearling bear cubs were following close behind. The man, seeing that I was watching them warily, assured me I had nothing to fear. It was twilight, but suddenly an undulating, green curtain of light spread across the sky. I turned to the man and in his stead was a magnificent bear with close-set eyes and a head so large that it filled my entire field of vision. Standing there together—the bear on his hind legs swaying ever so slightly—we watched the spectacle of light.

Paul listened intently and when I'd finished, said, "Well, Flo, that says it all." I hadn't the slightest idea what he meant. Later he told me that, at that moment, he knew he was the bear in my dream.

The next morning, as I picked up Noreen at the bed and breakfast to take her to the university, I dropped by Paul's room to say good-bye and deliver his honorarium. I thanked him and wished him well on his journey and informed him that a graduate student would take him to the airport. Paul was rearranging his belongings meticulously in a small satchel. Apparently everything that he needed for the coming months was contained in it and a briefcase for notes and books.

I left Paul in a somewhat distracted state with a far-away look in his eyes, which I attributed to his planning ahead for his next assignment. The vintage Paul Shepard was encapsulated in that parting: a thoughtful scholar concentrating on the moment, with belongings pared down to an absolute minimum.

During the next months, busy with chairing the affairs of the department, I tried to brush away intruding thoughts of Paul, but found myself looking in vain through the mail each day for a card from India. Although I had convinced myself that I would carry through with my latest plans to remain single for the rest of my life, I couldn't get him off my mind.

A hectic quarter ended and in June, and with grandson Jason in tow I escaped to the Hoback Basin for a week at sister DJ's cabin. Her school year of teaching had not yet ended and she generously offered her cabin to me for a brief respite. On the way, we stopped to visit my mother, and, as I entered her house the telephone rang. It was Paul. He had called my home and my granddaughter, Meredith, thinking he might catch me at my mother's on my way to the cabin, had given him the number. After his sojourn in India and Australia, he was driving across Nevada headed for his cabin in the Bitterroot Mountains of Montana and wondered if he might drop by for a visit.

Having given him somewhat nebulous directions, I was surprised the next day when he arrived at DJ's cabin in a beat-up blue Honda and a cloud of dust. Aside from the immediate attraction we felt for each other, there were other circumstances that helped to strengthen the relationship: He, from a family of sons, was a brother; I, from a family of daughters, was a sister. From the same generation and with similar academic backgrounds, we both shared a passion for the natural world.

Paul and I spent three days hiking, in conversation and going over our lives. The next day as he left, he kissed me firmly and said, "I'll be in touch." And so he was for the next eleven years, in spite of my aforementioned plans, until the day that death took him from my life as mysteriously as he had entered it.

Paul and I reduced our teaching schedules so that we could be together for most of the year. In awe of his profound knowledge, I expected that our life together would be one long, human ecology seminar. That was not to be. Witnessing his concentrated dedication to writing and research each day, I kept my distance and respected his silence while he was at his desk, which was a good part of each day from early morning until mid- afternoon.

On leaves and sabbaticals, we traveled on Paul's research forays or invited talks. Independent and on my own for fifteen years, at first I felt a bit threatened standing by this man in his limelight. I soon decided that I should not begrudge his moments of recognition, so deserved by his many years of scholarly work. I fully enjoyed and learned from each of his lectures and sincerely acknowledged and celebrated his well-deserved acclaim.

Although tolerant, gentle of demeanor, and a good listener, Paul was no pushover. His sense of ethics was well developed and when wronged, he asserted his position strongly. His incomparable wit punctuated each of my days with laughter. Independent, filled with radical ideas from years of research and rich experience, he was not inclined to change his mind or turn a project over to someone else to plan for him. It was clear to me from the beginning I'd have to run to catch up with this man.

After being partners for three years, in 1988 we invited our children and grandchildren to Thanksgiving dinner. Preceding our feast together, we recited our marriage vows with them as witnesses. The only person who cried was the judge who performed the ceremony. It was one of the happiest moments of my life.

During our life together we traveled worldwide. Each journey was meticulously planned in terms of his research for a book in process, as Paul led us to unbelievable places and incredible experiences. He was gathering information primarily for *The Others: How Animals Made us Human*. His thesis was that we evolved in conjunction with animals that taught us how to live on this planet. He was also seeking historical validation of the bear as the most important animal guide for Northern Hemisphere people.

When in 1990 we decided to build our cabin, I wondered if the planning might cause trouble between us, especially since Paul would not accept an architect's design. I could see that the construction of this cabin was a project he relished. I had certain requirements in terms of orientation to the sun and organization of space and he possessed a sense of aesthetics that I lack. We worked together well until we had something we both liked and a contractor who could build it. That fall during construction, when I had to return to Salt Lake City to my teaching, Paul stayed on to supervise the process.

We were proud of our little cabin and entertained many friends and family here for the next few years. Unfortunately Paul was unable to enjoy it for long before he was diagnosed with terminal lung cancer. Thanks to him, I've lived in the comforting and aesthetic ambience of the cabin ever since.

Whether across the oceans, in the solitude of his cottage in California, at my old home in Salt Lake City or in our cabin in the Hoback—and whether in health or on his deathbed—Paul remained essentially the same as the first time I'd met him: quiet, thoughtful, witty, focused, gentle, removed from the ordinary. Since Paul's death, through a decade of editing and publishing his last books and organizing his archives at Yale University, I have gained a clearer understanding of his profound knowledge and insight. But what I learned from him through his actions and demeanor was as important, and has become an example for how I try to live my life and hope to approach death.

Meeting Paul when I did was fortuitous for me. Having experienced failure and rejection as administrative head of our department, I was disillusioned with academia. Paul brought a fresh breath of air and multiple alternatives into my life. His wit brightened my days, even when he was close to death. He sincerely felt I had something to say and respected my opinion and always encouraged me to write my story. I like to think he'd be pleased with this attempt.

Paul approached ill health as he had each change in his life, with confidence and hope. He continued to do what was possible without bemoaning losses. Paul loved being in the company of others who shared his intellectual curiosity. During his illness, family and friends streamed in to see him. He died on July 12, 1996, with his daughter, Jane, my two daughters, Kathryn Ann and Lisi, and me at his side. Paul took his last breath as a storm approaching from across the salt flats of the Great Salt Lake blew through the open windows into his bedroom. The room vibrated with transformation. On the dresser, a lovely bouquet of delphiniums dropped its petals.

Paul Shepard (1990)

Paul ready for fishing   *Flo and Paul wedding (1988)*

Paul and Flo on
Sheenjek River
(1988)

Flo and Paul,
India (1989)

Paul on train,
India (1989)

· 11 ·

Silence

Winter slowly loosens its grip and gives way to spring, but not without a struggle. After a brief respite with clear days and blue skies, another storm sweeps in, erasing the fences, willows, sagebrush and gullies. The first weeks of March are cold and snowy. Although threatening, these days can also be thrilling and spectacularly beautiful. When snow falls quietly, layer upon layer, it adds to the stillness as does the landscape's muted tones of white, gray and sepia. Hard freezes solidify this quiet time and make it palpable. What sets winter apart from the spring I long for is not limited to the vagaries of the weather or the beauty. It is the silence.

In this winter-locked world I have given much thought to my responses to this supreme stillness. Max Picard claims that silence is fecund and much more than emptiness or a void that lacks sound. Instead, he asserts, it is a primary basic phenomenon, like love, loyalty, death and life that cannot be reduced to anything else. Although I don't entirely understand this proposition I do feel silence is irreducible.

To say this is a silent place is not to say it is devoid of sound. Outside, a pair of ravens exchanges caws as they pass overhead. Their calls and the swish of their heavy wing beats are broadcast on the cold, dense air as snow crunches under my snowshoes and the slightest breeze whistles past my ears. Trucks and cars, hidden from view behind high banks of snow deposited by the plow, occasionally churn along the crusty road. The chomp of my axe as I chop wood rebounds from the white surround. If I were blind, these place-based sounds would confirm my location.

In the cabin the fire crackles, the teakettle whistles, the refrigerator hums and the telephone rings. Water gushes from the faucet; steaks sizzle on the griddle. On very cold nights, the joists in the cabin crack and pop as they contract. I leave my window slightly ajar at night to let sounds of animals enter, along with fresh air, which protects me against asphyxiation from a smoldering log.

Animal and nature sounds penetrate the depth of stillness, but rather than breaking the silence, they deepen it. The nocturnal coyotes hunting around the cabin squabble and whine, especially when the moon is full. One sends out a howl, high-pitched and piercing, like a woman's scream. The unfamiliar screech of a short-eared owl startles me awake, its repeated call fading as it flies away across the basin. On their feeding grounds, elk mew. Mysterious calls and bumps in the night that I can't identify puzzle and bewilder and, sometimes, frighten me. But I welcome animal sounds; they are calling cards, signatures of being and presence. Such sounds—unlike noise created by inanimate machines and tools—resonate within, raise goose bumps and make me shiver.

Silence has its origin in a time when "everything was still pure Being," and consciousness grew out of this silence, postulates Picard. Not allowing evolution to enter into his phenomenology, he does not credit animals with the origin of our human consciousness and voice, as did Paul, who believed these characteristics developed within us because of our close association and evolution with animals. Their otherness, he asserted, brought our differences and similarities into view and led to our self-awareness. Paul believed that by watching animals, we learned to sing, dance, and care for our young. Picard, meanwhile, believes these attributes came to us out of primordial silence, and, I assume, likewise to animals.

Silence cannot be reduced, although it can be shattered or destroyed by noise. I often think of Nelson Mandela, whose honeycomb cell on Robben Island off Cape Town in South Africa I once visited. He was imprisoned there for a quarter of a century. When he was sent to a quarry to break rock each day, the silence was broken. Mandela must have welcomed returning to the sanctuary of his minute, quiet cell. Solitary confinement used as a form of torture, in his case, became a fecund time when he reconsidered his relationship to the troubled world, to which he was forbidden access. Bernie Krause informs us that the difference between human-caused mechanical noise and biophony, his word for the sounds of nature, is that the latter complement rather than disrupt the communication between living creatures, including our human experience of the non-human.

In this silent world I often think of my teen-age notion of becoming a nun. I am still attracted to buildings dedicated to spiritual life—monasteries, convents, temples and sanctuaries, often constructed in inspiring natural settings away from the din of civilization. In Guatemala while on sabbatical many years ago, my favorite place to read and write was the secluded and quiet ruin of an ancient convent, resplendent with red bougainvilleas still growing over immaculate white stucco walls. Accompanying

Paul in his search for remains of Artemis temples in Greece, I was most impressed by their common placement in hushed settings, overlooking the countryside.

Some spiritualists seek solitary rather than communal life. Thomas Merton was such a person. Others find their solitude in nature. Hermits find their places in caves or secluded sites. Saint Francis made nature his home and animals his companions. Saint Romedio befriended a bear and lived in a cave. Jesus spent forty days in the desert, and the last night before his crucifixion in a garden. This is not to say that peace and sacredness cannot be found in the presence of others. In India I saw a holy man in a saffron robe sitting in meditation on the steps to a temple with pilgrims streaming by. He lived in the holy solitude of his mind; his eyes reflected deep pools of being.

When hassled too much by daily life, we long for peace and quiet. But stony silence or deathly quiet foment unease. Picard suggests we respond thus because they remind us of death. He advises that such dark and silent moments should be welcomed rather than shunned since they carry the reality of our last definitive act, and are a preparation for it. He counsels us to view these moments as opportunities to prepare for death, something we only have the chance to do once. And he admonishes us to do it right, not making it unnecessarily difficult for our loved ones.

I take his counsel seriously. I have witnessed the great inconvenience foisted on children and loved ones by persons denying and attempting to stave off the inevitability of their deaths. In my experience, accompanying the dying as they enter that place of deep silence, when they accept its inevitability, also prepares us for our own. A word of caution, however: in attending the dying, one must be prepared for the great void left when the loved one's voice can no longer be heard.

A sound awakens me from deep sleep. It's four in the morning. I get out of bed, push open the casement window and stand shivering in the rush of cold air. The snowy landscape reflects the light of a waning moon. A dispersing jet trail and the Milky Way form a luminous cross in the sky. Coyotes call in the distance. But it is a less-familiar sound that draws me out of sleep. Carried on the cold, dense air, it echoes across the basin. Canada Geese! On their migration northward, the geese are heading for open water in Idaho or Montana or beyond. They know better than to stop in our ice-locked basin. As their sound fades, I return to the warmth of my bed. Aldo Leopold said it correctly: "One swallow does not make a summer, but one skein of geese, cleaving the murk of a March thaw, is the spring." I made it through the winter! *Primavera* beckons!

Although nature's messages are mixed as we move toward the vernal equinox, on clear days the depth of the snow is visibly decreasing: The blue top of the water spigot is beginning to show, as is the burn barrel. The sun, higher in the sky as it moves toward its zenith, no longer shines through the south clerestory windows, thus making the cabin harder to heat. I continue wearing my standard cold-weather uniform indoors, which converts rapidly for snowshoe walks when I exchange the skirt for insulated pants and the slippers for high, insulated boots.

Today is such a day, warm and sunny, a day of reprieve. Still not trusting the weather, I pack a windbreaker, a small survival blanket, water and an energy bar for insurance against an unforeseen mishap. Just because spring is on its way doesn't mean that flowers are blooming in Wyoming. It continues to be a very snowy and cold world. Although I head out early, the snow on the south slope of Clark Butte is already slippery and beginning to soften. For traction I utilize small patches of soil and sagebrush that are beginning to show as I sidestep slowly to the top. The summit retains a thick blanket of snow that covers the sagebrush and shrubs. To my surprise the usual medley of wintering birds—chickadees, nuthatches, juncos and Canada Jays—are joined by newly arrived Red-winged Blackbirds and American Robins, which have yet to visit the cabin environment where they summer. They stop over on the butte as they await the thaw that will clear their summer foraging and nesting grounds on the basin floor.

Making my way to Heartwood, I grasp the ropes of the swing and ease myself down on the seat that is now just above the surface of the snow. With legs straight I lift my snowshoes high, lean back, and swing slowly back and forth while examining the intricacies of the bark and branches above, where, I suspect, myriads of insects have over-wintered in the pinecones and needles collected in depressions. No tracks lead from the den under the tree where the snow has melted back, which tells me it provides protection for animals from summer's heat rather than from winter's cold.

Retracing my steps, I'm struck by how the sun's warmth mediates the force of winter winds, which deposited little drifts on the leeward side of small trees and reamed out wells around large trunks just as it did around the cabin. Twigs or leaves that have fallen on the snow are little passive solar collectors that melt into tiny depressions that retain their shapes. Animals use the warmth of the sun in many ways. Burrowing animals dig entrances facing east or south so they can benefit from the sun's warmth when they emerge. Many grazers spend a good portion of their winter on south-facing slopes absorbing the warmth of the sun to conserve energy as they nibble grasses uncovered by melting snow.

"Spring leaps forth in the North," wrote Margaret Murie in her memoir *Two in the Far North*. She was referring to Alaska, but the observation applies to the Rockies as well. As we approach April, changes occur quickly. Periodic snowstorms are interspersed with sunny days. Today I travel fifty miles north to meet with the staff of the Murie Center at Moose, in Grand Teton National Park. The center, known as "Conservation's Home," was for decades the original home base of Mardy and Olaus Murie, renowned naturalists and advocates for the designation of wilderness and the protection of the Arctic National Wildlife Refuge. The Murie Center continues their legacy. For years I've been involved with it and the Teton Science School, both situated in the Grand Teton National Park. I brought high school students and later university students to the science school for field studies.

The meeting moves quickly and on the way home I stop by the grocery store in Jackson. The drive back in late afternoon is enchanting. Compared to the Hoback Basin, Jackson Hole seems to be in some sort of a banana belt. Stands of golden willows are surging with sap and their brilliant yellow trunks stand out against the melting snow and patches of drab brown ground. On the out-skirts, the first Red-tailed Hawks I've seen this season are riding the thermals. Road-killed deer along the highway in the Hoback Canyon are fair warning for me to slow down. Drawn by the salt accumulated from winter snow removal, they congregate along the roadside and are often hit by cars. A pair of Canada Geese floats in open water where ice has melted on the Hoback River. In

deep concentration perched on a telephone wire, a Belted King-
fisher sits motionless, staring at a stretch of open water for signs
of life.

Back in the basin, Mountain Bluebirds flit past my car as I
turn into my parking area. I put on my snowshoes, pack the blue
toboggan with groceries and head for the cabin. Unlike previous
trips to Jackson when I arrived back after sunset, today I arrive in
late afternoon and face a new challenge. The temperature is above
freezing and with each step I break through snow and sink up to
my crotch in the soft layers of mushy corn snow and melt water.
False confidence builds as I find firm footing and instinctively begin to hurry, as if speeding will help. But stepping slowly or ginger-
ly makes no difference; I break through repeatedly. Extracting the
buried snowshoes is exhausting and, at times I lie back helplessly
in the snow, laughing at my predicament. My snowshoe trail is a
testament to the poor judgment of a greenhorn in a spring thaw.

As the struggle continues, the humor of the situation evap-
orates. Although the inconvenience seems comical, I realize it
could become life-threatening should I over-extend my strength
or suffer a heart attack. I've been at it for half an hour, yet with
each exhausting step the cabin seems to recede into the distance.
The strawberries I couldn't pass up in the grocery store look ridic-
ulous sitting on the top of the sled. I munch on a few as I rest and
imagine a tasty bowl for dessert. The sun is beginning to set and
I decide I'd better keep moving. Miraculously, as the sun disappears, the temperature drops and the snow freezes and supports
my weight. I can once more snowshoe easily over it.

As I approach the cabin, a huge striped skunk lumbers toward the deck. From the bumps in the night recently emanat-
ing from under the deck, I suspected I had a boarder. Very large,
jet-black, with a magnificent bushy tail, the skunk has two broad

white stripes down its back that meet on its head in an immaculate white skullcap. A beautiful creature, it waves its long tail in the air when it sees me. Awakened from its winter sleep, it must be hungry. Facing a paucity of rodents and insects, it probably appreciates my table scraps. The thick, beautiful winter coat gives it a roly-poly look, although after the cold winter, even with my handouts, it must be lean and hungry. I talk to it softly and wait until it waddles under the deck and disappears, then I stop for a moment to examine its tiny tracks that resemble a human hand or bear paw except for the very long claws on the forelimb print. Skunks mate around this time of year. Secretly, I hope my boarder is a male because, come summer, I'd rather not deal with a half-dozen or more little stinky critters (females may have litters with as many as ten) living under my deck. From my past experience with skunks, I have learned to give them a wide berth.

It was a cold spring day on the Boulder ranch when I discovered that I had no eggs for the cake I was baking. I was unable to leave mischievous Kathryn Ann and Matthew alone, so I put him in the playpen and wrapped Kathryn Ann in a jacket and carried her along. Once, thinking that Matthew would be safe for a few moments wandering about the childproof house while I ran out to fetch something, I returned to find him on the refrigerator! He had pushed his highchair next to it and climbed to the top. After that I called him my little Tensing Norgay after the Sherpa guide from the Himalayas.

At the chicken coop, I stood Kathryn Ann outside the door and asked her to please stand very still until I came back. As I started to gather eggs from the nests, I heard her saying "Kitty,

Kitty, Kitty." Since we had no cats on the ranch, I cut short the egg picking, rushed out and scooped her up just as a skunk sprayed us, soaking us with its acrid, nauseating scent. Coughing and gagging, I ran with her to the house, stripped off our clothes in the yard and hung them on the fence, brought the washtub into the kitchen (we had no bathroom), filled it with hot water from the reservoir in the cooking stove and tried my best to scrub off the musk. The house and our nostrils were saturated with the nauseous odor. I can't recall how I got dinner on the table or what became of the cake I had underway. After trying unsuccessfully to wash out the musk and air the clothes we'd been wearing, I finally gave up and threw them away.

Another memory of the Boulder ranch returns—of a spring day when just as I was about to set dinner on the table, a pick-up truck with three barking dogs in the back came driving down the road. An older couple came to the door and introduced themselves as Jennie and Walt McPherson. They lived nearby on the upper New Fork River. I invited them in and asked them to join us for dinner as I silently calculated how I could extend the meal for two more. Walt, sensing my dilemma, assured me, "Just open a can of pork and beans. There'll be plenty for all of us."

In the future they became frequent visitors, usually near mealtime. I kept a pantry shelf stocked with extra pork and beans and, after discovering Jennie's sweet tooth, with items needed for quick desserts, a pineapple upside-down cake or a fudge pudding that I could pop into the oven. This was before the days of packaged mixes. In anticipation of a regular Sunday afternoon visit, I would bake a special cake that Jennie favored. She and Walt often stayed until late at night. Although I repeatedly offered to fold down the couch for them to sleep on, they refused, but seemed never to want to leave!

Jennie was a woman of few words. Walt did the talking for both of them and, having been a government trapper, he had many stories to tell, especially about their winter adventures trapping in the high country. In late fall before heavy snows, in preparation for those winter months, Jennie and Walt would pack building supplies and staples into the mountains with horses. Locating a windfall where dead trees were plentiful, Walt hewed them with an axe into logs and built a one-room cabin furnished with simple crafted furniture and an inside/outside fireplace made of rocks. After gathering and stacking a good supply of firewood to last through the winter, they dug a pit in the floor of the cabin and buried the staples, which they had packed in: sugar, coffee, flour, lard, beans, salt pork, dried fruit and potatoes. They then closed the cabin tightly and rode back to their home where they arranged to have their horses winter-fed.

After several heavy snows and cold weather to consolidate it, they snowshoed with backpacks into their makeshift cabin and settled in for the winter. They trapped wolverine, mink and martens, stretched the skins on the cabin walls and supplemented their diet with meat from trapped animals as well as snowshoe hares and squirrels. Before the snow started to get "rotten" in the spring, they loaded their backpacks and headed on snowshoes for the valley where they would turn their talents to coyotes and beavers. When the snow had melted in the mountains, they'd return with packhorses to haul out the cached pelts.

In one of his adventure stories, Walt related how one winter on their way out they were caught in an unprecedented early thaw caused by a Chinook that persisted through several nights and kept temperatures above freezing. Getting out apparently was a trying ordeal during which they almost lost their lives working their way through miles of deep, rotten snow. My experience of being bogged down in soft snow makes me appreciate more fully their plight in the mountains, mired and struggling for a footing. Although Jennie and Walt passed on many years ago, they remain poignantly present to me this spring as models of courageous and independent individuals who settled in and loved this country.

Recently I tried to restore the cookbook I used in those days on the Boulder ranch, which looked as if it had been caught up in a tornado. I somehow pieced it back together and still refer to it occasionally. Along with paying homage to Jennie and Walt, I must also give credit to Betty Crocker and her *Picture Cook Book* for helping me through a long winter on the Boulder ranch. I tried, and somewhat perfected, every recipe in the book, from breads and cinnamon rolls to cream puffs and rhubarb pie. And, along with Betty Crocker, I must also thank my mother-in-law, Elise Krall, who provided the impetus for me to perfect my cooking.

From the moment I met Mrs. Krall (I could never call her Elise), she challenged me. She was a strong German woman, a professional and immaculate housekeeper and phenomenal cook. She first came to the United States as a nanny to a family in Connecticut, and then moved to Wyoming as a mail-order bride. She and her husband, Wilhelm Krall, homesteaded in the Fontenelle Basin. He was shot in an altercation over water rights and died of gangrene poisoning when Bob was just two years old. Mrs. Krall proved up on the homestead on her own and then moved to Kemmerer where she ran a boarding house. Straightforward and astute, industrious and competent, she didn't criticize me directly, but her actions when she visited spoke loudly: she always brought baked goods and cleaning cloths and washed the childrens' faces and hands shortly after she arrived. And she refused to talk to me for several months each time I became pregnant. I now see that her attitude toward me was justified. Insecure and depressed, I suffered her disapproval with consternation and silence. I am not especially proud of this since such silence speaks louder than words. After I had left Bob and moved to Salt Lake City and shortly before Mrs. Krall died, she wrote me a letter apologizing for her part in my distress during those years and wished me well.

Living out here in the open, I am constantly reminded of the tribal people who inhabited this area without any of the amenities we need to survive. With experience from previous years and knowledge of elders about migration, they probably kept records on bones, the most malleable but durable material they had at hand that could be transported with them. They also spent time creating artistic drawings and masterful rock constructs, often aligned with the sun on solstices. I doubt, however, that they counted the days as we do; instead I expect they prepared for migration when the sun rose at a certain point on the horizon or cast its light on a certain rock or through a cleft or on one of their constructs. From standing rocks in the Hebrides to mounds in the British Isles to petroglyphs in Chaco Canyon to temple ruins in Mexico and Latin America, I have stood in awe of the profound knowledge of earth processes and the cosmos shown by native predecessors on this planet.

In April a big thaw sets in. Days and nights are warm; water continuously drips off the roof. Brown patches of ground grow as snow disappears. Tiny Johnny jump-ups and green spears of daffodils appear in the flowerbeds. Each day, as the sun arcs higher in the sky, warmer days bring unanticipated transformations in colors, sounds and scents; I feel transported to some new land with little resemblance to my debarkation point, a long winter night ago. On clear calm days the warmth of the sun at midday feels therapeutic. Enticed to drag out a blanket, strip down and sunbathe, I remember the warnings of my dermatologist, who bemoans my sun-damaged skin, and I cast this indiscretion aside. After eating my breakfast on the south porch, I lean back against the cabin, close my eyes, enjoy the warmth and scent of spring and ease into a pleasant torpor.

On another spring day long ago in the privacy of the outhouse at the Opal School, I unfastened my garters and rolled down the thick, tan cotton socks to form firm round sausages around my ankles. The feeling of the cool air against my legs and the garters dangling freely from my vest sent a sensual shiver up my spine. Not simply an act of defiance, this was a serious transgression against my mother. Without the protective long socks, I could easily catch pneumonia!

The impulse, encouraged by the example of older girls with their surge toward independence primed by spring weather, felt all the more delightful for being forbidden. The thought of walking out to the south side of the schoolhouse where the snow had withdrawn to leave brown ground, and standing there barelegged in the deliciously warm sunshine, washed all guilt from my child's mind. With a devil-may-care attitude and throwing discretion to the wind, out I strode, my skinny knobby-kneed white legs exposed to the world and its elements.

Recess was too short for all we had to do. It was time for the pioneers and cowboys to regroup. Families established by the older girls gathered in the shack for spring-cleaning. We refurbished our households with more objects from the trash heap. Subsistence was the name of the game as we dug Indian potatoes in the sagebrush at the edge of the graveled playground. The long lacy leaves and creamy clusters of flowers harbored long, fleshy, starchy roots. Pioneers settling on this western land foraged for these tubers, as did indigenous natives, who gathered, roasted and ground them to meal. We dug the roots, scraped off the dirt, and ate them raw, gnawing on them as best we could. Concentrating on the task of survival, we paid little attention to the boys once more running around us, chasing and shooting each other dead.

Certain that Mamma would be displeased with my eating a root, I finally confessed to her. She surprised me when she showed great interest and asked me to walk with her in the sagebrush to show her the plant, which we dug up and tasted. At heart Mamma was a forager who used what was at hand in season. In the spring she cooked pigweeds that tasted somewhat like spinach and served dandelion greens in vinaigrette with crumbled bacon and hard-cooked eggs as a tasty green salad. She always had some sort of tea brewing to promote her health or heal her ailments, including flaxseed, bought in large quantities, or mallow and chamomile grown in her herb garden and dried.

By the second grade I had managed to learn to read and my favorite book was *Purr and Miew Kitten Stories*. This storybook about a cat family leading human lives especially enthralled me. At about the age of seven, along with the new teeth I was growing, I was gaining a new sense of myself as a unique individual, separating from mother and family, both physically and psychologically. It was a strange transitional time when this particular story about animals in human roles may have helped me navigate the ambiguity that I felt about my growing body and place in family and community.

After we began attending the Burgoon School, we walked home. The road from the bus stop during the thaw was muddy and more difficult to navigate with a car in the afternoon than in the morning when the ground was frozen. On the way, Barbara and I would often take a short-cut over the sagebrush terrace, following the course of melt water from remaining drifts, down a gully, over tiny waterfalls and through meanders where the water deposited silt in fragile riffles. Although I undoubtedly arrived home with muddy shoes, I recollect no reprimands. Perhaps Mamma, raised in a similar habitat but now bound with household duties, relived her childhood days vicariously through our carefree wanderings. Witnessing the leveling power of gravity, water and soil working together, although on a micro scale, may have founded my abiding interest in geomorphology.

In the spring of the fourth grade in the Burgoon School, Mamma selected an enrichment experience for me that would further complicate her traversing the muddy roads. Observing my admiration for my friend, Margaret Verne Flatterer, an accomplished tap dancer, Mamma decided that I should have lessons. Without coordination or sense of timing, still shy and inhibited, with the added stress of navigating the muddy roads with my mother, never an accomplished driver, I found the whole affair an ordeal. However, in the mixed-age group of children during the practices for the recital, I was absolutely fascinated by the flirting and carrying on of the older children, especially that of a handsome older cousin named Kenneth John.

A few years older than myself, Ken intrigued me with his friendly and uninhibited attitude, his musical talents (he played the trombone) and his intelligence. As we grew into adolescence, he occasionally worked for us in the hay field on our ranch. When I was in the tenth grade and we l lived in Kemmerer during the school year, Ken was hospitalized for weeks with pneumonia. I stopped by to visit him each morning on my way to school and prayed for his recovery at daily Mass. Upon graduation, he joined the Navy and visited me in Berkeley before he was deployed to the Pacific. I was heartbroken and concerned about his safe return. We exchanged letters during the war and, later, attended the University of Wyoming together. After earning a doctorate in ichthyology at the University of Wisconsin, he periodically visited Wyoming with his wife, Betsy. Our friendship continued as our careers as professors unfolded, his at Franklin and Marshall College in Pennsylvania. As with cousin Paul, he was an important friend during my growing-up years.

Cousins Paul and Ken bridged the gap between Mr. Hampton, my upper elementary teacher, and my future friendships with men. Whereas women acted as role models for my early development, platonic friendships with boys, and later in life, with male colleagues, helped me develop productive collaborative and egalitarian relationships with the opposite sex. Romantic relationships often seemed to develop a quid pro quo stance based on mutual needs and lack of maturity; non-romantic friendships with men augmented and enriched my life by helping me understand other ways of seeing and being.

Gray, overcast days give way to the dynamic play of light and dark above and below. High winds aloft push clouds across the sky and send their shadows racing over the landscape. Chinooks may visit us as early as January but are most common as we move through March. They seem to carry away the winter darkness and reawaken the anticipation I felt as a child with my face glued to the window, my expectations of warmer days to come unhampered by a sudden snowstorm.

During both equinoxes, the sun rises and sets at the same place on the horizon but life cycles are in a totally different stage of transition. In reverse to seasonal changes in the fall when life seems in freefall, in spring new life comes into being each day. With both seasons, I want the transitions to slow down so that I can fathom the changes. In the fall, I feel suspended, thankful for each precious moment of reprieve from the approaching cold. With the rapid changes in March, when snow still clings to the landscape, come vacillating moods: pure delight on warm days, impatience when they turn cold. As we move into April, the snow-gripped basin surrenders to a great thaw and vernal transformations.

Views from Clark Butte in March

With Bambi and cousins Linda and Alice (1933)

Tap dancer (1935)

· 12 ·

Sounds of Spring

Easter arrives and I decide to attend sunrise services at Saint Hubert the Hunter Church. About fifty people are present and we begin with a familiar song: "Morning has broken like the first morning, Blackbird has spoken like the first bird..." Then the reading: "Set your minds on things that are above, not on things that are on earth..." Silently I object to being asked to ignore the earth and I stare out the window at Red-winged Blackbirds, which on cue are singing in the willows near the church.

A little girl in a frilly, lavender dress sits next to me. Memories of my own children dressed in new outfits as we head for Easter Mass well up and lodge in my throat. On such a morning, their baskets would have been filled with brightly decorated eggs, chocolate bunnies, sweet-bread bunny faces and little surprises. Later there would be a special dinner shared with our extended family. I swallow hard and return to Saint Hubert's.

Following the service, the altar doors are closed and the church is converted into a social hall. The men cook and serve women and children a hearty breakfast of incomparable ham, eggs and pancakes. I leave the meeting with a full tummy and a fortified spirit. This is no time to feel downhearted and sorry for myself. Spring is here and life is returning to Hoback Basin.

It's a glorious day with a slight east breeze and a few scattered clouds. The surface of snow banks, lingering in the foothills, glistens with a quicksilver sheen. Except for drifts along the willows, snow has disappeared and brown ground begins turning green. With plenty of options before me, I put on my gloves and irrigation boots and get to work in the yard, cleaning up debris scattered by the wind, turning the compost pile, loosening the soil around the sprouting rhubarb plants and chopping kindling and firewood. A good head of water is running in the ditch.

At times like this, when Sometimes Creek was filled with meltwater from snow, the homesteaders must have felt as hopeful about the growing season as I am about raising a few wild ducks. With a plethora of water, I freely divert some to fill the ponds. Designed by Jack Doyle, an able wetland engineer, the plan works perfectly. As water fills the first pond, it spills over into the next, each on a slightly lower level until a broad feeder canal and all four shallow ponds are overflowing. The excess water drains back into the main canal and on to neighbors down ditch.

In a few days as the ponds fill, waterfowl begin appearing. An occasional Blue-winged or Cinnamon Teal join numerous Mallards and Green-winged Teals. Pintails, with immaculate white necks and breasts, stand out in the gathering. A low-flying pair of geese circle, land on my roof and exchange calls seemingly debating nesting sites. At sunset I get a close-up view of a lone male Lesser Scaup that has joined the group; his specula and rust-and-green head glow like colored lights.

The chorus of songbirds, building each day, awakens me gently in the mornings and lulls me to sleep in the twilight of the long evenings of spring. Frequenting the west porch, robins are building a nest on a ledge under the eaves as they do each year. The incessant chirping of males nudges me out of my warm bed. Likewise, male Western Meadowlarks sing from every fence post. Mountain Bluebirds dally playfully together and vie with Tree Swallows for the nesting boxes along the fence line. Songbirds abound and the choruses escalate each day. From my rooftop the geese continue their conversation.

On my walk up the draw this morning, I find sagebrush buttercups blooming at the edge of snowdrifts. Along drainages the emerald moss-like foliage of Hood's phlox, with spears of purple and green leaves, sprout up here and there. As I cross the low ridge that divides Clark Draw into its two drainages, the songs of mating boreal chorus frogs stop me short.

The amphibian chorus emanates from a little pool of meltwater being fed by a huge snowdrift. As I approach, the amphibian song (I refuse to call it croaking) ceases and everything becomes serenely quiet. I examine the edge of the water and find it teeming with peepers. As soon as I step a few feet away, they resume their chorus. Continuing up the draw, I enter the land of mating frogs; their songs, rising from each drainage and collection of snowmelt, cease when I draw near and begin again as I pass by. This proclamation of life brings back a childhood moment.

I shivered in my nightgown as I stood on tiptoes and looked over the sill of the open window of our upstairs bedroom. The cool breeze chilled my thin little girl's body. The window was small and high and opened inward. A screen was firmly attached on the outside and three metal rods had been placed across it, the window constructed according to Mamma's directions when the bedroom and bath were added to the log house. Her intent was to keep us as safe as possible up there by ourselves in our attic room.

This particular morning I lingered on, thrilled by the cadence of countless frogs in the irrigated meadows. That magical childhood moment, spiritual to the core, lodged in my immature consciousness, bonding me to the mysterious powers of nature. Spring had arrived with its life-giving cycles, and changes were occurring too rapidly for my child's mind to fathom. What I didn't comprehend was that it was water that made the difference.

At the Opal School, whether sunny or stormy, May Day was a time for celebration. We made baskets out of construction paper and then followed Miss Beyda into the sagebrush near the school in search of the first wild flowers to place in our baskets, mostly phlox and bluebells and a few sprigs of sage. When Mamma picked us up after school, we hid the baskets from her. At the ranch after she had entered the house, we placed the baskets on the doorstep, knocked on the door and ran away to hide. She came out and was appropriately surprised and delighted.

May Day is spring cross-quarter day and was historically celebrated by secular and religious groups: socialists, communists, anarchists, pagans and Christians. In my mother's day it was a holiday designated as International Workers Day and celebrated by union mine workers. The political fervor of past days was lost on me as I imagined myself in a pagan ceremony crowned with a wreath of flowers, dancing with others around a May Pole.

On a Saturday a week or so later when more flowers were in bloom, Mamma led a more productive wildflower walk. By then the snow had melted except for a few drifts on north-facing slopes. Her favorite flowers were the ephemeral but lovely lily-white evening primroses. They would fill the house with their sweet perfume until evening when they turned pink and wilted. This light-hearted flower hunt ushered in the critical activities of sheep ranching that would occupy us throughout the spring.

To add to our springtime challenges on the ranch, the Hams Fork River at the height of the thaw overflowed its banks. At its source in the Wyoming Range, it flowed from artesian Big Spring at the head of its West Fork, and gathered water from snowmelt from every creek and gully along its fifty-mile course before arriving at the ranch, roiling and seething with unconstrained power. When winter snow was heavy and the spring thaw fast, the river began flooding the road near the pole bridge over the river.

As the water inched up over the road, Dad parked our vehicles about a half-mile from the house on high ground on the other side of the railroad tracks. The house and yard were also on higher ground but water covered the road in between the house and bridge. We picked our way on dry patches and ditch banks to the bridge where water surged under and sometimes lapped over it. Steadying ourselves with a handrail, we worked our way across the crossbars that Dad had built on the trestle that carried the irrigation water across the bridge. As would be expected, Mamma supervised this treacherous daily passage out of fear that one of us might slip and meet her end in the rampaging river.

When Dad built the bridge, he secured it with steel cables anchored upstream to prevent the bridge from being washed away at flood time, but there was always the question of whether the cables would hold. He had built the bridge in the late summer when the river was low and probably had no notion of how high the water might rise after a winter with heavy snow in the mountains.

Floodwater crested toward the end of May, after which it slowly ebbed. By the summer's end the river was reduced to a trickle and the riverbed strewn with white, sun-dried rocks caked with dry moss. When the water stopped flowing, pools remained in meanders where the force of repeated floods had reamed out deep holes. In their depth, cold springs kept the pools full and invigorating, and bone chilling, for summer swims. But the dry streambed was weeks away. During these spring days, water was plentiful. It was irrigation time and frog-mating time, the moment for both amphibians and Dad to take advantage of the profusion of water.

Like the mating of frogs, ranching in the cold steppe country of Wyoming also requires fine-tuning, opportunism and a measure of just plain good luck to take full advantage of water while it's plentiful. As the raging river lowered and became manageable, Dad recruited his Italian comrades from town to help with the huge logs he had cut and hauled from the summer forest allotments. The crew lowered the logs into the outlet of the dam and the level of the water rose until it flowed through the head gate and into the Wright Ditch, named after the homesteader who had constructed it with horses. The ditch wound its way over high points of the meadows on the north side of the tracks. The Oregon Shortline Railroad, a branch of the Union Pacific completed in 1881, ran down the middle of the ranch, cutting it in two. In 1930 after buying the ranch, Dad applied for permission to build a canal under the railroad so that he could irrigate meadows on the south side of the tracks as well.

Homesteaders and ranchers like my father extended the natural meadows along the riverbanks. They grubbed the sagebrush, harrowed the soil, and planted it with English hay. Our ranch included about 200 acres of these hayfields, and about fifty times that much sagebrush grazing land, a modest holding in Wyoming for a self-sustaining sheep ranch that usually ran about 2,500 sheep. As with previous owners, my father did not have access to heavy-duty equipment or the money to level the fields, so they remained uneven with many natural depressions and archaic meanders and oxbows.

Long before the sun rose above the sagebrush knolls each day in May, Dad, in hip boots and with a shovel over his shoulder, set out on his irrigation rounds. He redistributed and directed water with little dams and ditches in an effort to soak every inch of hay meadow to insure the maximum growth possible. Over the course of about six weeks, the dry meadows morphed into a dense, sweet-smelling stand of hay. Not until the grasses had matured and growth slowed did Dad remove the logs from the dam and stop the flow of water in the Wright Ditch, thus allowing the meadows to dry in preparation for haying.

On my daily rounds of the ranch buildings in early childhood, I would often stop by the bunkhouse to sniff the tantalizing musky odors of Mason jars on the windowsill, containing a strange assortment of glands. Joe used musk glands as bait for attracting beaver and muskrats to his traps. The heavy scent followed him wherever he went, including into the house when he came to eat his meals. He trapped coyotes during the early spring but later his interests turned to beaver interfering with Dad's irrigation. They, as well as the muskrats, produced valuable pelts used to make fur coats for women. Joe skinned the animals he caught in his traps and stretched and tacked the pelts to the garage doors where they dried stiff as boards. He stacked them in a corner of the garage to await the scrutiny of Mr. Sardok, the entrepreneurial peddler, who, on one of his visits, would carefully examine each skin and set a price.

The process and perfection of irrigation as Dad envisioned it was embedded within a whole series of spring activities that were time- and season-bound and essential to our economic survival. Foremost among these was lambing, which occurred during the first weeks of May.

"May can make or break a sheep rancher," is a truism often repeated by cousin Josephine Angelo Julian, who had learned from her experience as a Wyoming sheep rancher for all of her long life. After graduation she married Don Julian, and together they raised a large family on their ranch. Their son Truman and his family manage the sheep outfit today. Until she was too old to do so, she killed an antelope and a deer every year to complement the lamb and beef from the ranch. We graduated from high school together and remained close friends until her death in March 2012 at the age of 87. She was a colorful woman, tough as nails, a dearest friend, and loved and respected by all.

Josephine knew that in the steppe country of southwestern Wyoming, weather during May can set the course and outcome of events for the next six months that will determine economic consequences in the fall. Good news at shipping time with numerous plump lambs depends upon moderate temperatures and precipitation in the spring, which invigorate growth of vegetation for birthing and nursing ewes and ensures the survival of newborns. That is not to say that a good winter is not important: one with sufficient but not excessive snowfall in both the mountains and on the desert. But with either a hard or mild winter, moderate precipitation and temperatures in May favor both good lambing and shearing conditions.

In April after the snow had begun to melt off the desert, the sheepherders trailed the sheep to the spring lambing grounds. For a week or two during the peak of lambing, Dad would camp out with the sheep. He'd return occasionally to the ranch for supplies and to bring back bum lambs that had been orphaned or were sickly. We welcomed them with loving arms and bottle-fed them, a task we continued throughout the summer.

No matter how careful the planning, success in lambing was determined by something beyond Dad's control: the weather. Drought or cold weather would stunt vegetative growth; severe snowstorms, although not usual, could decimate newborn lambs. Each year was a gamble and Dad just placed a bet on a good year and bit the bullet when it didn't happen. One year he made the headlines in a local newspapers when he saved his flock during a devastating storm by driving them into an abandoned mine.

Dad's plans for the sheep, from the beginning of lambing until they entered the forest allotments about the first of July for summer grazing in the Wyoming Range, were carefully orchestrated. The sheep would arrive on the lambing grounds heavy with lambs. Starting at one end, the herd was grazed slowly across its length. Ewes ready to give birth were cut out and left behind in a loose flock, called the drop herd, and watched carefully for lambs that had to be pulled or those that needed help with suckling.

Marauding coyotes, always a threat, were deterred by various means, including setting out scarecrows, lighting fires around the drop herd at night, shooting the coyotes on sight or poisoning them. As the lambs grew, the drop herds coalesced into larger herds and by the end of May lambing was pretty much over.

The next step, docking the lambs, was a ritual that required the help of the entire family and took place periodically over weekends when we were still in school. Early in the morning, Barbara and I took our usual positions hunkered down behind the cab of the old Ford truck loaded with all the equipment necessary for setting up makeshift pens. Dad, Mamma, DJ and Uncle Richard got into the cab and we rode to the lambing grounds where the sheepherders helped us set up the docking pens.

The process began by running about thirty sheep and their lambs from the main herd into a small coral. The lambs were separated from the ewes, which were counted and turned out but kept separated from the main herd. Dad and Mamma positioned themselves outside the docking pen, constructed with a wooden section with a narrow, table-like plank across the top.

Uncle Richard, a herder or two and we daughters wrangled the lambs: after catching one, we held its fore and hind legs securely together so that it couldn't wiggle as we waited in line. When it was our turn, if the lamb was a male, we placed it on its haunches, belly up on the plank in front of Dad. Dad grasped the scrotal sack, cut off the tip and then, squeezing it deeply, forced the two testicles to pop out. He clamped these in his teeth and pulled them out while pinching the sack together to stop the bleeding. Dad dropped the testicles into a pale of water nearby and grasped the tail, which he whacked off. With those operations executed, we turned the lamb over and placed its head on the plank, facing Dad, who sliced each ear with our earmark, a "slash and uppercut on the left ear and crop and underbit on the right."

We then moved the lamb down the plank to where Mamma stood with a brand, dripping with paint, ready to apply our mark to the lamb's back. We released each lamb gently after its ordeal, and it stood shivering and bleating in pain and distress. We immediately caught another—the point being to keep the process moving as quickly as possible—and continued in line until every little lambkin was left stunned and bleeding. The lambs were then released to the ewes that were milling around and bleating, and we separated another group of lambs to be docked. For a few days after docking, the herders carefully watched the sheep and lambs, as they mothered up, nursed and recovered.

Docking was a bloody process. With the slash of the knife, blood spurted in all directions from the lambs' ears and tails. By the end of the day we were caked with blood as if we had taken part in some massacre, which in a way we had. Before we could go home to wash, we had to dismantle and store the pens for the next docking event to take place in a few days. This routine continued over a couple of weeks with successive bands until all of the lambs were docked and the sheep consolidated into one large herd that would begin trailing to the summer allotments in the Wyoming Range.

After the day's work, we got back into the truck and Dad followed the dusty, bumpy primitive dirt roads back to the highway. Crouched behind the cab, Barbara and I watched through the rear window for oncoming cars. When one approached, we would stand up in unison like macabre specters, just as the car passed. The alarmed and horrified looks on the faces of bewildered passers-by set us in peals of laughter, and we would sit back down behind the cab to recover as we awaited our next victims. Back home, after cleaning up, we helped wash and trim the mountain oysters that Mamma sautéed in butter and onions—a tasty reward and hard-earned delicacy we savored for as many days as they lasted.

Shearing was another major spring event that had to be completed before the sheep were ready to trail to the summer range. It put a cap on the critical spring work with the sheep but, more importantly, it provided the first income of the year.

Buyers would have visited the ranch during the previous month to negotiate a contract with Dad for the price of wool per pound. He listened to the market reports on the radio each morning but, uncertain of the going rate offered in our area, he would go to town regularly to consult with buyers. It was a tense time for him: when he sold too soon and the prices rose, he was disappointed; when he negotiated a good price, he was pleased. The same process for selling lambs would be repeated late in the summer.

A shearing crew was contracted and they carried with them the necessary configuration of pens, tools, and men to complete the task as quickly as possible. They would set up near the lambing grounds and had their own cooks and living quarters. Mamma cooked meals for our herders and family in a cook tent nearby.

I remember those times most clearly as a teenager. Coming into womanhood, I found the work with this strange assortment of rough and tumble shearers quite fascinating. After shearing a sheep, the shearer tied the wool fleece together with twine and set it outside the pen. Paid by the number of sheep sheared each day, they vied to be the fastest and earn the most. In the early years they used hand-held shearing tools, which were later replaced by electrical ones. I helped gather the fleeces and carry them to a central location where a huge burlap woolsack was suspended from a wooden platform about twelve feet high. The sack was secured with a metal ring and a designated tromper would get into the sack. As fleeces were tossed up onto the platform, he would place them in the sack and stomp them down firmly. When the sack was stuffed full, it was lowered from the platform and the top sewn shut with a huge curved needle, sometimes by Mamma, and a new sack was secured and the process repeated. At the end of the day, the tromper's clothes were saturated with lanolin.

With anticipation, we watched the stack of woolsacks grow. After shearing had ended, Dad and Mamma would sit at the kitchen table in the evenings estimating the probable income. At docking time, they had a count on the numbers of lambs and sheep that had survived weather and coyotes; with luck, most would make it through the summer. They calculated the percentage of lambs-to-sheep to estimate birthing success. Since Dad selected sheep that had raised twins or triplets, it was usually over one hundred percent. The wool had been sold by then and the woolsacks were hauled to a warehouse and weighed. The average weight of wool per sheep was an important calculation in forecasting the spring income, as well as to compare with other years in an effort to improve productivity of the herds. A guess at the number of lambs that would survive the summer, how much they would weigh, and how much they would bring when sold would round out their calculations and give them an idea of where they stood with their finances. Our economic survival depended on the outcome of this round of seasonal activities. Although speculative, the calculations were approached with gravity. Having given it their all each year, Dad and Mamma were always optimistic that their efforts would pay off and reduce their debts. But on years of drought when growth was poor or when stormy weather occurred during lambing, they'd have to grimly count their losses and decide how to survive the current year and improve production in the next.

On the ranch, after a rain, Joe would leave in early morning and return with a gunnysack of mushrooms. They spoiled quickly so Uncle Richard helped Mamma wash and slice them in preparation for parboiling. Like all such seasonal harvests, we feasted on them for as long as they kept springing up, usually for about two weeks. Fried with butter and onions, they made delicious breakfasts.

By this time of year, the grass had begun turning green and the milk cows, which were kept and fed in corrals during the winter, were turned out to graze. In the summer Barbara and I rode out on horseback to gather the cows and then milk them. They grazed several miles away in the lower pasture. The sound of cowbells would lead us to where they were hiding in the thickets. After a rain, riding through the willows was like jumping into a cold shower. Wet branches brushed against us and chilled us to the bone. But the thought of a breakfast of sautéed mushrooms and onions with homemade bread, awaiting us after milking, urged us on. Occasionally to surprise our parents, we would rise very early, sneak out the window at the foot of the stairs, and complete the chores before our parents had awakened. After Barbara had gone off to college and married, I rode out for the cows. Later, DJ joined me, and after I had left home, she helped Mamma and, sometimes, took over this daily chore herself.

I haven't milked a cow in years, but the experience and sensations of milking still linger: the warm feeling and smell of the cow as I pushed my head into her groin, the shrill sound of the milk hitting the empty pail full force, the sweet vapors rising from the pail and the muffled sound as foam formed on top of the milk. The thickness of the foam was a measure of the skill of the milkmaid.

It's mushroom season in the Hoback Basin and no time for lying abed! It rained a bit last night and with a few nights above freezing, the Boletus mushrooms should be popping up in the sagebrush. The Hobacks, still sparkling white with snow, shine in the morning sun. Little freshets of water trickling from snow banks on the rims of ridges glisten in the sun but peter out before they can coalesce to form a head of water in the gullies. Basking in the sun's warmth on the east slope of Clark Butte, pronghorn does gather as they await the birth of their fawns. I dress, have a quick cup of tea and a piece of banana bread and head out the door for Clark Draw. I'm not as wise about gathering the mushrooms as some of my neighbors, who are more familiar with the places where they grow and usually get to them first. But it's always exciting to find the white caps pushing up through the soil and trailing off into the sagebrush or forming a fairy ring in a swale.

A week or two into May after the grand thaw in April, a trickle of water comes down the ditch, enough to keep only one pond filled. In early June when the irrigation of the meadows begins, the precious liquid in our ditches will be plentiful once more. The allocation of water is one of the most contested rights in the arid West where irrigation is necessary. Like me, most of the dozen or so residents in this small development own water rights, but that does not mean we get enough water where and when we need it. The flow is controlled by the rancher up ditch from us and is inconsistent. I'm beyond fighting over water rights so I let it go. Nonetheless, each year I count a few ducklings swimming in the one pond I keep filled.

On my walks each morning in spring, I can often hear the sandhill cranes calling, and then one day, "the cranes come planing down," as William Stafford described their landings so eloquently in his poem, "Watching Sandhill Cranes." Carl Hertel, a colleague and close friend of Paul's, read the poem at his graveside. On my walks, I hear and finally see a pair, strutting sedately through the sagebrush. Although they stand almost four feet tall, their color blends so well that I invariably have trouble spotting them. Their bugle always stirs me, and whenever I see two walking together, I think of Paul and Carl, now gone from this world, but returning to me in spirit when these magnificent creatures call.

A pair occasionally lands in the north meadow, privileging me with a courtship dance. And once when I was sitting with friends looking out at the meadow, a pair dropped down in front of the window and mated! Such pairs often stay for several days while considering nesting sites, but never remain. For their nests, they prefer the privacy of the sagebrush draws near seeps where they can probe for crustaceans and worms in the mud. Nonetheless, my spirit is invariably uplifted each morning or evening when I hear their calls.

At this time of year, bird song escalates with each day. As I walk through the sagebrush toward an aspen grove, the predominant territorial songs of the nesting birds, mostly sparrows, change as I cross each little knoll, swale, or drainage area. During our first springs at the cabin, Paul and I walked into the foothills early each morning to identify bird songs. As a child, he collected bird eggs, a hobby allowed in those days. He remembered their colors as the most beautiful he had ever seen in his life. He became a dedicated birder and falconer in his teens. In college, he was a teaching assistant in the ornithology course. With poor eyesight but keen hearing, Paul had remarkable aural memory. Since the birds in the West were new to him, after our walks he would play bird song tapes until he had identified each of the birds we had heard.

Now that Paul is gone, with neither his aptitude nor memory, I take along a little notebook and record bird songs in shorthand I've devised. Back at the cabin, I consult bird books and listen to the tapes, as he did. In the course of doing this each year, I have come to recognize a good number of species and their particular songs and nesting areas. When an unfamiliar song bursts forth, I am always challenged and excited.

Except for the White-crowned Sparrow with distinct white stripes on its head, the Chipping Sparrow with its rusty cap, and the Vesper Sparrow with white outer tail feathers, most of the notorious little brown birds that nest in this area are difficult for me to identify. Habitat is a clue. Song Sparrows and White-crowned Sparrows nest in the willows and Savannah Sparrows in the meadow near the cabin. Down along the Upper Hoback River Road in the willows we have seen Fox and Lincoln's Sparrows. Willow Flycatchers and Gray Catbirds with distinctive songs also occupy nesting sites in the willows near the cabin, to which they return each year.

As I walk from the cabin on up through the sagebrush, the melodious songs of the Western Meadowlark and the Vesper Sparrows are perhaps the most beautiful. The Brewer's Sparrow with its long and varied call, which seems to combine every burr, chip, trill, and warble in the bird book, is the most unique and delightful, almost matching the endless song of the Sage Thrasher that shares this habitat. Chipping, Grasshopper and Clay-colored Sparrows are less melodious but their calls are distinctive. Townsend's Solitaires and Say's Phoebes add their songs to this sagebrush chorus.

My destination this morning is a particular aspen grove nestled in a north-facing swale off the rim of Monument Ridge, a haven for cavity-nesting birds. Although many new shoots are emerging from old aspen clones, some conifers are invading the dead or dying aspen, which probably succumbed to some fungal or insect infestation. The snags provide a welcoming habitat for cavity-nesting birds. American Kestrels, Mountain Bluebirds, Tree Swallows, European Starlings, Red-breated Nuthatches, House Wrens and various woodpeckers take advantage of the hollow trunks. Once in this grove, as I leaned against a tree while scanning the dead stand for birds, I unconsciously tapped my fingers on the trunk and was startled by a buzzing sound like many tiny motors running deep in the tree. A Red-shafted Flicker, alarmed and scolding nearby, explained the source of its anxiety. The young tucked deep in the hollow mistook my tapping for their parents returning to feed them.

Ravens, already hatched and in family groups, search for food, including the eggs and young hatchlings of songbirds. They also make daily forays back and forth to the highway to feast on road kill. Red-tailed Hawks, nesting in the thick groves on Clark Butte, and soaring and calling above, have a choice of prey, including various small creatures that inhabit the underbrush and grassy areas, primarily the ubiquitous and prolific Uinta ground squirrel.

Male Unitas emerge first from hibernation in early April, followed a week or so later by the females. Mating occurs and females usually produce two litters through the summer. The adult females defend territories around their burrows where they conduct a kind of gardening, stimulating new growth that will be richer in nutrients than the first shoots, which they nibble and prune. After a brief time of nursing, the young emerge from the den. Quite precocious, but naïve and vulnerable, they are left on their own to forage. Although each individual lives independently, digging its own burrow, a litter will live communally in the same general territory as the maternal burrow. These ubiquitous rodents seem to have sentinels who position themselves on the tops of sagebrush and emit a high-pitched trilling warning call when I approach. I've often thought this might also be an invitation to predators in the area to a tasty meal.

Mortality of the naïve young Uintas is very high. The helter-skelter behaviors that make them easy prey may be an adaptation that winnows their population while feeding a great number of fellow creatures. They are easy prey for eagles, owls, and hawks with hungry nestlings, and are also readily available food for carnivores—coyotes, badgers, and foxes—which are still suckling their young in the dens. On the highway the Uinta ground squirrels seem suicidal as they time their crossings as cars approach. Their mashed remains provide food for scavengers—ravens and magpies and Golden Eagles—who habitually cruise the highways for roadkill. And at these times, the Uinta ground squirrels seem cannibalistic as they come to the highway to feed on the remains of road-killed cousins and often meet the same fate.

When I was a young girl on the ranch, my father put me to work trapping and killing ground squirrels that were boring holes in the ditches and redirecting his irrigation water. This summer I considered taking up this calling once more. The area around my cabin was infested with young ground squirrels scampering in all directions and eating every new sprout that emerged in my garden.

The proliferation was probably the result of a friendly relationship I had developed the previous year with what I presume was their mother. Emerging from the den, she claimed my porches as her territory. I could hear her running back and forth to a cache she was accumulating under my firewood stacked near the door. In the evenings as I ate dinner at the dining room table with the view of Clark Draw and the Hobacks before me, she would position herself, either sitting up or splayed on her tummy, watching me through the atrium doors. She was really begging to be tamed and would have eaten out of my hand. But not wanting to contribute to the further domestication of wild animals, I withheld my friendship.

Each evening after dinner, I'd go outdoors to water my flowerbeds around the cabin with a hand held sprinkler. It was a quiet, pensive time when I enjoyed the cool spray of water and lovely colors of the delphiniums and lupine in full bloom. One evening, standing there in a pensive mood, I looked down—and sitting on my boot enjoying the time with me was my friendly little ground squirrel. This cross-species incident leads me to conclude that if I am to succeed in growing a few vegetables, I'll have to do it by building a greenhouse, not by exterminating Uinta ground squirrels.

The badger, unlike me, is a formidable hunter of these little creatures. When on my walks I meet one staring at me through the sagebrush, I stop short. I've never heard of these creatures attacking humans, but, not taking any chances, I am cautious. Surreptitious, badgers are important players in the sagebrush steppe community as an effective control against the proliferation of ground squirrels, their primary prey. I've heard that a badger can dig faster than a ground squirrel can escape. Such diggings with the long, curved claws on their front paws leave telltale striations on the inside of newly excavated ground squirrel holes. Although their signs are everywhere, I rarely see a badger out and about, so when I'm lucky to encounter one, I freeze and watch it.

Truth be known, it is a strange-looking creature: squat, built close to the ground, its life closely associated with dirt and digging. This one freezes when it sees me approaching and stares at me through an opening in the brush. With short ears, its distinctive badges—patches of white and black on either side of a white stripe running the length of its face and forehead—give it a ferocious appearance. But when I observe it more closely with my binoculars, its mask-like appearance and snub nose and piercing black eyes take on a somewhat comical appearance, like a snoopy gossip that never lets anything pass unobserved. We eye each other until the big weasel is assured I am harmless and then lumbers away, its grizzly brindled body rolling along over the surface of the ground like some huge woolly worm.

The badger excavates large, deep burrows, usually on a slight slope where the entire area seems in upheaval as they form piles of new soil and create numerous entrances and exits. This helps to aerate the clay prairie soil that becomes solidly packed when undisturbed for years. The newly turned soil is a perfect seedbed for western wheatgrass, which by season's end grows three or four feet high around badger burrows.

In Wyoming and many other states, badgers are classified as varmints, along with coyotes, foxes and ground squirrels. Thus, they may be shot at anytime by anyone. Hunting and killing varmints is a kind of ethnic animal cleansing, one I definitely oppose. The classification is questionable if one considers how these creatures contribute to ecosystem balance. But there is no doubt that the large oval badger burrows are a menace to horses and their mounts and may cause bone-breaking spills for both.

The sound of the Hoback River, a quarter of a mile away, full and rushing with snowmelt, carries on the cool morning air and harmonizes with the melody of rivulets running in the ditches. The Western Meadowlark's beautiful call from all reaches initiates the dawn chorus as the world comes alive. Calls of the Long-billed Curlew from the wetlands across the Hoback punctuate the cackling of geese in the meadows and the bugling of Sandhill Cranes as they fly over in pairs. Beautiful and varied songs of sparrows and passerines rise from willows and sagebrush where they are establishing territories. From its perch on the highest branch, a Willow Flycatcher identifies its territory with a *fitz-bew*, as does the faithful Gray Catbird with *mew*. Bird song peaks in early morning, continues in little bursts during the day and rises again before dusk. We have to give credit to the male birds whose canorous concert is all the more enthralling, coming as it does after the long season of silence.

Sheep camp on lambing ground

Wool sacks after shearing

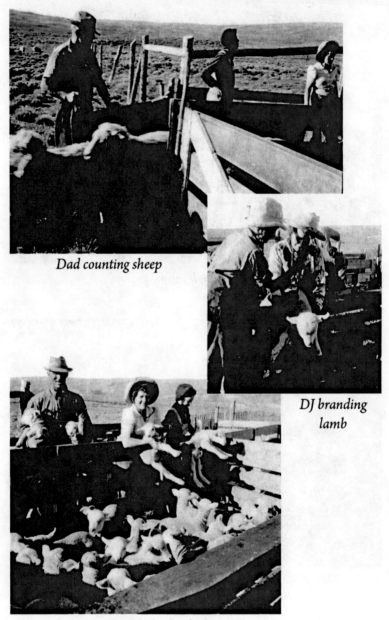

Dad counting sheep

DJ branding lamb

Separating lambs for docking

· 13 ·

Summer's Child

July, with its wildflowers and greenery, reminds me of my mother, summer's child. Matilda Rose Coletti Bertagnolli, Tilda to Dad and Tillie to friends, was born July 17, 1903 in Cumberland, Wyoming, to Louis and Teresa Coletti. My grandparents crossed the ocean the previous year from Monastero di Lanzo, an Alpine village in the Province of Piedmonte in the Italian/French Alps. He was thirty-one and she, twenty-one. Until their marriage, Grandpa Louis, one of the oldest of sixteen children, shared the responsibility with other siblings of caring for their large family.

At the end of the nineteenth century conditions for peasants in the Alpine region of northwestern Italy were similar to those in my father's homeland. Huge families and limited resources forced young men to leave in search of employment. Each spring, Louis and others from the village crossed over the alpine passes to work in coalmines in France. At the end of the nineteenth century, when burgeoning coal companies in Wyoming recruited miners from throughout the world, these young Italians were likely candidates.

In his 1850 journal, John Fremont first mentioned seeing coal in eroded banks in this area of Wyoming during one of his early expeditions. By the end of the nineteenth century, mining camps were springing up like mushrooms throughout the region in response to the energy demands of the Industrial Revolution. Louis and Teresa Coletti began their new life in the coal mining camp of Cumberland Number Two. About a dozen brothers and sisters and spouses had already sailed or would join them shortly. Grandma Coletti had only three siblings; two of these, a sister and a brother, immigrated to America. Another sister died early in life. Her brother, Guiseppe, was the only relative to return to Monastero to care for Great-grandmother Caterina, their widowed mother.

In a little over a decade, one-fourth of this immigrant family would be dead. Like other miners and their families, they succumbed to the Spanish flu and common illnesses such as pneumonia along with mine explosions and injuries and gunshot wounds. That more of them had not met their end in the numerous mine explosions—ninety men lost their lives in one alone—was remarkable.

In the winter, wind blew through the frame company houses in the shadow of the tipple, a long structure built on a raised area where coal, extracted by miners deep in the tunnels, was loaded into railway cars. Water was carried from a hydrant to the homes and later a bathhouse was built at the mines for the men. Without running water or bathrooms, the houses were nonetheless made comfortable and warm by people who knew how to make a home, even in a rock hut. Miners and their wives bought staples and necessities from a company commissary in each camp and from peddlers who came to the camp selling groceries and clothing.

With Mamma one day, I walked through the remnants of their home where the mining camp once stood. We gathered pieces of purple glass, lichen-encrusted boards from the house and old enamel-ware pots that remained from their days there. She remembered walking down the road toward the tipple each day to meet her father on his way home from work.

After working in the Cumberland mine for several years, Grandpa Coletti was presented with an opportunity. His brother John, a bachelor, had filed on a homestead and offered to transfer the claim to him. Grandpa accepted this generous offer, quit the mine in Cumberland and loaded Grandma, their five children and their belongings into a buck wagon. They drove twenty-five miles north to prove up on the homestead near the mining camp of Sublette perched on a ridge about a mile away.

Honed to a life as self-sustaining peasants, they must have rejoiced at the opportunity to live a simple, non-materialistic existence sustained primarily with homegrown provisions, much as they had in Italy. Milk cows, goats, and chickens contributed to the family's basic subsistence of cheese, milk, eggs, chicken and veal, supplemented by vegetables grown in their garden in the summer. Wheat and polenta flour, sugar, dried fruit, dried beans, potatoes and coffee would be purchased at the company store in Sublette where Grandpa continued to work in the mines. Johnny and Tony, teen-age sons and child laborers, worked with him and contributed to the amount of coal that Grandpa dug and was paid for each day. Meanwhile, Grandma, with the help of Mamma, carried on with the work of the homestead.

Mamma, the oldest, was an indispensable member of this family enterprise. In the summer she herded grazing cows and barefoot children over the sagebrush hills down toward Willow

Springs each day. She helped with the milking, making cheese, sewing, housework, and washing clothes with a scrub board. Kate, the sister closest to Mamma in age, could not be contained indoors with household chores; she favored outdoor work for the rest of her short life. As the other children came of age they also helped with ranch and household duties.

In summer the children ran barefoot; in winter they needed protection from the deep snow. Each fall a peddler with his wagon of dry goods stopped by the homestead, and Grandpa Louis bought work shoes for all the children, including the girls, overalls for the boys and a bolt of cotton cloth for making the girls' dresses.

Eventually Grandpa quit the mine to help Grandma with what became a home industry, a dairy of sorts. They subsisted on the small homestead and sold milk and goat cheese to the families in the Sublette mining camp. People from surrounding coal camps and Kemmerer came to their homestead to buy their delicious *tuma* cheese. Grandpa and Mamma went to Sublette several times a week in a little one-horse cart to deliver milk held in five-gallon metal cans. Miners' wives brought their own pitchers and empty lard cans to be filled with a dipper by Mamma.

Grandma Coletti was kind, reticent, patient, and loving. As she and Mamma worked together, Grandma taught her the skills of housekeeping and the art of preparing Piedmonte cuisine. She also inculcated values and genealogy of the family, knowledge of herbal medicines and treatment of diseases and a deeply religious Catholic mythology, including all the saints' feast days and their special areas of intervention.

Grandpa Coletti, on the other hand, taught Mamma something of the ambiguities of life. He brewed his own wine and at times became a heavy drinker. Although not violent when drunk, he raved and frightened the children who scattered like rabbits into the sagebrush.

His drinking problem seemed not to have altered my mother's love for him. He was basically a kind and gentle man who watched over his children, and on one blustery winter night, unable to get a doctor in time, delivered my Aunt Jennie into the world. Grandpa advised Mamma and the other children about the ways of the world and guarded her and her sisters against the advances of young men. Mamma remembered him as a good father, but was so impressed by his drinking that she abstained from alcohol for life.

When Mamma entered the first grade, she spoke only Italian. Because of family needs, she attended school sporadically. She always regretted not graduating from high school. In later years, after she and Dad had sold the ranch and moved to town in their retirement, Mamma earned her Graduate Education Diploma (G.E.D.).

On my wall hangs a cherished picture of my mother, a family portrait taken in 1919 when she was sixteen, about seven years after they had moved to the homestead. The eight children and Grandpa Louis stare at the camera with expressions of mixed bewilderment and seriousness. Not so for Mamma and Grandma, who appear assured and proud of this brood. One other son, Louis, was born after the picture was taken. My mother's left hand rests on young Jimmy's shoulder. Dry and chapped, with nails worn around the edges, her hands have the appearance of an older woman's. On her ring finger is a small Black Hills gold band with a garnet stone, given to her by the man she would marry.

The previous year, on a sunny July day in 1918, Mamma and Grandpa were at a homestead on Fontenelle Creek in the mountains above their ranch. They had purchased hay in the field, which they would cut, bale, and haul back to their barn for winter forage for their livestock. It was Mamma's job to lead a horse around and around the primitive baler to which it was tethered. After a tedious day in the sun she stayed the night with Pearl, a diminutive but sprightly schoolteacher who slept with a pistol under her pillow.

One day a handsome man with violet blue eyes and black hair, a red bandana around his neck, and a white Stetson hat cocked slightly to the side came riding through the meadows and stopped to observe the haying operation. A foreman for a large sheep outfit, he was on his way to the summer range to check on the flocks. Mesmerized by my mother, he sat on the baled hay and watched her. Before he rode off, he introduced himself. Either the sun or the strain of meeting Matt Bertagnolli, whom she sensed would be an intruder in her life, sent Mamma to bed with one of her first migraines. He stopped by to see her each time he passed the homestead and they soon became engaged.

That she proudly made public her troth to my father in the family portrait is appropriate. They were to marry the summer when the picture was taken. But during the ensuing year, three of her siblings became seriously ill: Jennie and Johnny with ruptured appendices, and the tiny one, Jimmy, with meningitis. Mamma provided the primary nursing care for these children, in and out of the hospital. As the summer approached, she postponed the wedding, not because of a change of heart, but as a response to the confusing mixture of exhaustion and responsibility she felt. Knowing how much she was needed at home, she could not leave her family at that time.

Mamma and Dad were married on September 3, 1921, and as far as I can surmise, were completely devoted to each other for their entire lives. Mamma always said that Dad, twelve years her senior, was a father and friend as well as a husband and lover. They had opposite but complementary personalities. Dad was ambitious and quick to anger, reach conclusions and retaliate if wronged. Curious and unafraid to take chances, he had an entrepreneurial and impulsive spirit. Mamma, on the other hand, was steady, serious, and slow to anger and make up her mind, somewhat of a skeptic and always forgiving. This combination of differences led to some lively discussions (upon which I often eavesdropped) but contributed to better mutual decisions in the long run. With a deep sense of responsibility and impeccable ethics, Mamma always stood fast to what she believed, but without losing her temper. "Tilda," Dad would say, "You are so stubboring!" Dad had his own version of the English language. Although they struggled at times to reach a decision, I never doubted their love for each other. They were conscientious about their duties to us children and to the successful operation of the ranch, and unconditionally devoted to each other.

Deeply bonded to her family and the welfare of her parents and siblings, Mamma was frequently nostalgic for them and the homestead. Separated for years from the family he loved dearly, Dad understood this longing in her. When roads were passable and the weather permitted, he would drive us to the Sublette ranch to visit our grandparents.

On our visits Mamma spent most of this precious time visiting with Grandma. I remember them conversing in Piedmontese, the Italian dialect spoken in Piedmonte, their region. They cried and laughed as they shared their present and past joys and sorrows. Although all of her siblings survived childhood, three of them, Johnny, Kate, and Tony, all died in their early thirties within three years of each other, from illnesses easily cured today.

These tragic deaths left my mother and grandmother bereft. I remember hearing the deep concern in my father's voice as Mamma mourned the death of Aunt Kate: "Tilda, if you don't stop crying, you are going to hurt the baby." At five, I didn't understand the implications of what he was saying, that my mother was pregnant with my little sister. But I remember the gentleness in his voice and his deep concern.

DJ's arrival a few months later was somewhat of a surprise to me. We had gone to Ogden to Aunt Minica's for Mamma's delivery, and when she came home from the hospital, I was puzzled by this tiny new addition with long, dark hair. I asked Mamma if I could lie down with them when she was resting in bed. But when Mamma asked if I wanted to touch the baby I declined and said that she scared me. I must have suspected that this new little creature would usurp my position as the youngest in our family.

As Mamma and Grandma sat in conversation on our visits, we children surveyed the homestead. It stood in a little meadow in a sea of sagebrush at the foot of Oyster Ridge where the coal camp, Sublette, by then a ghost town, once thrived. We explored the large barn and substantial hay shed for storing winter forage. A spigot of water, piped from a spring in the meadow above, flowed continuously into a huge trough. The frame house was small, with a long porch with chairs for sitting along its length. The cellar under the house carried the heady scent of aging cheese and wine. The kitchen was welcoming and filled with the aromas of roasting kid laced with garlic, baked bread, freshly brewed coffee and pound cake displayed on the sideboard.

When we arrived and as we left, we were enveloped in love: Grandpa ruffled our hair, pinched our cheeks and hugged us. His full handlebar mustache made his kisses memorable. Grandma took us in with a look filled with love, awe and delight. I remember her studying me intensely with a mixture of interest and amusement. And I now look back at this grandmother with recognition of my similar responses when I greet my own grandchildren and great grandchildren with feelings of awe and thanksgiving for such marvelous beings.

At times when she felt lonely, but travel to the homestead was impossible, Mamma would sit on her bedroom floor with boxes of photographs she had taken from storage in the trunk in her walk-in closet. With us children gathered around she would identify the people in each picture and explain the context and occasion. Sometimes she opened a jar of cherries preserved in grappa that she had stored in her closet. Although our uneducated palates did not favor the taste, it was clear they represented something quite important to her. We did our best to show appreciation for this strange treat.

In the pictures, Mamma wore lovely dresses with circular or short pleated skirts with her beautiful long hair set in waves around her face and ringlets pulled back and held with a clasp. She would sometimes take several fox furs out of her trunk and put them around our necks or let us try on a beautiful brown velvet coat with fur on the neck, sleeves and hem. Mamma never mentioned the bootlegging days, undoubtedly the time when the clothes had been purchased. I doubt that she wanted to return to those days but I expect, in the throes of the Depression, pondered how dramatically her life had changed.

On other days, when rain had slowed work on the ranch and she grew restless, Mamma would prepare special treats for us. In the middle of the afternoon, we'd find ourselves seated around the oil-clothed table waiting patiently for the delicacies she was concocting: *zambione*, a frothy Italian dessert of whipped eggs and wine, or paper-thin crepes rolled with strawberry jam, singed with a hot poker and dusted with powdered sugar. We had no idea what initiated the treats but responded with enthusiasm and appreciation.

With her knowledge brought from the homestead, Mamma timed the breeding of milk cows with the seasons and broke young heifers for milking. She attended and assisted with the birth of each calf, sometimes staying with the cow throughout the night. After the birth, she would whisk the calf away before the cow could see or smell it. She would then drench her hands and arms in the fluids from the placenta and let the cow smell and lick them. This afterbirth ritual bonded the cow to Mamma, a surrogate for the calf. I remember when Dolly, a lovely Jersey, would come with a taut udder to the fence around our ranch house and bellow for Mamma to come milk her.

Mamma's peasant-like love for farm animals translated to other species. She always had a pet dog, which shared our household. We looked forward to the boxes of chicks she bought by mail order as well as those hatched from brooding hens. She raised a menagerie of turkeys, chickens, ducks and geese and was amazed when one of the goslings that hatched looked very much like a Canada Goose. Apparently a wild gander had stopped by the ranch on his way north in the spring. In accord with its wild nature, the hybrid flew off with a migrating flock in the fall but returned for a brief visit for several years.

Once Dad brought home a fawn he had found on the lambing grounds. He assumed its mother had abandoned it, but more likely, the doe had just bedded it there before she went off to browse. Similar to pronghorns in their behavior, mule deer fawns will lie quietly until the does return. Mamma named the little creature Bambi and raised it on a bottle. As summer approached it ranged around the yard but loved to come into the house. When allowed to do so, it would go directly to Mamma's bedroom and jump on her bed and curl up for a nap. As it grew, it ranged farther away. One day it disappeared and after a thorough search by all of us, Uncle Richard found it dead on the railroad tracks. Adept at jumping fences, it had no notion of the lethal power of trains.

In the spring of 1954 Dad and Mamma were driving a truckload of supplies to the Boulder ranch, where Bob, our children and I were then living, when Dad became very ill. Dad refused to go back to Kemmerer and instructed Mamma to drive the truck on to our ranch. When they arrived, I called a doctor, who came immediately, but, since Dad had no chest pain, misdiagnosed his weakness and nausea as a problem with high blood pressure. Dad was obviously seriously ill and the next day, Bob drove him and Mamma back to Kemmerer to their doctor and then to the hospital where he was diagnosed with a massive heart attack. These were the days before heart surgery, when the only treatment for heart attacks was bed rest, and the doctor ordered Dad to remain in the hospital for six weeks.

At the time, I was expecting my third child and as the time for delivery drew near I went to Kemmerer to birth the baby. I was overdue, so the doctor sent me to the hospital to take castor oil, used at the time to induce labor. The hospital was small and my room was just a few doors from Dad's. Through the night as the pains increased, I kept very quiet so as not to alarm him. As morning approached so did the time of delivery. The nurse on duty had apparently concluded that the baby would arrive on the next shift, after she was off duty at 7 a.m. At 6 a.m., however, I knew the baby was on her way and I buzzed the nurse, took her firmly by the wrist and ordered her to get me to the delivery room. Lisi arrived as the nurse wheeled me into the room where the maternity nurse was scurrying about. I sat up and looked at my new baby girl who had pretty much arrived unassisted. The doctor came rushing in after it was all over. As I think back on Lisi's unassisted entrance into the world, I see her carrying on in like manner throughout her life. Her very best gift, when she turned six was a two-wheel bicycle on which she explored the neighborhood with friends. Since that day, she's been an explorer of places and ideas.

Dad was in the hospital for six weeks but never recovered fully from the heart attack. DJ, then an elementary teacher, came home for the summer to help Joe Dona and Mamma with the ranch work. During Dad's long recovery at home, Mamma devotedly nursed him back to health with special diets and loving care. She had always been totally involved in the running of the ranch and its management and finances. She shouldered the serious financial problems they faced as well as the work of the ranch with amazing fortitude. The following year, when it became obvious that Dad would never recover his health, they sold the Boulder ranch and Bob and I moved to the Hams Fork ranch to help them. My fourth child, Bobby, was born that fall. Although he was a frail infant at birth, with the guidance of a pediatrician in Salt Lake City, I was able to nurse him to health.

Before Dad had suffered the heart attack, forever planning ways to make a little money, he had been building a lambing shed. He estimated that with a small band of sheep, kept on the ranch, lambed early and protected in the shed, he could raise prime lambs by the following fall, which would bring in much needed funds. In March, the sheep began lambing and we followed his plan. Dad, Bob, Mamma and I took shifts watching over the lambing ewes. I took the midnight shift and every half-hour would go to the coral to see if any had given birth or were in labor. It was always thrilling to walk into the coral and hear the bleating of a newborn lamb. With the mother following close behind, I'd carry the newborn into the shed to a pen, prepared with straw for bedding and hay in a manger. In between checking on the sheep, I kept a good fire going in the kitchen and baked bread or cookies or rocked Bobby after his feedings.

The money we earned was well worth the effort. With our united effort and the sale of the Boulder ranch, Mamma and Dad were able to pay off most of their debts. In 1958, facing the reality that they could no longer manage the Hams Fork ranch, they sold it and retired. Bob and I and our four children moved back to our home in Kemmerer where Bob found work.

Although Dad's health continued to wane, he and Mamma enjoyed his last years. They spent six months in Europe with relatives that Mamma had met only by mail. They traveled often to visit friends and relatives and camped out on the LaBarge Creek and the Hams Fork River in the summer where Dad enjoyed fishing.

Sitting on a bookshelf near my desk is a large green ceramic frog made for me by Mamma in the summer of 1965. When I cup the figurine in my hands I sense the touch of her hands fashioning it. She made it for me during the summer following Dad's death. He died suddenly one night in March when they were watching his favorite television show, "I Love Lucy," with their dear friends, Anna and Joe Dona, who by then had married.

Mamma's grief was so profound that I feared for her mind. Although Dad had been seriously ill for a decade, she apparently had never considered life without him. After the burial, grandchildren took turns staying with Mamma to keep her company in the evenings. In early June, as I was preparing to leave for Pullman, Washington to begin my masters degree at Washington State University, I invited her to accompany me. Mamma declined, saying that she did not feel able to watch my children. I assured her this wasn't my intent and suggested that the change of scene would be good for her. Mamma finally agreed to join us.

I did my best to make it a good summer for her. With a National Science Foundation scholarship I had sufficient subsistence funds for the family. I enrolled the four children in theater and physical fitness day camps and Mamma in a ceramics class. She spent long hours at this craft, in the mornings in classes and in the afternoons working on her projects in the ceramics facility open for student use. On weekends, I drove her and the children through the beautiful Palouse countryside of southeastern Washington or to the lakes and forests of nearby Idaho for picnics and rock hunts. At the end of the summer, we loaded boxes of vases, cookie jars, dishes and little ceramic animals she had fashioned for Christmas presents into the Plymouth station wagon. Molding the clay and painting these creations somehow filled a part of Mamma's empty heart. She began opening up and letting the world re-enter. She later thanked me for that summer, which she said, "saved her life."

Mamma was a widow for thirty years after dad's death, but she never forgot him for a moment. She told me repeatedly that when he died, the light faded from her life. She had been his partner in every sense of the word. The only time he had not heeded her counsel was in the phosphate mine fiasco, but Mamma never held this big mistake against him. Forgiveness was her strongest trait. After his heart attack, Dad knew that he would not live long and had wisely planned for her financial independence after his death.

Through her last years, Mamma was devoted to family, church and good works. She registered for extension courses, joined the local historical and homemakers clubs and gardened, growing beautiful flowers. She traveled to Italy and Europe nine times, each time accompanied by one of her daughters or grand-daughters. She visited me frequently in Salt Lake City, and each summer I took her on a sentimental journey back to the mountains she loved when the flowers were in bloom.

When she began failing, Barbara, who had retired, took Mamma into her home, with DJ and me taking her for a week each month. Devotion to children and grandchildren flowed from Mamma in a steady stream until her death in her ninetieth year. Toward the end her mind slipped away but she retained her sweet and loving nature. In summer, when the balsamroot has turned the hillsides golden, I see her walking through the foothills.

The church and its ancient belfry dominate the tiny square in the Alpine village of Monastero de Lanzo, Italy. Even before the introduction, the keeper of the keys looks familiar to us. Although a distant cousin—a great grandson of one of Grandpa Coletti's brothers—the family resemblance is remarkable. He opens the magnificent wooden doors with an enormous key and we enter the peaceful ambience of the church. Light streams through the stained glass windows onto an ornate blue and dark walnut altar trimmed with gold. The wooden pews are smooth and lustrous from years of wear. Our footsteps echo as we walk across the marble floor. Above the altar hangs a faded painting depicting Saint Michael slaying the dragon. Our grandparents were married in this church. To the side is a font where generations of my maternal ancestors were baptized.

On my first visit to this village with my mother, when we came to see her cousin Vittoria, I watched them holding hands and talking in their native Piedmontese like long-lost sisters. They were amazingly similar in appearance and affect. Now both are deceased, and I have planned this visit with my sisters, Barbara and DJ, and daughter Lisi, our very adept driver. She takes naturally to the Italian way of negotiating tortuous roads, which, at times, keeps me on the edge of my seat.

Teresa, Vittoria's daughter, and her son, Juan Paulo and his family, met us at our hotel in Lanzo this morning, and we followed their car up the winding road to where Grandma and Grandpa Coletti were born. We are in the montane foothills of the French-Italian Alps in the Piedmonte Province near Turino, its capitol.

This high, rugged country, dissected by many isolated valleys, provided refuge for peasants and various religious groups down through the ages. Vestiges of old monasteries and convents still exist, some used today as retreat centers. Historically, diverse conquerors, explorers, and missionaries, including Hannibal, Constantine and Saint Paul, made their way over the Alpine passes into France.

Our cousins' summer home is in Monastero di Lanzo, the birthplace of my maternal ancestors. Their large stone dwelling is contiguous with similar buildings along a narrow cobbled street. We park our cars, walk past a water fountain and enter a lovely garden that extends up a hill, planted with fruit trees, berry bushes, a great variety of flowers and vegetables and, to our surprise, a kiwi tree. Although deep in snow in the winter, in summer the climate is moderated by the Mediterranean Sea. The interior of their summer home is finished with tiled floors and white plastered walls and furnished with dark walnut furniture. To the side is a fireplace for cold days.

Warm and friendly, my mother's kin immediately make us at home. I can understand Italian, but am minimally conversant. But Juan Paul and his wife Marcella understand a little English, so we are able to communicate with one another. The day has been carefully planned for us and the first order of business is a walking tour of Monastero. The cobbled street forms a narrow winding passage between rows of two-story apartment-like dwellings. Built originally to hold very large, extended families, the homes and lands are passed down from generation to generation. Some of the residents live here throughout the year, but most come for weekends or the summer. Our destination is Great-grandmother Caterina's apartment. Unlike most of the dwellings that have been preserved and restored with stonewalls shored up against the pull of gravity, hers is dark and crumbling. The shambles of the minute cubicle with its tiny window and fireplace reveal the humble and stark reality of her existence.

We return to our relatives' summer home for a delicious meal. We begin with antipasti and wedges of tuma cheese at various stages of aging, which carry a familiar flavor of those made by Mamma and Grandma Theresa. Handmade ravioli followed by veal scaloppini are served with lettuce salad from their garden, fresh-baked bread and red wine. Fruit and more cheeses are served and then a delicate pastry served with espresso. As an exclamation point to a delicious meal, we are offered tiny liqueur

294 • SOMETIMES CREEK

glasses of grappa, which carries the familiar taste of Dad's home brew.

Following dinner, Gian Paulo escorts us up an unimproved road to Alpine meadows where our ancestors herded their cows each summer. They lived in diminutive stone huts made of slabs of mica schist and built on stilts on steep slopes, which provided a walk-in space under the house for making and storing cheese. At the end of the summer they hauled carts of cheese to Lanzo for sale. As some still do today, they carried loads of harvested grasses and flowers from the Alpine meadows on their backs, wrapped in canvas or packed in hand carts to their barns in Monastero to store for winterfeed. They also kept sheep in these meadows and spun woolen yarn, which they knitted or wove into apparel. Here, as in Monastero, properties and little huts are passed down through families and restored as tiny summer cottages.

The Sancutario di Santa Anastasia, an ancient chapel and historic site, stands above the scattering of crumbling rock huts. Colorful paintings by local artists adorn its whitewashed walls. With primitive simplicity, the depictions record various near-death scenarios of the faithful whose prayers were answered by the intercession of Saint Anastasia, who, as a young girl, once lived in this village. According to the pictorial documentation, she has been kept very busy. The village is either a very dangerous place to live, or the residents are extremely accident-prone. The folk-art paintings illustrate people being gored by bulls, crushed by cave-ins, falling off roofs or into wells, injured in a variety of auto accidents or undergoing surgery.

From the sanctuary, Gian Paulo escorts us along a rough and rocky dirt road to the top of a high mountain to a hiker's hostel where drifts of snow still linger. Here we are treated to a grand view, apple strudel and café lattes. Circling back down the high mountain road past rock huts and goat herds, I realize this was the sort of setting for the book about one of my girlhood heroines, Heidi, and portrayed in tear-jerking perfection by Shirley Temple in a movie. As I'm sure my mother did each time she visited, I resolve to return another day. Like the old rock huts, family memories must constantly be shored up before they disappear.

Coletti family on homestead, Tillie far left, c. 1912

Coletti family, Tillie back row second from left, c. 1919

Grandma and Grandpa Coletti on homestead porch

1921   *1928*

Dad and daughters, with cousin Phons and Jackie, c. 1939

Mamma with Mary Bertagnolli and children

Bertagnolli family, 1938

*Dad and Mamma
picking flowers in
the Wyoming Range
(1962)*

*Mamma and best
friend, Anna Dona
(1981)*

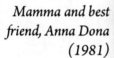

Mom at the old Coletti homestead (1990)

· 14 ·

Crossing the Divide

It's midsummer in Bridger-Teton National Forest and the mountains are in bloom. Clusters of yellow and magenta monkey flowers adorn springs while lavender elephantheads carpet the lush, boggy meadows. Accents of ivory-colored columbines sprinkled among flowering snowberry and buffaloberry bushes form the understory beneath conifers heavy with cones. Stalks of green gentian stand like sentinels on the ecotones of forests and meadows carpeted with yellow balsamroot.

On a sentimental journey, with sisters Barbara and DJ, we are driving up the LaBarge Creek Road. I am pleased that they accepted my invitation for this summer excursion—one I often took with Mamma during her last years, to this place she cherished.

We sisters haven't traversed this route together since we were children, yet the landscape is amazingly familiar, as is the road that remains relatively unimproved. This is a good sign as far as we're concerned. As we drive along, I stop periodically as they snap pictures. Simultaneously we recognize the family campsite selected by Dad at the edge of the forest and conveniently near LaBarge Creek.

At this glorious time of year our parents often packed us into the truck for a summer camp-out near our sheep allotments in the Wyoming Range. Thanks to Dad's fastidious attention to irrigating, the hay had grown lush and the fields were drying in preparation for haying. With all equipment in order and Joe Dona covering the daily chores, Mamma and Dad prepared for a much-awaited vacation to "The Mountains" where we hoped the sheep and lambs were thriving.

Finally, after much anticipation, we watched as our parents carefully arranged boxes of food, camping equipment and clothes on the bed of the truck, leaving a space behind the cab where Barbara and I would ride. With everything ready, they tucked us in, bound a canvas tarp over the rack, and Dad, Mamma, Uncle Richard and DJ got into the cab. At last we were packed and on our way over gravel roads to the place where Dad would set up our camp.

While there, the camp jack would meet Dad with a horse and they would ride out to the herd to count the blacks. One black sheep per one hundred gave a quick estimate of whether the herd was intact. If the herd had not met with any mishaps, such as mixing with another band of sheep or being scattered by a marauding bear, Dad would return and spend the remaining days fishing in the nearby streams, helping Mamma prepare meals or taking us on hikes or rides to some of his special places.

I park at the view area overlooking LaBarge Meadows, and we set up camp chairs and unpack our lunch. From our perch, we savor the food and the scene below, a lush willowed bottom, crisscrossed by the meandering stream. This was a stopover for immigrants following the Lander Cut-off of the Oregon Trail. Here they staked their horses and cows to graze as they themselves rested, bathed in the cool stream, washed clothes and regrouped for their final push to Utah, Idaho or California. Some 62,000 immigrants stopped here in the mid-1800s. On their way to gold, religious freedom or an independent agrarian life elsewhere, they had no intention of settling permanently in this part of the Rockies. Like us, they were just stopping over for a refreshing moment.

After eating lunch, we sit and enjoy the beautiful summer day that draws me back to a memorable moment. "Do you remember the day Dad showed us the divide?" I ask. Barbara and DJ recollect the tree we found that had fallen over another and bounced when we sat on it. Dad trimmed and shaped it with seats that made a make-believe horse. And they remember the ranches we constructed in the thick beds of needles under the trees, populated with little animals made of pinecones. But neither of them recalls that particular event that remains so lucid in my mind. We pack up and as we resume our journey I reconstruct for them the scenario of that long-ago day.

Early that morning, Dad, as usual, had built a roaring fire. Barbara and I descended from our blankets in the bed of the truck, arranged there to assure Mamma that we would be safe throughout the night. We dressed by the fire and then watched Dad prepare breakfast. By that time he had already brewed coffee and had served a cup to Mamma, who lingered with DJ in their warm bed. From his solicitous care of Mamma, I surmised that Dad had planned this camping trip as a rest for her away from household and ranch duties as well as a vacation for us. The smell of bacon and eggs cooked on a camp stove and potatoes fried in a Dutch oven over hot coals soon brought Mamma, DJ and Uncle Richard, who was sleeping in another tent, to the table.

At breakfast Dad announced that he was going to take us to a very important place that day. After eating and camp cleanup, we took our usual places in the truck. Barbara and I were allowed to stand behind the cab to monitor our progress. The old truck bumped its way down the dirt road into LaBarge Meadows, heavy with the sweet scent of growing grass and wet soil, and then lumbered up to a high rocky ridge where Dad parked.

We disembarked and followed him along the crest of the ridge where he stopped and with the verve of an explorer announced, "This is a divide." Pointing to the sloping, nondescript drainage on the east side of the ridge, Dad explained how the melting snow and rain that fell there, with water from springs along the way, formed LaBarge Creek, which flowed by our campsite. That stream, he said, emptied into the Green River, which we had seen on our way to our camp, and kept going south until it joined the Colorado River. I learned later that its waters emptied into the Sea of Cortez off Mexican shores. On the west side of this little divide, he explained further, snowmelt, run-off and coalescing tributaries formed Greys River, which flowed north into the Snake River to eventually confluence with the Columbia River and thence, on to the Pacific Ocean. At the time, with only a rudimentary understanding of geography, I couldn't comprehend the significance of this division of waters, but I was nonetheless in awe that two different rivers flowing in opposite directions could begin at the same place.

After I had reconstructed Dad's lesson of the day, Barbara, DJ and I walk to our parked car and stop to study a historical marker. It informs us that we are standing on the Tri-basin Divide that sends waters from this region into the Snake River Basin, the Green River Basin and the Great Basin. Back in the car, we continue our circular journey by following the Greys River Road out of Bridger-Teton National Forest. At Alpine Junction we buy ice cream cones to sustain us through the final leg of our journey through the Snake River Canyon, where busloads of tourists are floating the whitewater. This is where explorer George Price Hunt, leader of the Astor party, made another of his miscalculations.

Encouraged by the size of the Snake River at its confluence with the Hoback River, Hunt surmised that, at last, he had found a water route to the Pacific. Despite the advice of John Hoback and his Shoshone guides that this portion of the Snake was not navigable, he set the French boat-makers to work buildings canoes, the purpose for which he had recruited them in Canada. After embarking, his men, unable to maneuver the treacherous rapids in the hand-hewn canoes, wrecked with loss of lives and provisions. John Hoback then led Hunt and the party by land over Teton Pass and on into what is now Idaho. It would take Hunt and his party another year of hardship before he finally reached his destination at Astoria on the Pacific coast, the center for fur trading established by John Jacob Astor.

In Astoria, John Stuart had been waiting for Hunt's arrival. Also hired by John Jacob Astor, Stuart was commissioned to sail around South America to Astoria to await the arrival of Hunt and prepare for an overland journey back to Saint Louis. After almost three years en route, Hunt finally arrived. John Stuart, with eight men, left Astoria and arrived back in St. Louis in six months. Utilizing his own good sense and information from Hunt, together

306 · Sometimes Creek

with the advice of native guides, Stuart led his men over what is now called South Pass where the Wind River Mountains taper off onto the plains. The route Stuart forged would become the Oregon Trail to be followed by pioneers until the transcontinental railroad was built.

Finally back in the Hoback Basin, tired and content, I drop my sisters off at DJ's cabin and head for mine. As I mull over our day's journey I am struck by the enduring memory of the divide experience. It may have been the genesis of an impulse that has drawn me through the years, with students and children, to various watersheds in the West.

In the early 1960s I had reached a divide in my own life, one that would send me into new territory. I was not a part of the great progressive movement of that decade and change did not come to me in one spiritual epiphany. It came after many dark nights. But throughout setbacks and recovery, my study and love of the natural world became a constant beacon. And teaching was my saving grace.

In late spring of 1963, I found an advertisement in my school mailbox describing a two-week field course at the Audubon Camp of the West to be held that summer in the Wind River Mountains. It offered recertification credit for teachers, which I needed. I asked my mother and sisters to care for my children while I attended and after school was dismissed, on my own for the first time in over a decade, I headed out. I took the Farson Cut-off Road to Dubois, Wyoming and from there followed a rocky road to Trail Lake Ranch in the foothills of the Wind River Mountains.

The instructors were magnificent teachers and the participants inspiring activists. The common premise of the classes on ecology, geology, invertebrates, mammals and birds was that land, water and other creatures are a necessary and inseparable part of our human experience. I left the camp committed to bringing innovation to my classroom and to making my teaching interesting and relevant for students. I decided then to go on to graduate studies and, after increasing my knowledge of the natural world, to return to teach at the Audubon Camp. It was then that I applied for a National Science Foundation scholarship and was accepted at Washington State University in Pullman, Washington, where I would earn my masters degree.

The assumption for the scholarships, that increasing teachers' scientific knowledge would improve their teaching, proved true for me. Just as important were the examples of three exceptional professors: Dr. David Rahm in geomorphology, Dr. Rexford Daubenmire in plant ecology and Dr. Harvey Miller in botany. Their thorough knowledge, passion for their fields and innovative instruction motivated me to become a better teacher.

Dr. Rahm's use of spectacular slides, taken from his airplane to complement his lectures, inspired me to photograph Wyoming landforms and ecology for use in my classes. One day I decided to create a student inquiry that replicated one used by Dr. Rahm. While explaining the deposition of sedimentary layers, he constructed a peanut butter and jam sandwich, naming each layer of the sandwich according to a geological formation. He then folded the sandwich in two, took a bite out of the center and, holding it up to us, showed us how the sequence of sedimentary layers (bread, jam and peanut butter) were reversed where the "earth's crust" had been warped back upon itself. This, he told us, was similar to a reversed sequence in a geological formation we might encounter in roadcuts or eroded mountains.

I ordered bread, chunky peanut butter and strawberry jam for an activity for my freshman earth science class. Students would construct the sandwich model with each of the layers representing a geological strata found in our area. After recording the sequence and completing the worksheet, they would eat their models. At the same time, in an effort to provide living specimens for the high school biology classes studying the structures of flowering plants, I ordered gladiolas. When the principal called me into the office to ask me for an explanation for ordering these materials for my classes, I huffed out of his office, mumbling something about teaching the rest of the year on pond water.

Occasionally I had utilized an overgrazed pasture bordering the school for my biology classes. Now motivated to follow through on my response to the principal, I made the area the primary focus for my biology students. On the first visit I sat with the class on the hillside overlooking the area as we discussed what students saw in the little swale below us. On following days I gave them time to explore and draw a map of the area. By that time they had become acquainted and interested in the area, and I then asked them to select a site for individual or team study. I explained that, with their cooperation, we would use this area throughout the year to study the ecosystem that was their home ground. With the exception of a small spring, which we would explore as a group in the winter, they could choose any site for study. Throughout the school year, I explained, students would be studying chosen sites and recording observations and data in a bound efficiency notebook.

The biology classroom was in a wing of the school with a door to the outside. I suggested students keep old shoes in the locker to be used in the field to avoid tracking in mud or dirt that would give the janitors extra work. I made it clear that I would write no excuses if they were late for their next classes. They would be free to come and go to the site during the class whenever necessary to gather data, but they had to do so quietly to avoid disturbing other classes. Set up as a subversive collaboration between us, students acted responsibly and appreciated the freedom. I proceeded with the plan without notifying the principal or asking his permission.

The curriculum required much thought and preparation on my part, since I was committed to students mastering all concepts covered in a traditional biology course. It required individual instruction and coordination of materials and resources as well as providing lectures, writing and reading assignments and tests on concepts at appropriate times. I required a term paper, collaboratively planned with an English teacher.

The bookshelves in the biology room were filled with reference books checked out from the library as well as several versions of the "new" biology being introduced in schools. This was the time when nations were competing in their explorations of space. In an effort to improve the teaching of high school and math curriculums, the U.S. Department of Education had commissioned scientists, professors and exceptional high school teachers to write new texts for all courses. Three versions were available with different emphases in molecular, genetic or environmental biology. I also recruited the help of natural resources scientists from federal and state agencies in the community, who generously supplied reference materials for students and helped us fathom the amazingly diverse flora and fauna in those few acres of sagebrush steppe. In the winter, I designed units on invertebrates and microorganisms using samples students had collected from the spring and soil.

Positive responses from high school students motivated me to recommend that the school district purchase this land for an outdoor laboratory for all grades. The school board did so and the few acres were set aside as KOLAB, the Kemmerer Outdoor Laboratory. Over the next year, with a small state grant, I purchased necessary field equipment for elementary classrooms and conducted in-service workshops for teachers, grades one through six. That spring, the halls and rooms of the elementary school were decorated with drawings of birds, butterflies, animals and plants the children had seen in the KOLAB. Independently, the enthusiastic teachers had designed a teacher's guide for its use.

During this time a representative from the National Association of Biology Teachers observed my classroom and I was named an outstanding biology teacher in Wyoming. I felt honored and thrilled at a school assembly when I was presented with a microscope by the association. I put the beautiful instrument to immediate use, when, along with students, I studied the fresh water ecology of the little spring in KOLAB. The research gathered became the topic of my master's paper and my first publication, "Mudhole Ecology."

I was told that after the award at a school assembly, a school board member remarked with some passion, "Hell, we've been trying to fire that woman ever since we hired her."

During my years as a teacher, I had been a constant thorn in the school board's side. When I was first hired, no salary scale was published and contracts were negotiated individually and arbitrarily. Several teachers and I joined the state education association and formed a local teachers' organization. We met with the school board and negotiated a published salary schedule and hiring procedures, even though this jeopardized our own positions.

After having achieved success in teaching and overcoming depression, I felt I had my feet on the ground when another threat entered my life. Sexual harassment was not a subject the school board would have understood in those days. Their assessment, and that of most men and women of that era, was that when it occurred, the woman was asking for it. When I rejected the advances of a supervisor, he removed me from committee assignments, which I considered the lifeblood of my professional development and an avenue for institutional change. This blow, coupled with continuing problems with my marriage, forced me to come to grips with the reality of my untenable situation. I applied for and received a graduate fellowship in the Department of Educational Studies at the University of Utah. In mid-life with my teenage children, Matthew, Lisi, and Bobby (by this time, Kathryn Ann had married) and with twelve years of teaching experience, I left husband, home and high school teaching to pursue a doctorate in education with a minor in ecology.

This plan was no surprise to my husband, since I had discussed separation with him, but it shocked my family and community. I asked my three children, who were reluctant to leave their home and school, to give it a try for a year. If, at the end of the trial, they were unhappy with their new school and situation, I promised I would return to Wyoming with them. I enrolled them in Catholic schools and, luckily for me, they took to them and their new friends.

The children spent time with their father on weekends and vacations, but, in retrospect, I now appreciate more fully the consequences of the absence of a father from their daily lives. Matthew had to take on more responsibilities. Lisi was very close to her father, and the separation created a void in her life. Bobby, the youngest, just entering the eighth grade, was most affected. He had always been a quiet and thoughtful child, secure in the comfort of our home. An image of him as a child replays in my mind as I watched him outside the kitchen window one sunny summer day. He had on shorts and was barefoot and bare-chested and was playing with horned toads he had captured and was keeping as pets. He was lying on his back on the lawn with a horned toad crawling across his chest. He seemed absolutely enraptured by the moment, feeling the sun's warmth, the movement of his little friend on his skin, the firm ground of home under him. He was completely grounded in place. The move undoubtedly uprooted him. But it brought me the possibility of fulfillment for the rest of my life and for that I am grateful to my good-hearted children.

During the next four summers, I fulfilled my dream to return to the Audubon Camp of the West as an instructor. Photography, which enhanced my study of nature and teaching, became a passion. Inching my way around a waterfall on Torrey Creek where dippers nested in the spray and incredible energy of the falling water, I suddenly felt very vulnerable and alone. Not a benign little intermittent stream such as Sometimes Creek, this was a mass of energy seething with power and destruction. Realizing how close I was to the edge, I carefully crept back to the safe haven of terra firma. I knew then that there was no one guiding my safe passage over the challenges of mid-life and, for the sake of my children and myself, I had to assume a more cautious and thoughtful perspective.

In 1972, at forty-six, I completed my PhD in education and ecology and was appointed assistant professor in the Department of Educational Studies at the University of Utah. That spring Bob and I walked into a lawyer's office and finalized our divorce. And at Mass one Sunday, when the priest attributed the problems of troubled youth to their divorced mothers, I walked out of the church and never returned.

The 1970s were opportune years to be in teacher education. Consciousness of environmental, feminist and equity issues infused educational reform. I involved college students, preparing to be teachers, in meaningful classroom experiences that complemented university courses. A plethora of books that critiqued schools for stifling the intellect and imagination of children provided me with inspiration and encouragement to innovate.

Of particular interest to me was Paulo Friere's *Pedagogy of the Oppressed*, in which he documented his work with illiterate adults in Brazil. His book provided the template for what I called Generative Thematic Modules, developed by education students around contemporary issues of particular concern to high school students. With the cooperation of a trusting high school principal, education students taught these modules to disaffected high school students, who were essentially in-school dropouts. The success of these modules, developed over several years, led to formalized alternative high school programs. Upon graduation and certification, many of these education students became teachers in the high school programs where they trained future alternative teachers.

After completing his doctorate at Ohio State University, Robert Bullough, a former student and the first teacher in STEP, an alternative high school program we created, joined our faculty at the University of Utah. He encouraged colleague Ladd Holt and me to attend meetings of *The Journal of Curriculum Theorizing*, whose intent was reconceptualizing education. William F. Pinar, Janet Miller and Madeline Grumet were the first organizers of conferences that later became the Bergamo Conferences,

314 · SOMETIMES CREEK

which I attended each year. Their acceptance of my instructional methods and publication of my personal narratives on teaching were invaluable to me as an academic.

During the ensuing years, I became a dedicated environmental activist and encouraged graduate students to become involved in ecological issues. We were familiar presences at public meetings and hearings for environmental impact statements, where we made a case for preserving the integrity of wild lands. Within the context of a generic class I developed and labeled "Field Studies in Environmental Education," I often selected study areas where students could gather data to support preservation. As president of the Utah Audubon Society, I served on many state and federal committees, always making the case for the protection of nonhuman creatures and their habitats. I remember one meeting in particular where I was the only member objecting to the U. S. Army's proposal to test a new unmanned aircraft, the Drone, for surveillance and target practice on the West Desert in Utah. I made the case that such stealth activities were immoral and besides would upset the nesting of raptors on the Newfoundland Mountains where testing was proposed. In recent years and armed conflicts, the common use of these unmanned weapons hasn't escaped my notice.

When a group was proposing a new organization, the Utah Wilderness Association, whose specific purpose was to protect wild lands within the state, I sponsored a fund-raising event at the university for their support. Edward Abbey and Barry Lopez were invited speakers. They were a great success and brought in a crowd of environmentalists from surrounding states. On the following Monday, I was called to the Dean's office to explain why he was receiving calls from legislators complaining of the involvement of the university in controversial environmental issues.

Undeterred, I spent the next decade designing workshops and seminars for graduate students, many of them teachers who melded activism and bioregional knowledge. Some lasted for weeks in the summer and became topics for my personal narratives, which I compiled in my book, *Ecotone*. A memorable field studies course was a writing workshop in Arches National Park in 1976 with Edward Abbey, which he suggested we call "On the Rocks." He had published his *Desert Solitaire* as I was beginning my doctoral studies and his book was (and still is) an inspiration to me. The year before the workshop, he published *The Monkey Wrench Gang*, which was causing quite a stir. Each day, after a long day of hiking in the park, we all met at sunset under a great ledge to listen to Abbey, backlit by the evening sky, as he read or talked to us. One evening in response to comments and criticisms from feminists concerning his sexist depictions of women in this last book, he replied, "It's sure funny how as it gets darker, the questions get harder."

As my ecological perspective matured in graduate studies and later in my teaching, various streams of discourse fed into and expanded this interest. A growing interest in dwelling rightly within my bioregion was furthered by my friendship with Dolores LaChapelle, whom I had met on Earth Day in 1980. After that meeting she was my guest during February of each year when she skied with old friends at the Alta ski resort. During these visits, Dolores also conducted workshops for my students and mini-seminars with me around our dinner table each evening. Her keen intellect and passionate dedication to deep ecology and non-consumptive living within a bioregion forced my rational-minded interest in the form and function of land and its creatures to a higher level of ethical consideration. She pointed out that nature was not the object of my study but an entity of which I was a part. We humans and other creatures all counted the same.

The inspiring poetry of Gary Snyder, who visited the University and area several times, impressed me as he admonished us to live in harmony on this "Turtle Island" home. The fierce criticisms of social ecologist Ivan Illich, also a repeated campus visitor, and his book, *Deschooling Society*, led me to question my own behavior and the mores of the materialistic society I had accepted as a given. Through his books, Paul Shepard's critical human ecology presented new questions and insights into our genetic affiliation to other creatures and this earth as primal home. After we became partners, I benefited from his presence and deep ecological knowledge. In California with him, an added gift was his friendship and conversations with colleagues such as Carl Hertel and Lucien Marquis as well as Ivan Illich, who were frequent guests at his home.

Throughout these new encounters, the formative experience bestowed by my father guided me unconsciously as I planned workshops along headwaters and courses of the Green and Colorado Rivers. Over the years, backpacking or floating rivers with children, college students and teachers, or on my own, I followed the course of the Green River from its head in the Wind River Mountains to its confluence with the Colorado in Utah and on to its delta in the Gulf of Mexico.

Standing on the divide that day with my sisters, my mind zoomed in and out, close up and far away, from the past into the present. I went from the little child looking with awe at the divide deemed so important by her father to a teenager with concerns for her appearance and boys, to a young woman making a rational choice to marry to satisfy her needs for children and a man, to a mature woman finding fulfillment in teaching and nature to the present older woman standing with her sisters, looking back. Out of that past come driving forces in my life: deeply complex and binding relationships with my children, thrilling and gratifying friendships with men and women, fulfilling and challenging teaching experiences and an expanding and mysterious spiritual and cognitive relationship with the natural world.

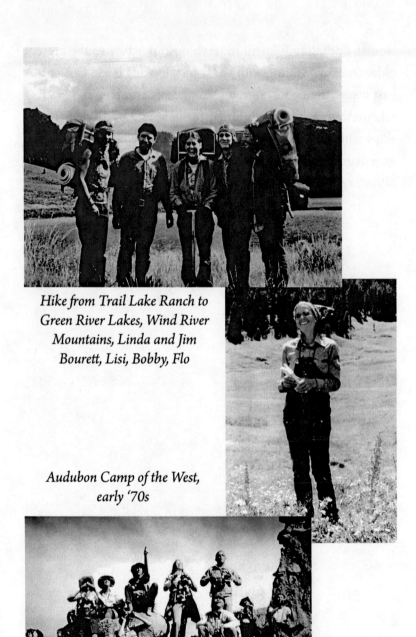

Hike from Trail Lake Ranch to
Green River Lakes, Wind River
Mountains, Linda and Jim
Bourett, Lisi, Bobby, Flo

Audubon Camp of the West,
early '70s

Environmental Field Studies

Dark Canyon,
Utah (1978)

Navajo Reservation (1979)

*"On the Rocks" Field Studies in Arches National Park
with Edward Abbey (1976)*

· 15 ·

Going Home

W*elcome to Wyoming.* Each time I cross the state line as I drive
to my cabin from Salt Lake City, I take the greeting personally.
The journey back through my childhood landscape is always a
pilgrimage of sorts, and today it holds special meaning for me.
My time at the cabin in the Hoback Basin has about ended for
this year and I won't be spending another winter there. After a
quick trip to the city, I'm returning to the Hoback Basin to spend
a few more weeks before the snow starts building. Today, instead
of driving the three hundred miles back to the cabin as quickly
as possible, I've decided to take the entire day for a sentimental
journey to revisit significant places that helped shape my past.

Topographic features for me are much like the sacred sites
for aboriginal people on their walkabouts. The familiar landscape
draws up an origin myth of sorts, wherein I have traced the history of my Italian ancestors who settled in Wyoming in the twentieth century. Today I retrace their path, one followed before them
by explorers and pioneers.

Past the University of Utah, where I taught for twenty-seven years, and through the Wasatch Mountains, I follow in reverse Brigham Young's route with the first Mormon settlers into the Great Basin—and the one I took with my three teen-aged children in 1969 when I began my doctoral program. Although at the time I had no intention of making a permanent home in Salt Lake City, I've lived there ever since.

Up out of the valley and through farmland along the Weber River, Interstate 80 winds its way to Echo Junction, where extra engines are added to pull freight trains up the steep two thousand-foot grade to Evanston, just inside the Wyoming border. This passage through the sensuous red rocks of the Jurassic Period provide a transition from the Great Basin topography to Wyoming's austere sagebrush habitat. The welcoming sign on the Wyoming state line always fills me with the same anticipation and pride I felt as a child upon returning to Wyoming after visiting relatives in Utah.

On through Evanston and still climbing, I turn off the interstate onto Highway 189-N and enter a broad strike valley of sagebrush steppe bordered on either side by eroded tilted strata dotted with junipers. With that turn, I take a deep breath. Although it looks like the middle of nowhere to most strangers, it feels like home to me.

Instead of immigrant trails, the broad valley is now crisscrossed with pipelines carrying gas and oil from the Overthrust Belt. Called Fossil Basin by geologists, this expanse is known as the Cumberland Flats, or just the Flats, to locals. Contrasting examples of what some define as progress can be seen where black veins of coal in eroded strata were first noticed by explorers passing through. Wind generators whirl on the western skyline and revegetated scars of the coal strip-mine trace the crest of the ridge on my left. At its base, a coal-fired power plant belches smoke from its stacks. Huge copper-colored pipes are stacked along the roadside for constructing more pipelines for transporting the ever-increasing production of natural gas and oil to all parts of the country from this region.

Not only a mineral resource, the Flats are also a repository of cultural and natural history. On their seasonal migrations to the mountains in the spring and to wintering grounds in Utah or Idaho in the fall, Shoshones camped among the junipers on the ridges. There, with my first husband, Bob Krall and our young children, I spent many pleasant outings searching for ancient campsites and artifacts. A remnant of a buffalo jump still exists at the base of one of the cliffs, where native people drove these magnificent animals to their death, then dried their meat for winter subsistence. Traces of wagon tracks on a branch of the Oregon Trail are still discernible as they head to old Fort Bridger, the site of my first memorable field trip with my beloved sixth grade teacher, Mr. Hampton.

With magnificent vistas and an ever-changing sky above, the treeless steppe holds surprises at every season. Now into September, grasses have turned yellow and migrating birds are moving through. Pronghorn bucks herd their harems on the slopes. Golden Eagles and Common Ravens cruise the highway searching for road-killed handouts.

On winter days, ground blizzards often obliterate this stretch of highway with a sea of flowing snow that makes for a treacherous drive. During such cold days, pronghorns and mule deer gather on south-facing slopes, as Snow Buntings and Horned Larks forage along the roadside.

Clusters of drop herds of domestic sheep with newborn lambs and patches of blue flax form a mosaic across the steppe as it greens up in the spring. Coyotes pop up in the sagebrush as they hunt ground squirrels as well as newborn lambs. Birds abound and ducks float on reservoirs. Breeding Golden Eagles tumble in the sky. Sandhill Cranes, disoriented by sudden snow squalls, plane down on forced landings.

Most of the headstones in a small cemetery off to the side of the highway identify children and young adults who perished during the Spanish flu epidemic of 1918. A few more miles down the road, blackened remnants of an old mine tipple mark the site of Cumberland Number Two, one of the first coal camps opened in the region where my grandparents first settled and my mother was born. On my last walk there with Mamma, she led me to the site of her home, where we searched the scattered middens for remnants of the past.

The highway leads up an incline and then descends into the narrow Hams Fork River valley. Three small towns, less than a mile apart, are clustered along the river's banks. Bordered by the mining towns of Diamondville on the south and Frontier on the north, Kemmerer continues to be a center for services for the surrounding communities.

Down the main street of Diamondville I can see no sign of the Burgoon School that I attended so long ago. And I surmise that the Diamond Bakery—established by Dad as a front for his thriving bootlegging enterprise—once stood on a lot now occupied by the post office. The Mountain States Trading Company, where our girls' sixth grade secret society hid their treasure, has disappeared.

On to Kemmerer and down Sage Avenue I pass our home during my first marriage, where we raised our four children. Bright red crab apples dangle from branches of four thriving trees planted by my father, one for each of my children. On to Cedar Avenue,

I drive by the small brick bungalow built by my parents, where I was born in 1926. In a few blocks I pass the home of Mamma and Dad after they sold the Hams Fork ranch and retired. The schools I attended where I later taught junior high school science have been razed. St. Patrick's church, minus its stained glass windows, still stands to serve another faith.

On up the road on the outskirts of town I visit the cemetery on a knoll overlooking the valley and Oyster Ridge to the east. My first stop is at Paul's grave. He chose to be buried here among my relatives where he knew he would not be forgotten. And just beyond are the graves of my parents and stillborn brother.

Pronghorns graze peacefully amidst gravestones, and Red-tailed Hawks call from the cottonwoods. For as long as I can remember, my family members have joined relatives here on Decoration Day (Memorial Day) to pay homage to the dead. Each year since our parent's passing, we sisters walk with our children, carrying flowers to the graves as we collectively reconstruct our genealogy and locate the gravesites of some forty relatives. Afterward, we gather at the senior center for dinner, where an impromptu reunion takes place with relatives, classmates and friends.

On hasty returns to my Bondurant cabin after visiting the Kemmerer cemetery, I typically continue through Kemmerer past the golf course and through the old mining town of Frontier, now the site of a conference center and corporate business offices. The company store and diminutive miners' houses that once occupied this space have been moved or torn down and the lots sold. Then I usually contour the switchbacks out of the Hams Fork Valley and cross Oyster Ridge where it angles off to the northwest into the Upper Fontenelle Basin. In that basin, my blue-eyed father first met and fell in love with my brown-eyed mother. On to Willow Springs, where my mother as a child herded milk cows and

328 • SOMETIMES CREEK

children each day, a dirt road angles off to the north and leads to my grandparent's old homestead. On the crest of the ridge above it, is the ghost town of Sublette where my grandfather and mother sold milk and cheese to the miners. The only building still standing is the jailhouse.

When taking this route, I continue on down the highway, skirt Round Mountain, and enter the Green River Basin. But today I modify my typical route out of Kemmerer and, after visiting the cemetery, I circle back through a housing development to the high school where I once taught. I drive past the recreation center and park near recently built grade and middle schools. On down a boardwalk, I enter KOLAB, now very different from the over-grazed pasture studied by my biology students. Fenced and protected from grazing for 43 years since I left Kemmerer, it has grown into a healthy and diverse steppe habitat for study by children in grades K through 12.

Back in my car, I circle back to the highway and follow it twelve miles east through the lower Hams Fork valley. During the school years when I road the bus over this route, I chose a window seat on the side where I traced the course of the meandering river back and forth across the valley, a topographic meditation of sorts. Isolated ox-bows, created where the Oregon Shortline Railroad bisected the valley offered me an example of the effects of technological development on the land and its resources.

As I turn off the highway onto a dirt road and head to the ranch, I realize why, on our yearly outings, Mamma didn't want to come back here. And I now understand more fully Eileen Dockham's tearful response when we drove to her home place. Old foundations and crumbling ruins are heart-wrenching and reinforce the fact that parents and childhood are gone. For a moment, I consider turning back—but, reconsidering, force myself to drive on.

Several homes with small plots of land, for people wanting to live in the country and keep a few horses, have sprouted up along the way. Crossing the railroad tracks and skirting our swimming hole, I drive over a sturdy new bridge and ease past the corrals and barns into the yard. The outhouse built by the WPA during the Great Depression stands upright and sturdy as ever. Several large excavating machines are parked nearby. The verdant slough of childhood adventures no longer exists; a bulldozer, which leveled the pond and uprooted the willows that surrounded it, stands nearby. The barricade of buildings Dad built along the west side of the house still stands and so does the cellar whose doors hang askew, allowing me to peer in at the dark interior, so frightening to me as a child.

I circle the house several times peering in the windows at old furniture and peeling wallpaper. The roof seems to have held up and I wonder why the house hasn't been kept up and occupied. It could still make someone a good home. Cottonwood trees, planted as shoots by Dad and watered regularly by Uncle Richard, are enormous but in various stages of decay. A Red-tailed Hawk screeches at me from a dead limb and then lifts into the sky.

Although I know that the natural destiny of humans and their structures is to return to the earth, the deteriorating buildings consolidate deep, dense memories and leave me feeling lost. Nonetheless, I'm bolstered by the steady state of the sagebrush-covered hills and meadows along the Hams Fork River, which remain as undisturbed as my roots to this place.

With a sigh of resignation, I get into the car and head away. Ahead on a hillside overlooking the ranch, a new home has been built near a sandstone outcrop that we daughters called the "Rock of Gibraltar." It was the site for summer evening bonfires and roasted hot dogs and marshmallows. We loved to explore its intricate eroded structure and the sandy areas under overhangs littered with flint chips and charcoal from ancient campfires.

Retracing my route to the highway, I drive on to Opal, where the Opal Mercantile, still a sturdy brick building, stands empty and abandoned, its front windows broken and boarded over. A sign, "Liquor Store," hangs above the covered windows of the old hotel lobby where I spent many delightful days when we were houseguests of Stella Petrie. I drive across the railroad tracks and follow several roads amidst old homes and trailer houses and abandoned cars where the Opal schoolhouse once stood. Off to the west, I see the house of my dear childhood friend, Rae Roberson, now occupied by the Larson family who owns it as well as our old ranch. The pine trees have grown taller than the sturdy two-story house.

With my survey of Opal completed, I head down the Opal Cut-off. During my childhood, it was a rollercoaster, stomach-upsetting gravel road with miles of steppe stretching as far as one could see. Now massive refining facilities and gas wells scatter over the landscape. But in spite of the modern distractions and a much-improved road, this place draws up memories. I'm taken back to that little girl riding along in the old truck with Dad as we headed for the mountains to check on the sheep herds—or with family on our way to a summer camp-out as well as driving with Barbara on one of our adventures.

One evening, I accompanied her on an assignment to drive supplies to a sheep camp in this area. As we chugged along over the seemingly endless rises and dips, we worked ourselves into quite a frenzy, convinced that we were in a "twilight zone" and would never reach our destination. When the sheep camp finally appeared on a distant ridge, we were elated and flooded with relief. Barbara, the oldest daughter but a young teen-ager, was trusted with such tasks that often exceeded her ability and experience.

I recall another adventure with her and the old truck. Instructed by our parents to feed sheep in the lower pasture, and accompanied by John Pearson, a Swedish carpenter employed on the ranch to remodel the old ranch house, Barbara drove the truck to the upper meadow. There John loaded the truck's box high with hay, on which he perched for the ride to the lower pasture. As we started down the steep road that led to the pasture, the truck began picking up speed. Confused, Barbara stepped on the clutch instead of the brake, and the truck raced out of control across the meadow. When we hit a bump, the entire load shifted over the cab, obstructing our view. When Barbara finally applied the brakes and brought the truck to a stop, we jumped out of the truck to see what had happened to John. Bewildered, he finally emerged from under the load of hay and exclaimed, "Yumpin Yiminy, Barbara, you nearly killed us." It was then we realized that she had finally brought the truck to a stop on the very edge of the riverbank.

Although John was one of many hired men who stayed on the ranch at various times during our childhood, Barbara and I remember him fondly. He'd come into the kitchen early each morning, looking for a "cup of coffa," brewed by my mother to bring him to consciousness. He was pleasant, and often downright funny and seemed to cheer the people around him. In the evening he played polkas on his accordion as Barbara and I danced.

As with many of the hired men who worked on ranches or sheepherding, he was a heavy drinker when he was in town. But on the ranch as he remodeled the house for Mamma, he was a star boarder. It took two years before John had satisfied all of my mother's expectations for a modern house.

Back on the Opal Cut-off, I've traveled to where it joins Highway
189 and enters the Green River Basin. As I drive north, mountain ranges rise up around the horizon: the Uintas in the distance
to the southeast on the Utah border, the Wind Rivers running
from east to north, the Gros Ventres due north and the Wyoming
Range to the west.

The highway descends into the Green River valley along
the Seedskadee Dam, misconceived in the notorious "Wreckla-
mation" days. Colorful Eocene sandstone and shale cliffs frame
the water, which on clear days reflects a robin-egg blue sky;
when cloudy, it is steel gray. In spite of mounting opposition to
the building of the dam in those days, it was built. Much to our
dismay, as the water backed up it covered several large productive ranches. As the dam filled, the weight of the water deformed
the underlying pliable sandstone and shale layers, and created a
rollercoaster track out of the new road that had to be completely
rebuilt. We wondered how a dam constructed on such malleable
layers could hold. As a matter of fact, it didn't. For years, much
effort and money was spent staunching the leaks that developed.
Thankfully, with mounting opposition from ranchers and environmentalists, future dams planned for tributaries of the Green
River were abandoned.

Beyond the Seedskadee Dam and its impounded water, haying
has ended on the extensive cattle ranches throughout the broad
Green River Basin. Long before explorers and trappers came
about two hundred years ago, native people inhabited this basin.
The Sheepeaters, horseless hunters lived year-round in the surrounding mountains, foraging on roots and berries and subsist-
ing primarily on mountain sheep. The Shoshone tribes followed
the migratory wild herds to the mountains in spring and back to
warmer climes in the fall.

Water for daily survival was the primary concern of explorers and pioneers who followed Indian trails through this territory and across the divides to California and the Southwest. Fifty years later, another imperative entered entrepreneurial minds. Somewhere in these reaches lay rich mineral rewards available for the taking. The development of land and minerals was considered the Manifest Destiny of the expansionist movement. Since that time, America's conquistadors of one sort or another—from explorers to beaver trappers and buffalo hunters, to homesteaders and ranchers, to miners and companies for energy exploration and extraction, to recreation seekers—have marched into, across and out of this land, reaping what they could. A few, who came to love the place, stayed on.

Maintaining healthy ecosystems and preserving the resources for future generations would seem to be a matter of primary importance to everyone. But profit, not preservation, is the goal of exploiters. And activists concerned with social justice and animal rights, while responsive to the needs of humans, are sometimes unable to discern the connection between the problems they try to solve and the degradation of ecosystems. As I slow down to let a speeding Halliburton truck pass by, I find it hard to believe that my frugal, ecological lifestyle, which is now a mindset, makes any difference in the glut of unregulated consumption and extraction on this land. I remain an advocate of wilderness because it is the template for conservation and restoration.

The negative effects of mindless over-development in the Green River Basin—loss of winter wildlife habitat and increased noise pollution that disrupt mating and birthing grounds of wild animals—have undoubtedly affected the viability of all wildlife in the region. And just as animals experience negative effects from the degradation of their environment, so humans also suffer from health problems and loss of quality of life caused by soil, air and water pollution. Sadly, the increase in wealth brought into a community with such development does not translate into happier and healthier lives for its residents. Social services are stretched, the sense of place eroded for human inhabitants and the integrity of the land and its creatures compromised.

During my drive north, the majestic Wind River Mountains dominate the horizon. On some days when pollution is high, they are barely visible, but on windy days, their ramparts shine. At a point where the Green River makes a great arc to the south, I pass the site near Daniel Junction where fur company rendezvous were held each summer in the early 1800s. This is a historic site where trappers and Native Americans traded beaver pelts with fur companies for supplies needed for the coming year.

I turn west on Highway 189-191, and after a stop for a cone piled high with huckleberry ice cream, I begin the final leg of my journey home. Embraced by the Wind Rivers on my right and Wyoming Range on the left, I cross the Green River one last time. After successfully traversing Union Pass guided by the trapper John Hoback, explorer George Price Hunt and his Astorians camped here to replenish their supplies and trade with a gathering of Shoshone tribes who were collaboratively hunting and drying meat for their move to their winter grounds. Hoback, and two fellow trappers on their way back to their homes in Kentucky, had met Hunt and his party on the Missouri River. After advising Hunt to abandon his plans to continue on the Missouri River where the Blackfoot Indians were hostile, Hoback agreed to guide the Astorians over the Wind River Mountains by way of Union Pass to the Snake River. As things turned out, Hoback and his companions would never return to their homes. They eventually met ignominious ends at the hands of tribal people retaliating for the murder of one of their braves.

As I crest the East Rim and the Hoback Basin falls away below, the beauty and majesty of the place lift my spirits. The road winds downward past conifers, aspen and willows and, with one last broad curve, enters the Hoback Basin. Bales of hay dot the meadows. Making a quick stop at the post office for my mail, I drive down the highway, across the Hoback River, turn onto the graveled Upper Hoback River Road and follow it to my turn-off. Through an opening in the willows, I see my cabin back-dropped by the Hoback Mountains.

Water is running in the ditch and the pond is full. As it has been for me, this would also have been a good summer for those settled along Sometimes Creek. Apparently satisfied with having the place to themselves, pronghorns are resting around my cabin. Beyond is Clark Butte, where I trust Heartwood still stands strong on its summit. I park the car in front of the cabin, climb the stairs to the porch, unlock the door, and enter the cabin's welcoming ambience. Once more, I'm home. All things considered, it has been a remarkable journey.

Bertagnolli sisters

Photo by Joni Dietz

Bibliography

Abbey, Edward. *The Monkey Wrench Gang*. Philadelphia: Lippin-
cott, 1975.

Abbey, Edward. *Desert Solitaire, A Season in the Wilderness*. New
York: McGraw-Hill, 1965.

Bachelard, Gaston. *The Poetics of Space*. Boston: Beacon Press,
1994.

Barrett, G. Kemmerer. *Wyoming, The Founding of an Independent
Coal Town (1897-1902)*. Kemmerer: Quealy Services, Inc.,
1975.

Bates, Marston. *The Forest and the Sea, a Look at the Economy
of Nature and the Ecology of Man*. Boston: Random House,
1960.

Bodsworth, Fred. *The Last of the Curlews*. Toronto: McClelland
& Stewart, 1954.

Casey, Edward S. *Getting Back into Place*. Bloomington: Indiana
University Press, 1993.

Casey, Edward S. *Remembering, A Phenomenological Study*.
Bloomington: Indiana University Press, 1987.

Chawla, Louise. *In the First Country of Places: Nature, Poetry, and Childhood Memory.* New York: State University of New York Press, 1994.

Cobb, Edith. *The Ecology of Imagination of Childhood.* New York: Columbia University Press, 1977.

Cole, John W. and Eric R. Wolf. *The Hidden Frontier, Ecology and Ethnicity in an Alpine Valley.* Berkeley, California: University of California Press, 1999.

Coletti, Anthony. *The Cumberland Saga* (unpublished). Ames, Iowa, 1978.

Craighead, Jr., Frank C. *For Everything There is a Season.* Helena, Montana: Falcon Press, 1994.

Csikszentmihalyi, Mihaly. *Flow: The Psychology of Optimal Experience.* New York: Harper and Row, 1990.

Csikszentmihalyi, Mihaly and Eugene Halton. *The Meaning of Things, Domestic symbols and the self.* Cambridge: Cambridge University Press, 1981.

Derrida, Jacques. *The Ear of the Other, Otobiograpphy, Transference,* Translation. English Ed. by Christie V. McDonald, translated by Peggy Kamuf. New York: Schocken Books, 1985.

Dewey, John. *Experience and Education.* New York: Collier Books, 1979.

Dewey, John. *The School and Society.* Chicago: The University of Chicago Press, 1900.

Eiseley, Loren. *The Immense Journey, An Imaginative Naturalist Explains the Mysteries of Man and Nature.* Vintage: 1959.

Fleckinger, Angelika. *Ötzi, the Iceman.* Bolzano: Folio Vienna, 2003.

Freire, Paulo. *Pedagogy of the Oppressed.* New York: Herder and Herder, 1970.

Groutage, Lorenzo. *Wyoming Mine Run*. Salt Lake City, Utah: Paragon Press, 1981.

Halfpenny, James C. and Roy Douglas Ozanne. *Winter Ecology*. Boulder, Colorado: Johnson Books, 1989.

Halton, Eugene. *The Great Brain Suck*. Chicago: University of Chicago Press, 2008.

Hart, Roger. *Children's Experience of Place*. New York: Irvington Publishers, 1979.

Hensley, Nathan. *Curriculum Studies Gone Wild*. Peter Lang Publishers, Inc., 2011.

Illich, Ivan. *H_2O and the Waters of Forgetfulness*. Dallas, Texas: The Dallas Institute of Humanities and Culture, 1985.

Illich, Ivan. *De-schooling Society*. New York: Harper and Row, 1971.

The Junior Classics. Volume VIII, Animal and Nature Stories. New York: P. F. Collier and Son Company, 1912.

Krall, Florence R. *Ecotone, Wayfaring on the Margin*. Albany: SUNY Press, 1994.

Krall, Florence R. "Living Metaphors." *Journal of Curriculum Theorizing*, 1979. Reprinted in William F. Pinar, *Contemporary Curriculum Discourses*. New York: Peter Lang, 1999, 1-5.

Krall, Florence R. "On the Rocks." *Southwestern American Literature*. Southwest Texas University, 1995. 21(1) (1995): 19-22.

Krall, Florence R. "Navajo Tapestry." *The Journal of Curriculum Theorizing*. Ed. William R. Pinar. Rochester: The University of Rochester, 3(2) (1982): 165-208.

Krall, Florence R. "Mudhole Ecology," *The American Biology Teacher*. September 1970.

Krall, Lisi. *Proving Up, Domesticating Land in U.S. History*. Albany: SUNY Press. 2010.

LaChapelle, Dolores. *Earth Wisdom*. Silverton, Colorado: Guild of Tutors Press, 1978.

LaChapelle, Dolores and Janet Bourque. *Earth Festivals*. Silverton, Colorado: Finn Hill Arts, 1973.

Leopold, Aldo. *A Sand County Almanac*. London: Oxford University Press, 1949.

McPhee, John. *Rising from the Plains*. New York: Farrar, Straus & Giroux, 1986.

Merleau-Ponti, Maurice. *The Prose of the World*. Evanston: Northwestern University Press, 1973.

Murie, Margaret E. *Two in the Far North*. New York: Alfred A. Knopf, 1957.

Nabhan, Gary Paul and Stephen J. Trimble. *The Geography of Childhood: Why Children Need Wild Places*. Boston: Beacon Press, Concord Library, 1995.

Ortega, Y. Gasset. *On Love, Aspects of a Single Theme*. Translated by Toby Talbot. Cleveland and New York: Meridian Books, The World Publishing Company, 1957.

Picard, Max. *The World of Silence*. Boston: Henry Regenery Company, 1964.

Rybczynski, Witold. *Home, A Short History of an Idea*. New York: Penguin Books, 1986.

Searles, Harold F. *The Nonhuman Environment*. New York: International Universities Press, 1960.

Serres, Michel. "The Natural Contract," *Critical Inquiry*. (1992).

Shepard, Paul. *Coming Home to the Pleistocene*. Ed. Florence R. Shepard. Washington, D.C.: Island Press/Shearwater Books, 1998.

Shepard, Paul. *The Others: How Animals Made Us Human*. Washington, D.C.: Island Press/Shearwater Books, 1996.

Shepard, Paul. *The Sacred Paw, The Bear in Nature, Myth, and Literature*. New York: Viking Penguin, Inc., 1985.

Shepard, Paul. *Nature and Madness*. San Francisco: Sierra Club Books, 1982.

Snow, Don. "A Huckleberry Testament," an essay presented at the Sitka Symposium, "Gifts of Nature, Gifts of Culture: Who Owns the Commons?" presented by The Island Institute. <http://www.islandinstitutealaska.org/> (2008).

Snyder, Gary. *Turtle Island*. New York: A New Dimensions Book, 1969.

Sobel, David. *Place-Based Education: Connecting Classrooms and Communities*. Great Barrington, Massachusetts: The Orion Society and the Myrin Institute, 2004.

Stolzenburg, Will. *Where the Wild Things Were: Life, Death, and Ecological Wreckage in a Land of Vanishing Predators*. New York: Bloomsbury, 2008.

Stuart, John. *The Discovery of the Oregon Trail, Robert Stuart's Narratives*. Ed. Philip Ashton Rollins. New York: Edward Eberstadt and Sons, 1935.

Teilhard de Chardin, Pierre. *The Phenomenon of Man*. New York: Harper Perennial, 1976.

War Dead WWII. <http://warchronicle.com/numbers/WWII/deaths.htm>

Worster, Donald. *Rivers of Empire*. New York: Pantheon Books, 1985.

Throughout the writing of the book, various field guides have helped me identify and understand what I've observed in nature. The list that follows includes some of the books, which have been most helpful.

Erlich, Paul R., David S. Dobkin and Darryl Wheye. *The Birder's Handbook: A Field Guide to the Natural History of North American Birds.* New York: Simon and Schuster, Inc., 1988.

Kershaw, Linda, Andy MacKinnon, and Jim Pojar. *Plants of the Rocky Mountains.* Edmonton: Lone Pine Publishing, 1998.

Nelson, Ruth Ashton. *Handbook of Rocky Mountain Plants.* Tucson, Arizona: Dale Stuart King, 1969.

Petersen Field Guide Series including:

Clark, William S. and Brian K. Wheeler. *Hawks.* Boston: Houghton Millflin Company, 1987.

Craighead, John J., Frank C. Craighead, Jr., and Ray J. Davis. *A Field Guide to Rocky Mountain Wildflowers.* Boston: Houghton Millflin Company, 1963.

Peterson, Roger Tory. *Western Birds.* Boston: Houghton Millflin Company, 1990.

Stebbins, Robert C. *A Guide to Western Reptiles and Amphibians.* Boston: Houghton Millflin Company, 1966.

Sibley, David Allen. *The Sibley Guide to Birds.* New York: Alfred A. Knopf, 2000.

Stokes Nature Guides including:

Stokes, Donald. *A Guide to Bird Behavior, Vol.I.* Boston: Little Brown and Company, 1979.

Stokes, Donald and Lillian Stokes. *A Guide to Bird Behavior. Vol. II.* Boston: Little Brown and Company, 1983.

Stokes, Donald and Lillian Stokes. *A Guide to Bird Behavior, Vol. III.* Boston: Little Brown and Company, 1989.

Zeveloff, Samuel I. *Mammals of the Intermountain West.* With original paintings and drawings by Farrell R. Collett. Salt Lake City, Utah: The University of Utah, 1988.

• • •

Acknowledgements

I owe the successful completion of this book to the unconditional support and assistance of many people, but two, Kathryn Ann Morton and Susan Marsh, were particularly helpful. Daughter Kathryn Ann was always there with love and encouragement and technical skill with photos and construction of the map. Susan Marsh, writer, photographer and natural scientist with incomparable knowledge of place, never turned me away as I repeatedly solicited her assistance and advice. Her photos of the Hoback Basin grace the cover and the chapters and her final copy-editing brought the book to completion. Daughter, Lisi Krall, with her honesty and keen mind, provided an important critical perspective.

First readers, besides ever-present daughters and Susan, helped me immeasurably with the many iterations of the manuscript. Dixie Snow, a gracious neighbor and dear friend, offered support and encouragement on an early version. Liz Haslam's comments and questions and Judy Rollins's editorial critique provided the basis for substantive improvements on a first draft. Dawn Marano's course in creative non-fiction and her masterful critique and suggestions helped me see new possibilities for the text.

In a final reading Casey Walker offered incomparable insights and encouragement. Dear friends, Carolyn Petersen, with her careful reading and questions, and David Petersen, with his editing, prepared the way for me to Raven's Eye Press. And David, with his e-mails, and my children, with their phone calls, helped me through the long winter at the cabin when this book first took form.

Former students, who taught me more than I did them, and colleagues and friends who have enriched and influenced my thoughts and writing include: Ligia Albuquerque, Ramona Allen, Bill Baker, Edward Brady, Jim and Linda Bourett, Robert Bullough, Tom Butler, Michael Caley, Bob Chance, Fran and Ron Chilcote, Jorge Conessa-Sevilla, Matt Dali, Barbara Dean, Terry Deal, Joan Degiorgio, Lori Diefenbacher, Susan Edgerton, Fred Edwards, Calvin Evans, Jacquie Martinez Ferrall, Linda Filippi, Doug Gregory, Madeline Grumet, Stella and Rich Hageman, Shirley Hager, Eugene Halton, Earl Harmer, Kim Heimsath, David Holmes, Amy Howard, Thomas Kemp, Gary Kiren, Bernie and Kat Krause, Louie Landgren, Nola Lodge, Greg Marsden, Jeff Metcalf, Janet Miller, Cecil Miskel, Jeanne Moe, Diane Nofs Nova, Max Oelschlaeger, John Organ, Susan Perry, William Pinar, Walter Prothero, Barbara Ras, Chip Rawlins, Nancy Shea, Dona Smart, Jeff Soder, David Taylor, Ann Logan Weaver, Terry Tempest Williams, and Greg Zeigler.

Dear friends and colleagues, now deceased, Carolyn Benne, Aaron Boswell, Ladd Holt, Josephine Angelo Julian, Dolores LaChapelle, Ron Padgham and Dottie Tupper inspired me in life and remain as close to my thoughts and writing as they were when they walked beside me. And my late husband, Paul Shepard, instructs and guides me each day. The late Dr. Floyd Clark and Dr. George Baxter, exceptional professors at the University of Wyoming during my undergraduate studies, first sparked my interest in zoology.

Edward Casey with his book *Remembering* first started me on this journey. Lindsay Nyquist, who formatted the book and designed the cover, and Ken Wright, editor at Raven's Eye Press who published it, were instrumental in bringing *Sometimes Creek* to completion. Scott Leeper gave me the idea for the title when he told me about Sometimes Creek, an intermittent stream that once flowed through my property.

Finally, without the generosity of my good-hearted children, Matt, Lisi and Bobby Krall, I would not have been able to start a new life and career.

I have included some revised excerpts from my previously published essays and books including:

"A View from Clark Butte." *The Journal of the American Association for Curriculum Studies.* 6 (2010).

"Crossing the Divide." *The Eighth World Wilderness Congress.* Anchorage, Alaska: USDA Forest Service Proceedings, RMRS-P-49 (2007).

"Riding the Bear." *The Trumpeter, The Journal of Ecosophy.* ed. Michael Caley. 23 (3) (2007). And in the *The Poetics of Wilderness.* ed. Roger Dunsmore. Missoula, Montana: The Univeristy of Montana Wilderness Institute, 2001.

"The Shape of Things." *Heart Shots, Women Write About Hunting.* ed. Mary Zeiss Stange. Mechanicsburg, Pennsylvania: Stackpole Books, 2003.

"Coming Home to the Wild." *Wild Earth, Wild Ideas for a World out of Balance.* ed. Tom Butler. Minneapolis, Minnesota: Milkweed Editions, 2002.

"Heartwood." *Northern Lights.* (2000).

"Paul Shepard: Thinking Animal and Tender Omnivore." *The Wild Duck Review.* 3(3) (1997).

Ecotone. *Wayfaring on the Margins.* Albany: SUNY Press, 1994.

"Reunion." *Northern Lights.* 6(2) (1990).

• • •

Press

Raven's Eye Press
Rediscovering the West
www.ravenseyepress.com

Man Swarm and the Killing of Wildlife
by Dave Foreman

The Monkey Wrench Dad:
Dispatches from the
Backyard Frontline
by Ken Wright

Racks: A Natural History of
Antlers and the Animals That
Wear Them
by David Petersen

Ghost Grizzlies: Does the Great
Bear Still Haunt Colorado?
by David Petersen

How Delicate These Arches:
Footnotes from the Four Corners
by David Feela

Visit www.ravenseyepress.com
for a complete listing of our titles.

CPSIA information can be obtained at www.ICGtesting.com
Printed in the USA
LVOW061427190912

299407LV00003B/1/P